Higher Education and Regions

GLOBALLY COMPETITIVE, LOCALLY ENGAGED

D1570410

OECD

ORGANISATION FOR ECONOMIC CO-OPERATION AND DEVELOPMENT

ORGANISATION FOR ECONOMIC CO-OPERATION AND DEVELOPMENT

The OECD is a unique forum where the governments of 30 democracies work together to address the economic, social and environmental challenges of globalisation. The OECD is also at the forefront of efforts to understand and to help governments respond to new developments and concerns, such as corporate governance, the information economy and the challenges of an ageing population. The Organisation provides a setting where governments can compare policy experiences, seek answers to common problems, identify good practice and work to co-ordinate domestic and international policies.

The OECD member countries are: Australia, Austria, Belgium, Canada, the Czech Republic, Denmark, Finland, France, Germany, Greece, Hungary, Iceland, Ireland, Italy, Japan, Korea, Luxembourg, Mexico, the Netherlands, New Zealand, Norway, Poland, Portugal, the Slovak Republic, Spain, Sweden, Switzerland, Turkey, the United Kingdom and the United States. The Commission of the European Communities takes part in the work of the OECD.

OECD Publishing disseminates widely the results of the Organisation's statistics gathering and research on economic, social and environmental issues, as well as the conventions, guidelines and standards agreed by its members.

This work is published on the responsibility of the Secretary-General of the OECD. The opinions expressed and arguments employed herein do not necessarily reflect the official views of the Organisation or of the governments of its member countries.

Also available in French under the title:
Enseignement supérieur et régions
CONCURRENCE MONDIALE, ENGAGEMENT LOCAL
La Educación Superior y las Regiones
GLOBALMENTE COMPETITIVOS, LOCALMENTE COMPROMETIDOS

Foreword

A*fter decades of expansion in higher education, policy attention in OECD countries has begun to focus on the outcomes of higher education, its quality, relevance and impact. Consequently, there is also stronger interest in how higher education contributes to regional development. In recent years there have been many initiatives across OECD countries to mobilise higher education in support of regional economic, social and cultural development. The key questions in this context include the following: What is higher education's regional engagement all about? What are its drivers and barriers? What does it mean for the governance and management of higher education institutions, for regions and for nations? And how does regional engagement fit with the pursuit of world class academic excellence?*

The OECD Programme for Institutional Management in Higher Education (IMHE) addressed some of these issues in the 1999 report entitled The Response of Higher Education Institutions to Regional Needs. *The OECD Centre for Education Research and Innovation (CERI) continued this work with its 2001 report* Cities and Regions in the New Learning Economy *with focus on the role of the regions in the promotion of learning, innovation, productivity and economic performance.*

The current report has a focus on the regions and the contribution that higher education can make to regional development in a globalising knowledge economy. The report draws from the earlier reports, OECD territorial reviews and, in particular, from the extensive thematic review project entitled Supporting the Contribution of Higher Education Institutions to Regional Development. *This review project, managed by the IMHE in collaboration with the OECD Directorate for Public Governance and Territorial Development (GOV), sought answers to how issues relating to higher education institutions and their regional engagement were addressed in 14 regions across 12 countries.*

The review sought information on institutional, regional and national strategies, policies and activities in order to understand the rationales, stages of development and drivers and barriers to higher education institutions' regional engagement. In doing this it addressed a wide range of questions. Higher education institutions were asked to critically evaluate, with their regional partners and in the context of national higher education and regional policies, how effective they were in contributing to the development of their regions. How did their research contribute to regional innovation? What was the role of teaching and learning in the development of human capital? How did they contribute to social, cultural and environmental development? What was the role of the higher education institutions in building regional capacity to act in an increasingly competitive global economy?

The review was designed not only to elucidate good practice, policy guidance and international trends more generally, but also to support partnership building in the regions. It had a strong developmental focus. Therefore, the participants were not only higher education institutions, but also their regions including public authorities which are responsible for territorial and higher education development at the national and regional scale. The selection included nine European regions; two each from Latin America and Asia-Pacific and one from North America. The regions range from rural to metropolitan and from peripheral to central. The higher education institutions include not only research-intensive, but also vocational and professionally oriented institutions. At the national level, the review embraced devolved as well as highly centralised governance systems.

While the review of these regions provides no one-size-fits-all solution, it does point to important general issues that need to be considered by higher education institutions, their local and regional stakeholders and national governments. This review has provided an important dimension to our work on higher education and territorial policy, and the questions it raises will be addressed in follow-up work.

The project was led by, and accountable through, a Steering Group comprising three partners: IMHE (part of the OECD Directorate for Education), the Directorate for Public Governance and Territorial Development (GOV) and the Higher Education Funding Council in England (HEFCE). HEFCE and Fundación CYD (Spain) sponsored the project. We are grateful to the Korean Ministry of Education and Human Resource Development for loaning us Kiyong Byun to manage the first phase of the project; and to the City of Turku for supporting Jaana Puukka who was the project manager during the second and final phase. The academic leader of the project was John Goddard (University of Newcastle upon Tyne) and, he and Jaana Puukka (OECD/ IMHE), Chris Duke (RMIT), Patrick Dubarle (OECD/GOV) and Paul Benneworth (University of Newcastle upon Tyne) have contributed to the writing of this book. It is published under the responsibility of the Secretary-General of the OECD.

Barbara Ischinger

Director for Education

Odile Sallard

Director of Public Governance and
Territorial Development

HIGHER EDUCATION AND REGIONS: GLOBALLY COMPETITIVE, LOCALLY ENGAGED – ISBN 978-92-64-03414-3 – © OECD 2007

Acknowledgements

This study would not have been possible without the substantial contributions made by the regions, the participating institutions and the regional stakeholders. Many dozens of institutions and uncounted hundreds of individuals were involved in the review project throughout the fourteen regions and beyond. We are indebted to the regional coordinators and the chairs and members of the regional steering groups and committees which were established specifically for the project. Several of these are continuing following through the recommendations from the peer reviews.

We also wish to thank Peer Review Team Members who visited the 14 regions and the members of the project task group and steering group. The study enjoyed extensive inputs by experts who followed the analysis and gave their comments and views at various stages. We wish to acknowledge their invaluable contribution.

We wish to thank the Higher Education Funding Council in England (HEFCE) and Fundación CYD for sponsoring the project. The Korean Ministry of Education and Human Resources Development and the City of Turku as well as Turku University of Applied Sciences are thanked for the secondments of the project managers.

Finally, we wish to acknowledge the help and support of the many colleagues in the OECD who have contributed to this study.

Table of Contents

Executive summary   11

Chapter 1. **Introductory Remarks**   19
    Introduction   20
    The OECD study   23
    Note   28

Chapter 2. **Drivers for Regional Engagement**   29
    Evolving perspectives on regional development and the place
    of higher education   31
    Evolving perspectives on higher education and the role of regions   35
    Synthesis: higher educations institutions tying down the global
    in the local   39
    Note   43

Chapter 3. **Barriers to Regional Engagement of Higher Education**   45
    Higher education, science and technology and labour market policy   46
    Funding regional engagement   51
    Regional structures and governance   56
    Governance, leadership and management of higher education . . .   58
    Conclusions   63
    Notes   64

Chapter 4. **The Regions and their Higher Education Institutions**   67
    Australia   68
    Brazil   71
    Canada   74
    Denmark   78
    Finland   82
    Korea   85
    Mexico   88
    The Netherlands   91
    Norway   94
    Spain   96
    Sweden   101
    United Kingdom: England   105
    Cross-border co-operation between Denmark and Sweden   108

Conclusions 111

Notes 113

Chapter 5. **Contribution of Higher Education to Regional Business Innovation: Overcoming the Barriers** 117

Enhancing the engagement potential of higher education institutions 122

Policy practices and instruments 130

Conclusions 140

Notes 141

Chapter 6. **Contribution of Higher Education to Regional Human Capital Formation: Overcoming the Barriers** 143

Widening access 145

Improving the balance between labour market supply and demand 151

Attracting talent to the region and retaining it 158

Strategic co-ordination of the regional human capital system 160

Conclusions: managing the regional human capital system 162

Notes 163

Chapter 7. **Contribution of Higher Education to Social, Cultural and Environmental Development: Overcoming the Barriers** 165

Health and welfare 167

Culture and creative industries 171

Environmental sustainability 173

The case of Nuevo León in Mexico 177

Conclusions: from entrepreneurial university to the socially engaged university 177

Notes 180

Chapter 8. **Building Capacity for Co-operation Between Higher Education and Regions** 181

The higher education pillar 182

The regional pillar 192

Putting the bridge in place 195

Realising the potential of higher education to contribute to regional development 198

Notes 199

Chapter 9. **Pointers for Future Development** 201

Central governments 202

Regional and local authorities 203

Higher education institutions 204

HIGHER EDUCATION AND REGIONS: GLOBALLY COMPETITIVE, LOCALLY ENGAGED – ISBN 978-92-64-03414-3 – © OECD 2007

Annex A. **OECD Project on Supporting the Contribution of Higher Education Institutions to Regional Development** 207

Annex B. **Selected OECD Countries' Characteristics and Innovation-Based Policies Targeting at the Regional Engagement of Higher Education Institutions** 221

Bibliography 233

List of boxes

2.1. Universities of Applied Sciences in Switzerland 37
3.1. The New University for Regional Innovation (NURI) in Korea 46
5.1. Examples of industrial liaison programmes in OECD countries . . . 125
5.2. Three cluster model programmes 128
5.3. Twente TOP programme 131
5.4. Entry points for SMEs to the university knowledge base 133
5.5. Upgrading the existing industry base in Castellon, Spain, and North East England 135
5.6. Science and technology cities 137
5.7. Higher education networks supporting the growth of knowledge-based economy 139
6.1. Higher Education Equity Programs in Australia 146
6.2. Paraná, Brazil: Higher education expansion driven by the local authority 147
6.3. L'Université de Moncton: A symbol of cultural pride and catalyst of local economic development 148
6.4. Widening access through distance education in remote areas . . . 150
6.5. Widening access in the North East England 152
6.6. Balancing between labour market supply and demand 153
6.7. Work-based learning 155
6.8. Targeted development programmes in response to regional needs 156
6.9. Embedding regional engagement in core curriculum 157
6.10. Enhancing entrepreneurship 159
6.11. Fast Forward high potential management development programme 160
7.1. Jyväskylä conjoint effort to respond to the challenges of ageing population 169
7.2. Cultural and creative industries in region building 174
7.3. Institute for Sustainability, Health and Regional Engagement (iSHARE) 176
7.4. Mandatory social service for higher education students in Mexico 178
8.1. Higher education management at the Jyväskylä University of Applied Sciences: supporting regional engagement 183
8.2. Rewarding staff for regional engagement 185
8.3. Regions of Knowledge 187

9

8.4. Higher education regional associations supporting regional
     development in the North East of England and Öresund region . . 188
8.5. Atlantic Canada Opportunities Agency (ACOA) 193
8.6. Examples of strategic co-operation in regions 195
8.7. Central government initiatives supporting the regional agenda
     of higher education institutions 196

List of tables

3.1. External engagement of higher education institutions 63
5.1. Perceived importance of alternative channels
     of knowledge transfer from university to industry 120
5.2. Research and innovative activities performed by universities
     in selected European countries 120
5.3. Sources of information and knowledge for innovation activities
     in UK manufacturing (year 2000) 121
5.4. Policy trends supporting clusters and regional innovation systems 123
5.5. Co-operation of firms with research institutions in connection
     with product innovation according to the size of firms:
     in percentage 132
B.1. Selected OECD countries' characteristics and innovation-based
     policies targeting at the regional engagement of higher education
     institutions 222

List of figures

2.1. Closed model of HEI/region interface 40
2.2. National policies impacting on HEI/regional relations 41
2.3. Regionally engaged multi-modal and multi-scalar HEI 42
7.1. Regenerating the region adapted from Barnley's model 167

ISBN 978-92-64-03414-3
Higher Education and Regions:
Globally Competitive, Locally Engaged
© OECD 2007

Executive Summary

In order to be competitive in the globalising knowledge economy, the OECD countries need to invest in their innovation systems at the national and regional levels. As countries are turning their production towards value-added segments and knowledge-intensive products and services, there is greater dependency on access to new technologies, knowledge and skills. And, with the parallel processes of globalisation and localisation, the local availability of knowledge and skills is becoming increasingly important. OECD countries are thus putting considerable emphasis on meeting regional development goals, by nurturing the unique assets and circumstances of each region, particularly in developing knowledge-based industries. As key sources of knowledge and innovation, higher education institutions (HEIs) can be central to this process.

In the past, neither public policy nor the higher education institutions themselves have tended to focus strategically on the contribution that they can make to the development of the regions where they are located. Particularly for older, traditional HEIs, the emphasis has often been on serving national goals or on the pursuit of knowledge with little regard for the surrounding environment. This is now changing. To be able to play their regional role, HEIs must do more than simply educate and research – they must engage with others in their regions, provide opportunities for lifelong learning and contribute to the development of knowledge-intensive jobs which will enable graduates to find local employment and remain in their communities. This has implications for all aspects of these institutions' activities – teaching, research and service to the community and for the policy and regulatory framework in which they operate.

How can higher education institutions live up to this challenge? This publication explores the policy measures and institutional reforms that can help them to do so. It considers regional engagement of higher education in several dimensions, notably: *knowledge creation* through research and technology transfer; *knowledge transfer* through education and human resources development and *cultural and community development,* which can, among other things, create the conditions in which innovation thrives. This study draws from a review of 14 regions across 12 countries as well as OECD territorial reviews, which broaden the scope of the study to a wider OECD area.

11

The review project was launched as a response to the initiatives seeking to mobilise higher education in support of regional economic, social and cultural development. The aim was to synthesise this experience in order to guide HEIs and regional and national governments. The project was designed to assist with building capacity for conjoint working between HEIs and regional stakeholders.

Stronger focus on regions

Examples of higher education helping to serve the needs of local economies can be found in various countries in the past 150 years. However, these links have been sporadic rather than systematic. This has changed dramatically with recent expansion of higher education, particularly in the non-university sector, which in some cases has consciously aimed to address regional disparities and to widen access. Another important factor changing the context of regional development has been a switch towards more indigenous development, which emphasises the building of skills, entrepreneurialism and innovation within regions. Growing efforts have been made to remove barriers to the application of research, which obliges HEIs to become involved in innovation. Policy responses which initially focused on enhancing the capacity for technological innovation through technology transfer and interactions between HEIs and private industry have now widened to include public services, social and organisational innovation, and to engage HEIs in the wider social fabric of which they are part.

Regions and HEIs are building partnerships based on shared interest which is principally economic. From the perspective of agencies promoting city and regional development, HEIs have become a key resource. They can help serve regional development most obviously by contributing to a region's comparative advantage in knowledge-based industries and to its human capital base, but also for example by helping to generate new businesses, by contributing to tax revenues and by providing content and audience for local cultural programmes. From the perspective of HEIs, regional involvement has a range of benefits. The local area brings business to institutions in a variety of forms, including student enrolments and payments for research, consultancy and training. At the same time, a thriving region creates an environment in which higher education can also thrive, helping institutions to attract and retain staff and students.

Barriers

In the regions involved in the OECD study, partnerships are being developed between HEIs and the public and private sector to mobilise higher education in support of regional development. While the case for engagement is patchy, it is becoming acknowledged across a wide range of HEIs in most regions. The partnerships, which are in most cases at early stages, are often bottom-up initiatives with limited support from central governments. The early stages are characterised by numerous small scale and short term projects championed by key individuals. The environment for higher education to engage in regional development across OECD countries remains highly variable.

More active engagement is constrained by the orientation of public policy, inadequate funding and incentives, limits to leadership within HEIs, and the limited capacity of local and regional agents to get involved with higher education. Regional engagement strategies of HEIs depend on the role the HEI chooses for itself and the leadership role it adopts. The governance, leadership and management of HEIs can constrain active engagement. Also, traditional academic values give little weight to engaging with local communities. Institutional structures within HEIs offer limited incentives or resources to pursue activity that serves the region.

National higher education systems may impose regulations that reduce the capacity of HEIs to engage regionally. Administrative-based higher education systems leave little room for institutional autonomy and flexibility. In many unitary countries, higher education policy does not include an explicit regional dimension. Ministries of Education need to balance between conflicting policy priorities and may show limited interest in HEIs' regional engagement. Applied research and development and meeting skill needs in the local labour market are left to institutions which often lack a well-established tradition in research or infrastructure to support it. Even when engagement with business and the community has been recognised and laid upon HEIs as a "duty" by national governments, it has remained a "third task", not explicitly linked to the core functions of research and teaching.

Funding and incentive structures often provide limited support for regional engagement. HEIs are faced with competition, new tasks and pressures to reduce cost notably by the central authorities. This context does not necessarily favour an enhanced regional role for HEIs. Research is generally funded on a geographically neutral basis or aims to create critical mass. HEIs can seek to diversify their funding sources and turn to private external funds but are faced with legal constraints in doing this. A strong focus on excellence when allocating research budgets may result in concentration in advanced regions which is often considered necessary in the face of increasing global competition within the HE sector. Funding for teaching is weakly oriented towards building human capital in deprived regions and higher education's role in aiding community development is not systematically funded. Regional engagement is generally not supported by major incentives or monitoring of outcomes. The related metrics are underdeveloped, retrospective or do not take account of developmental work that may lead to future income or services in the public interest.

Regional structures and governance are in many instances ill-suited to furthering the regional agenda of HEIs. The territorial coverage of local and regional government is constrained to serving fixed constituencies, whereas higher education needs to define its sphere of influence in a flexible way. Local governments do not always have responsibilities that allow them to engage freely in economic development. HEIs and firms often experience significant gaps in their collaborative relations: academics may be uninterested in tackling seemingly mundane problems and/or failing to deliver solutions on time or to budget while firms may lack sufficient information to track down the appropriate expertise within the HEIs. Restrictions on publishing research results also set constraints.

Overcoming barriers

Overcoming barriers to promoting innovation with a regional focus

Despite the existing constraints, the new tasks of HEIs have increased as countries have reinforced the HEI apparatus in relation to firms and regional economies. The policies have had a common goal: to transform each HEI into an engine for growth. The efforts have often been indirect *i.e.* granting enhanced autonomy to HEIs and improving framework conditions and incentives to co-operate with the private sector. Two prominent ways have been: enhancing the role of tertiary education within regional innovation systems and enhancing the participation of HEIs in cluster type initiatives. Temporary incentives have been developed in the form of grants, calls for projects or joint programmes. Policies have often prioritised the uptake and development of high technologies, while mechanisms to support social entrepreneurship and innovation for wider needs of excluded groups in rural areas and inner cities have been limited. There has also been less emphasis on services, which account for 70% of the workforce in the OECD countries.

Case studies from different countries show how a regional dimension can be integrated into public investment in the science base in HEIs. For example in France, Finland, Japan, Mexico and the United Kingdom national governments have taken steps to identify and support regional centres of innovation. Examples from Öresund cross-border region and from Atlantic Canada illustrate how HEIs can work together to improve and diversify their supply of services for local and regional firms. Small and medium-sized enterprises (SMEs) do not always find it easy to work with large HEIs or to engage in the wider research issues raised in universities. Creating access points can help smooth this process. Case studies illustrate how this is done in the North East of England with a "Knowledge House" which provides a common entry point to five universities and in Georgia Tech which has 13 regional offices throughout the state. HEIs can also potentially play a key role in bringing global players into a local context in order to attract inward investment. Whether it is the University Jaume I in Valencia in Spain helping to transform the traditional SME-based ceramic tile industry to a global leader or the University of Sunderland in the UK participating in an alliance that helps to make Nissan's new car plant the most productive in Europe, higher education is starting to realise the pivotal part it can play.

Overcoming barriers to developing human capital within regions

Higher education can contribute to human capital development in the region through educating a wider range of individuals in the local area, ensuring that they are employable when they leave education, helping local employers by responding to new skills requirements, ensuring that employees go on learning by supporting continuous professional development, and helping attract talent from outside. Widening access to higher education is a national as well as a regional task, but the regional dimension is particularly significant in countries with wide disparities. Some countries, for example Australia, have introduced a specific regional dimension to the higher education equity initiatives. Given that one-third of working age adults in the OECD countries have low skills, up-skilling and lifelong learning are particular challenges. In Finland, the Provincial University of Lapland has pooled the expertise of four HEIs to reach out to remote communities in co-operation with regional stakeholders.

HEIs can also improve the balance between labour market supply and demand. This requires labour market intelligence and sustained links with local businesses, communities and authorities. Work-based learning programmes, such as the Family Firm system in the Dongseo University in Busan, represent person-embodied knowledge transfer which often culminates in job creation and promote links between SMEs and HEIs. Aalborg University in Denmark and many new HEIs have built their education provision around Problem Based Learning which guarantees a high degree of co-operation with the society and the private sector. HEIs are also increasingly creating entrepreneurship programmes. The emergence of a well functioning human capital system in the region as distinct for a number of disconnected components requires some degree of co-ordination and steering, not least between different stages of education. Co-operation among HEIs can bring numerous advantages including critical mass in competing with other regions, improvement of pathways that involve enrolment at multiple institutions and the sharing of learning through the dissemination of best practice.

Overcoming barriers to promoting the social, cultural and environmental development of regions

Regional development is not only about helping business thrive: wider forms of development both serve economic goals and are ends in themselves. HEIs have long seen service to the community as part of their role, yet this function is often underdeveloped. Few OECD countries have encouraged this type of activity through legislation and incentives. The mandatory social service for higher education students in Mexico provides an interesting model for countries seeking to mobilise higher education towards social goals.

Many HEIs have a strong involvement with health, and this can be turned to community use – for example the universities in Northeast England work with the Strategic Health Authority to address public health issues in the region. Higher education can be well placed to analyse and address social needs in deprived areas. For example in Central Finland the Jyväskylä University of Applied Sciences is working with a wide range of stakeholders to develop social innovation to help long-term unemployed people back into work. In the cultural domain, the contribution made by culture to quality of life, the attraction of creative talent and the growth of creative industries are all part of regional development. Higher education can be a major player in internationalising their regions and making them more diverse and multicultural, but often not enough is made of international links in this regard. High profile initiatives can help to coalesce efforts in this area, for example, in the European context, the bids to become European Capitals of Culture have worked to this direction. Higher education institutions can also play a significant role in environmental development, for example by mustering expertise and by demonstrating good practice.

Building capacity for engagement

In regional engagement much depends on the institutional leadership and entrepreneurialism of HEIs. Mainstreaming the regional agenda and scaling up the institutional capacity from individual good practice cases to a well-developed system requires senior management teams able to deliver the corporate response expected by regional stakeholders, modern management and administration systems (human resources management system and financial management system underpinned by modern ICT systems), transversal mechanisms that link teaching, research and third task activities and cut across disciplinary boundaries, permanent structures that enhance regional engagement (*e.g.* regional development offices and single entry points to HE expertise, such as Knowledge House in the North East England) and sufficient incentives, for example by making regional engagement a consideration in hiring and reward systems as has been done in the University of Sunshine Coast in Australia. There is also a need to ensure that units established to link the HEIs to the region, such as science parks, centres of continuing education and knowledge transfer centres do not act as barriers to the academic heartland or provide an excuse for detachment. Finally, there is a need to acknowledge that regional engagement can enhance the core missions of teaching and research and that the region can be seen as a laboratory for research projects, a provider of work experience for students and a source of financial resources to enhance the global competitiveness of the institution.

HEIs play an important role in partnering with regional stakeholders. Many OECD countries have strengthened this role through requiring higher education governance to include regional representation and encouraging the participation of HEIs in regional governance structures. Some countries, *e.g.* the UK and Finland, have also encouraged closer co-operation between HEIs in the region (joint degrees, programmes, research programmes, strategies, higher education regional associations, one stop shops for industry collaboration). Partnership structures linking HEIs have been developed for example in Öresund region, where a loose consortium of 14 universities not only pools research and teaching efforts but also helps to provide necessary co-ordination across two countries with different education, labour and administrative systems. Stronger commitment can be achieved when HEIs are mobilised not only in the preparation but also in the implementation of regional strategies backed up with necessary financial resources. A crucial step is to create well-functioning co-ordinating bodies at the regional level that comprise the key regional actors including private sector and that take a long-term wider view of regional development, not just focusing on economic but also social, cultural and environmental development.

HEIs can play a key role in joining up a wide range of national policies at the regional level. These policies include science and technology, industry, education and skills, health, culture and sport, environmental sustainability and social inclusion. OECD countries which wish to mobilise their higher education system or part of it in support of regional development, need to ensure that the higher education policy which embraces teaching, research and third task activities include an explicit regional dimension. Countries also need to create beneficial framework conditions such as strengthened institutional autonomy that support more entrepreneurial HEIs and their co-operation with enterprises, and supportive incentive structures including long term core funding as well as additional strategic funding schemes. The search for indicators and benchmarking mechanisms has remained a weakness in many countries. Even if measuring is difficult and controversial, engagement policies will not improve without sound evaluation processes.

The concluding chapter contains pointers for the future directed at national and regional governments and higher education institutions.

ISBN 978-92-64-03414-3
Higher Education and Regions:
Globally Competitive, Locally Engaged
© OECD 2007

Chapter 1

Introductory Remarks

This chapter briefly illustrates the various dimensions of regional engagement of higher education and provides a definition for this activity. It describes the OECD study encompassing intensive analysis of higher education institutions' engagement at regional level. It explains the aims and the methodology of the thematic review including self evaluation and external evaluation. It highlights the developmental focus of the OECD study and the aim to support partnership building in the participating regions.

Introduction

Regional economies depend on the interplay between a number of factors. Obvious features include the natural resource base, physical infrastructure, the environment, existing and emerging businesses and the skill base of the population. However, other factors including their tradition and history, the explicit policy frameworks for regional development and the availability of education and lifelong learning opportunities are becoming critical factors in enhancing regional competitiveness and economic performance.

With some notable exceptions, higher education institutions, particularly research-intensive universities, have traditionally tended to be self-contained entities focused on the creation and development of basic knowledge for the national and/or the global economy with limited emphasis on local and regional needs. This has, however, changed recently. The active involvement of national governments and supra-national organisations such as the European Union in setting regional policy frameworks and incentives and/or infrastructure to achieve regional development goals has impacted on the higher education sector. The recognition that higher education can play a key role in development is now a fundamental underpinning of most economic development strategies, both at international, national and regional level. It is becoming recognised that the two perspectives – the national/international and the regional/local – can be complementary, reinforcing one another. The issue is often more a question of balance than of substitution.

Impact on regional economics

Higher education makes considerable direct economic contribution to the local and regional economy. Higher education institutions are employers and customers as well as suppliers of goods and services. Their staff and student expenditure have a direct effect on income and employment in the cities and regions. Higher education institutions can also widen the tax base. At the same time, they are consumers of local government services and local firms' products. These interactions are sometimes called backward linkages (Felsenstein, 1996). In regions with a well represented higher education sector the contribution to the regional GDP can be significant. For example, in peripheral regions, the expenditure of higher education institutions may range from 2 to 4% of regional GDP.[1]

While the backward linkages are important to regional development, there are also indirect impacts linked to human capital, pool of knowledge and attractiveness of the local area. Emerging models of regional development emphasise development that is based on unique assets and circumstances of the region as well as the development of knowledge-based industries. This has resulted in a re-examination of the role of higher education institutions in the regions. A knowledge-based or learning economy requires a larger number of graduates and an employment orientation in teaching. It also requires the provision of lifelong learning opportunities for a wide variety of traditional and non-traditional learners. Moreover, if higher education institutions want to contribute to regional economic development, they must do more than simply educate – they must engage with the regions and contribute to the development of knowledge-intensive jobs which will enable graduates to find local employment and remain in their communities. They must also respond to the needs of the established firms in terms of skills upgrading and technology transfer. Higher education institutions are thus expected to be involved not only in the creation of knowledge, but also in the application of knowledge, often with their local and regional communities. They are expected to take an interdisciplinary approach to their activities and engage in partnerships with industry, with communities and with a wide variety of stakeholders. These factors impact on all aspects of the role of the higher education institution – teaching, research and community service.

Higher education and cities

While much policy development in this field has involved central governments, there is scope for action at the metro-regional level, which combines both the physical proximity at which collaboration is easiest and the sufficient scale to capture synergetic effect and diversity. Cities and city-regions have interest in supporting local higher education institution's regional involvement. They benefit from the presence of a higher education institution, which represents not only a main asset but could be a magnet to inward investment and talent. Flagship areas of expertise of local higher education institutions can be highlighted by city authorities in branding their city as centres of entrepreneurship, innovation and creativity.

Partnerships between city-regions and higher education institutions are particularly fruitful in three domains: first, matching supply and demand in the local labour market; second, promoting local economic development; and third, contributing to regional systems of governance.

Metropolitan regions often face shortages in highly skilled workers because of insufficient or maladjusted local skill supply or brain drain. Cities and their higher education institutions can gather labour market intelligence and identify how the labour market needs can be met by higher education.

They can also jointly develop new models of decision-making which increase economic competitiveness and reduce social exclusion (ODPM, 2004). Higher education institutions have the potential to provide support, expert analysis and guidance for cities. Thus, they can also promote and facilitate the decentralisation and devolution process through developing linkages within the broader city-region.

Strategic partnerships between the cities and their urban research-intensive universities serve as a vehicle for sharing experience and providing common policy responses. These coalitions seek to make a positive difference in urban environments. They can also take the form of sub-regional alliances with communities and agencies to deliver economic, physical and social regeneration project. Frameworks such as science cities help to link and reorganise research units and centres of excellence with regional industries and strength.

With the processes of globalisation and localisation, the local availability of knowledge and skills is becoming increasingly important. In the globalising knowledge economy higher education institutions are seen as sources of knowledge and innovation and engines of growth, making contributions to the economic, social and cultural development of their societies. This has meant new expectations to be fulfilled by higher education institutions. The question is how to translate them into relevant policy measures and institutional reforms.

In this publication regional engagement of higher education refers to a number of dimensions, including:

- knowledge creation in the region through research and its exploitation via technology transfer (spin out companies, intellectual property rights and consultancy);
- human capital formation and knowledge transfer (localisation of learning process by work-based learning, graduate employment in the region, continuing education, professional development and lifelong learning activities);
- cultural and community development contributing to the milieu, social cohesion and sustainable development on which innovation in the region depends.

The need for greater regional engagement and mutual development of capabilities is becoming widely acknowledged. Many OECD countries have strengthened the regional role and contribution of higher education. Often, the regional mission has been characterised as a part of a "third task" or social obligation of higher education institutions. There is, however, a growing recognition that the third task must be integrated with longer-standing teaching and research functions if higher education's contribution to students' learning, to knowledge exploitation by business, and to civil society in the region is to be maximised.

Where do we stand now? What is higher education's regional engagement all about? What are its drivers and barriers? What does it mean to the governance and management of higher education institutions, regions and nations? And how does regional engagement fit with the pursuit of world class academic excellence? This publication seeks to address these questions, drawing from the OECD territorial reviews and the 14 regional self-evaluation and peer review reports of the current study.

This publication gives an overview of the drivers for and barriers against regional engagement of higher education. It then focuses on how these barriers can be overcome through mobilising higher education to participate in regional innovation systems, to enhance human capital formation and to contribute to the social, cultural and environmental development in the region. It then moves to look in capacity building and the ways higher education and development systems can be built in the regions. Finally, it presents some pointers for the future for national and regional governments as well as higher education institutions.

The OECD study

In 2004, following the reports of *The Response of Higher Education Institutions to Regional Needs* (OECD/IMHE, 1999) and *Cities and Regions in the New Learning Economy* (OECD, 2001a), the OECD Programme on Institutional Management in Higher Education (IMHE) in collaboration with the OECD Public Governance and Territorial Development Committee (GOV) embarked upon a study to improve understanding of international trends and practice relating to higher education institutions and their regional engagement.

Central to the study was an in-depth comparative review of 14 regions across 12 countries, which was launched as a response to a wide range of initiatives across OECD countries to mobilise higher education in support of regional development. The review project, which was carried out in 2005-2007, had the aim to synthesise this experience into a coherent body of policy and practice that could guide institutional, regional, national and supranational reforms and relevant policy measures including investment decisions seeking to enhance the connection of higher education to regional communities. Current practice needed to be analysed and evaluated with sensitivity to various national and regional contexts. At the same time, the review project was designed to assist with capacity-building in each country/region through providing a structured opportunity for dialogue between higher education institutions and regional stakeholders; and clarifying roles and responsibilities.

The review project was primarily qualitative in nature, covering a wide range of topics and requesting supporting documentation. While regional development is often thought of in economic terms only, the OECD template guiding the self-evaluation process suggested a wider interpretation. It asked higher education institutions to critically evaluate with their regional partners and in the context of national higher education and regional policies how effective they were in contributing to the development of their regions. Thus key aspects of the self evaluation were organised under the following headings (see questionnaire in Annex A):

- contribution of research to regional innovation;
- role of teaching and learning in the development of human capital;
- higher education institutions' contribution to social, cultural and environmental development;
- the role of higher education institutions in building regional capacity to act in an increasingly competitive global economy.

The renewed focus on higher education and innovation as a driver of regional competitivity was echoed by the Public Governance and Territorial Development Directorate which ran a supporting and interlinked study *The Contributions of Higher Education Institutions to Regional Development* (OECD, 2006a) on the theme drawing from materials accumulated in the territorial reviews exercises and from the experience and case studies of the IMHE review. At the same time the Education and Training Policy Division of the Directorate for Education was conducting national Tertiary Education Reviews in 24 countries (OECD, 2008, forthcoming). These also looked at regional engagement and development, but from a national policy rather than a regional/territorial perspective. The co-operation contributed to a continuing dialectic between territorial development and higher education and between the governance and development of regions and the role and management of higher education institutions. The synergy and collaboration between the three areas and lines of activity and the differences in methodology contributed a wealth of experience for mutual benefit. As a result, this publication draws from all of these sources.

The project steering group was comprised of Jannette Cheong (HEFCE), John Goddard (University of Newcastle upon Tyne), Mario Pezzini (OECD/GOV), José-Ginés Mora Ruiz (Technical University of Valencia) and Richard Yelland (OECD/IMHE). There was also a Task Group including Peter Arbo (University of Tromsø), Patrick Dubarle (OECD/GOV), Chris Duke (RMIT), Steve Garlick (University of Sunshine Coast and Swinburne University of Technology), John Goddard (University of Newcastle upon Tyne), Jaana Puukka (OECD/IMHE) and John Rushforth ((University of West England). The project was managed by IMHE.

Participating regions

The project has embraced 14 regions from 11 OECD countries and 1 non-OECD country:

Asia-Pacific:	Busan (Korea) and Sunshine-Fraser Coast (Australia)
Europe:	Canary Islands (Spain), Jutland-Funen (Denmark), the Jyväskylä region (Finland), the North East of England, the Öresund Region (Sweden-Denmark), the Mid-Norwegian region Trøndelag, Twente (the Netherlands), Valencia region (Spain) and Värmland (Sweden)
Latin America:	The State of Nuévo León (Mexico) and northern Paraná (Brazil)
North America:	Atlantic Canada

The regions range from rural to metropolitan and from peripheral to central regions. The higher education institutions include not only research-intensive, but also vocational and professionally oriented institutions. At the national level, the review embraced devolved as well as highly centralised territorial and higher education governance systems.

The project sought to have participating regions with a recognisable regional identity (whether as a formally constituted administrative region or in some other way) and some history of working with higher education institutions. This was not applicable in all of the cases. Similarly, it sought to embrace all higher education institutions operating in the region in order to identify the impact of the entire higher education sector and the division of tasks and key partners. Again, this was not applicable in all of the cases.

The intention was to put the regional agenda in primary position in the project rather than build it around the needs of higher education institutions. This proved challenging for a number of reasons. "The region" is a diverse, fast evolving and problematic notion. It was not always clear what constituted a region; this varies by country and part of the world as well as within single locations. The European Union, for example, has triggered the creation of EU-specific regions for certain purposes that do not correspond to historic and governance regions in some member countries. There is also no standard OECD-wide definition and meaning of region. Forms of governance and devolution vary greatly across and between both unitary and federal systems. In some regions all higher education institutions were not included in the scope of the review. In most cases exclusion was due to the tensions within the binary system of education or the high number of higher education institutions which would have made the project coordination unmanageable. Notwithstanding the above caveats, a range of regional, national and institutional settings has been embraced by the project. (Chapter 4 gives a more in-depth account of the regions participating in the review.)

The regions included in the project were not selected on the basis of a predetermined classification but rather to exhibit a wide variety of economic, social and cultural conditions and to reflect different trajectories of development. This allows for an examination of the relationship between regions and their higher education sector providing empirical underpinning to the issues addressed by the project. The self-evaluation and peer review reports also provide a rich set of examples of structures and processes facilitating regional engagement. As each of the case regions has undergone a review process, the case studies also permit an in-depth examination of the nature and impacts of partnership building.

Developmental focus: seeking to empower the regions

The methodology chosen for the study was a thematic review which was influenced not only by other OECD reviews, but also the development-oriented evaluation projects commissioned by the Finnish Higher Education Evaluation Council. The methodology consisted of the following elements:

- a common framework for regional self-evaluation developed by the OECD task group;
- a Self-Evaluation Report by the regional consortium using OECD guidelines;
- a site visit by international Peer Review Team;
- a Peer Review Report and a response from the region;
- analysis and synthesis by OECD task group drawing upon regional case studies.

There was also a commissioned literature review which looked into the historical trends in higher education working with the regions (Arbo and Benneworth, 2007).

The focus of the study was on collaborative working between higher education institutions and their regional partners. It sought to establish a regional learning and capacity-building process. This made it necessary to engage in participatory learning within and between regions. Thus, the study sought to make an active intervention in the participating regions. As a way to enforce the partnership-building process, the OECD project guidelines requested the participating regions to build up regional steering committees with representation from the key stakeholders in the public, private and not-for-profit sector. The steering committees were charged with the role of driving the review process and partnership building in their regions.

In practice, the regions were at different stages of maturity in capacity building. While for some regions the OECD project was the first opportunity to bring together the higher education institutions and stakeholders to discuss the development of the region, some already had – to a larger or smaller extent – operational mechanisms in place for that purpose. For example, in England the existing higher education regional association in the region, known as Universities for the North East or Unis4NE, took the responsibility for coordinating the exercise. In Busan, Korea, the Regional Innovation System Committee assumed the role of the Regional Steering committee.

The region produced a self-evaluation review, using the project template (Annex A). Self-evaluations often constituted extensive collaborative research, data assemblage and, at best, in-depth analysis. They resulted in two things: new understanding and insights into regional conditions and development issues and problems; and a basis for ongoing dialogue and collaboration which did not exist before. In many regions the self-evaluation phase was a learning and capacity-building event in itself.

The self-evaluation process was followed by a Peer Review. Peer Review visits were carried out between October 2005 and October 2006. The Peer Review Teams of four each comprised a team coordinator from or on behalf of the project planning team in OECD, with three others: two international experts, one the lead evaluator, and a national expert from the country (but not the region) being reviewed. Based on the week long review visit, the Self-Evaluation Report and other information each Peer Review Team prepared a report analysing the situation and providing policy and practice advice to higher education institutions, and the regional and national governments. A number of regional and national seminars were organised to disseminate the outcomes of the reviews.

The notion of *peers* was central to the methodology and to the process of capacity building. The OECD review sought not to be a judgemental inspection ranking against other regions; it was peer review in the sense of being developmental, suggesting other approaches and reflecting experiences and approaches tried elsewhere. Despite the OECD guidelines, there was a recurrent tension between academic-led or practitioner-led and between a qualitative, holistic orientation towards the empirical work and its analysis and a quest for more quantitative measures that would satisfy scrutiny in terms of essentially economic audit.

The project displayed a natural evolution – beginning with centralised control towards a network in which communication and knowledge-making flows in all directions, with the centre serving as one anchor-point and clearing house. This evolution can be traced through the various dissemination meetings and the widening circles of participation that characterised the biography of the project. The wider peer learning developed as regions engaged with the work, their teams met with others, and intra- and inter-regional activities broadened the circle of those involved.

Note

1. Economic weights of higher education institutions are estimated by multiplier values and employment impact using an input/output model. For example, the local impact of Norwegian University of Technology and the two university colleges is about NOK 4.3 billion annually. In the North East of England, the five HEIs contribute to 2.3% of the regional GDP with a total of 14 000 employees and 90 000 students. In central regions, the spending impact is usually lower in relative terms but still significant. University of California's impact on the regional economy was estimated at around USD 15 billion in 2002 (1% of the Californian GDP), with a rate of return of 3.9 for every dollar spent in state funded research.

ISBN 978-92-64-03414-3
Higher Education and Regions:
Globally Competitive, Locally Engaged
© OECD 2007

Chapter 2

Drivers for Regional Engagement

This chapter explores why higher education institutions are becoming more engaged with the cities and regions in which they are located and why such communities are seeking to mobilise higher education to support their economic, social and cultural development. It describes the changes in the territorial development policy and higher education policy which contribute to the stronger focus on the interplay between higher education and their regions. Finally, it provides a conceptual framework for the synthesis of the interests of higher education institutions and regions in the context of globalising knowledge economy.

Higher education institutions (HEIs) are increasingly engaged with the cities and regions in which they are located. At the same time, these communities are seeking to mobilise higher education to support their economic, social and cultural development. The emerging partnerships arise from a growing appreciation of shared interests.

At a basic level this shared interest is principally economic. In the face of declining national public resources for higher education HEIs are seeking:

- local support for their global aspirations in research and student recruitment;
- increased student enrolments from the local population;
- additional income from services provided to local businesses through consultancy and professional training;
- the indirect benefits of a local environment that can attract and retain creative academics and motivated students.

For those agencies charged with city and regional development higher education institutions are:

- major businesses generating tax and other revenues;
- global gateways in terms of marketing and attracting inward investment in the private sector;
- generators of new businesses and sources of advice and expertise for multiple purposes including support for existing businesses;
- enhancers of local human capital through graduate retention and professional updating of the existing workforce and lifelong learning including distance and e-learning;
- providers of content and audience for local cultural programmes.

From a HEI perspective, regional engagement is an outward and visible sign of the third task or public service role of higher education, through which the institution can demonstrate its contribution to civil society. Through such endeavours higher education institutions are able to provide concrete evidence of the value that higher education and research add to public investment in it. From a city and regional perspective, higher education institutions, particularly in highly centralised states, can be key local agencies able to bring together within the territory different national interests in science and technology, industrial performance, education and skills, health, social inclusion and culture.

This chapter seeks to substantiate these high level generalisations by reference to the academic literature review on the regional contribution of higher education institutions commissioned by IMHE (Arbo and Benneworth, 2006). It first examines the drivers for *reaching in* to higher education from within the domain of urban and regional policy. The drivers from within higher education for *reaching out* from higher education institutions to their surrounding cities and regions are then reviewed. Finally, the interests of higher education institutions and regions are brought together in the context of globalising knowledge economy.

Evolving perspectives on regional development and the place of higher education

Traditionally territorial development has been geared towards redistribution of resources to reduce regional disparities. The outcomes of these policies have often been disappointing. Scattered subsidies have become too diluted to sustain economic take-off while more selective redistribution has faced obstacles. Recently, these policies have been overhauled in most countries. The policy focus has shifted from supporting lagging regions and distressed areas, and there is now a stronger focus on unlocking the potential for development with emphasis on improved competitiveness and comparative advantages in the regions. In this context, higher education institutions are playing an increasingly important role as providers of knowledge, facilitators of cluster development and key actors in regional innovation systems.

The discussion adopts a historical perspective to help understand how policy and practice has evolved and how past periods have shaped the current structure of higher education institutions and regional policy.

Reducing regional disparities

The post-World War II regional policy in the OECD countries emphasised the need for intervention by the nation state to reduce disparities between central and peripheral regions. This intervention found justification in economic theories of development based on principles of "circular and cumulative causation" (Myrdal, 1957). These theories refuted neo-classical theories regarding the mobility of factors of production leading, in the long run, to regional convergence. Rather it was argued, that without state intervention, the operation of the free market would result in rich central regions getting richer and poor peripheral regions getting poorer (Kaldor, 1970). Public intervention took the form of financial support for established industries in peripheral regions and the attraction of mobile investment in order to absorb surplus labour. There were also measures to equalise living standards between regions, including standards of primary and secondary education.

Significantly, higher education did not enter into the panoply of regional policy interventions. Many higher education institutions in Europe which had developed to serve traditional industries during the latter part of the 19th and first half of the 20th century were incorporated into national systems of higher education. In this process their local ties were weakened. While there was a diversity of experience and many higher education institutions continued to have a strong regional role, higher education in general was not conceived as an instrument in post-war redistributive regional policy.

In the United States uneven regional development was not a federal responsibility but individual states did support public universities in serving the needs of their territories building on the land grant tradition established in the 19th century. Indeed, state investment in higher education to tackle industrial decline in New England and to attract new Federal investment in areas facing structural adjustment in agriculture in California laid the foundation for subsequent high technology corridors such as Route 128 and Silicon Valley.

In the dominions of the British Commonwealth (Canada and Australia) where a federal structure of government was established, higher education played a key role in the development of the cities which were the gateways to the individual states and laid the foundations for the so-called "sandstone" universities in each of the state capitals of Australia. Regional problems were (and remain) essentially problems of underdeveloped city hinterlands and rural areas. Outside of the so-called "developed world" the priority of nation building around national capitals contributed to rising regional disparities with national universities being one of the magnets for internal migration.

The European post-war consensus around the need for state intervention to reduce core/periphery regional disparities broke down during the 1970s. This was associated with the onset of structural adjustment problems in advanced economies and the rejection of the post-war Keynesian models of economic regulation. These structural adjustment problems had particularly severe impacts on cities, including those in some core regions. The emergence of so-called "rust belts" linked to traditional industries such as coal and steel, heavy engineering and textiles which were now facing competition from newly industrialised countries; and the related decline of mobile investment seeking lower cost sites within industrialised countries, undermined the basis of redistributive regional policy.

Regional innovation policy

In response to the crisis, the emphasis in territorial and industrial policy switched towards indigenous development focussed on small and medium-sized enterprises (SMEs) with a particular emphasis on the role of innovation in raising their competitiveness (Rothwell and Zegveld, 1982; Birch, 1987).

Traditional regional policy had focussed on attracting branch factories in search of lower labour costs to support production of goods reaching the end of their product life cycle. Indigenous development policy in contrast focused on new products and the introduction of new manufacturing processes into SMEs.

This shift of emphasis opened the way for links into the research base in local higher education institutions. It also coincided in the US with the passing of the Bayh-Dole Act in 1980 which empowered universities to commercialise their own intellectual property. During the 1980s a growing body of academic literature underpinned the case for local or "bottom up" public intervention in the supply side of the local environment supporting (or inhibiting) innovation. Studies of the so-called "third Italy" indicated that networks of traded and untraded interdependencies between SMEs could provide a fertile environment for innovation in traditional industries outside established urban agglomerations (Piore and Sabel, 1984; Brusco 1986). Whereas in Italy these networks did not involve higher education institutions, the experience of Silicon Valley in California and Route 128 in New England assumed totemic significance in relation to the possibility of creating new industrial districts or regenerating older districts through strong links with research-intensive universities.

Learning regions and industrial clusters

Moving into the 1990s, the range of supply-side factors that regional policy makers deemed to be influencing economic performance widened. Most significantly education and skills and the tacit knowledge gained through work-based learning became embodied in the concept of the "learning region" (Morgan, 1997; Malmberg and Maskell, 1997). This had resonances with the growing appreciation that innovation is not necessarily a linear process and can involve close interaction between producers and users, interactions which are best conducted face to face. Moreover, the role of students and graduates in "knowledge transfer on legs" and establishing the social relations between researchers and the business in which they work becomes increasingly apparent. (See *e.g.* Audretsch and Feldman, 1996; Kline and Rosenberg, 1986.)

During the 1990s these perspectives began to be formally adopted in public policies to foster the development of "industrial clusters" rooted in particular places. The concept of the industrial cluster recognises that innovation is seldom isolated but systemic with the industrial cluster acting as a reduced scale innovation system. Clusters, in this instance, encompass strategic alliances of higher education institutions, research institutes, knowledge-intensive business services, bridging institutions and customers. Cluster success requires and encourages flows of talented individuals, including students and graduates, and the creation of vibrant and exciting places. Higher education institutions can play a role in the development of clusters through:

● science-based discovery and new business formation;

● direct advice to firms to enhance management capabilities;

● provision of skilled labour;

● consumption of specialist supplies;

● knowledge dissemination to related industries down the supply chain;

● advice on policy and regulation to national and regional agencies.

Within the cluster the higher education institutions assume an entrepreneurial role while firms develop an academic dimension. The emphasis is on a spiral model of interaction where a number of channels feed into the process including research links (the creation of new knowledge), information transfer (selling existing knowledge) and people-based transfer (students and staff) as well as spin-offs. In this model specialised centres and cluster discourse can provide a focus for both higher education institutions and the business community. It involves embedding engagement in the core business processes of both higher education institutions and industry. (See Porter, 1990, 1998, 2003.)

Territorial development policy now: The demands on higher education

Throughout the OECD there is a convergence of innovation and territorial development policy. This is placing new demands on higher education institutions as innovation policy becomes more comprehensive. There is increased emphasis on education and training, employability, the quality and skills of the workforce and lifelong learning. People and human resources are being brought into focus. There is recognition that initiatives to foster innovation and competitiveness need to take account of challenges of urban and regional variations in unemployment, poverty and exclusion in a multi-cultural society. There are also aspirations to establish and foster creative and enterprising places where people and companies want to locate. Thus many towns and cities have been inspired by reflections on the new "creative class" and the global competition for talent which has led to increasing investment on place marketing and the branding of cities as "a nice place to live" (Florida, 2002).

In summary, regional policy which was redefined and narrowed down to technological innovation policy is now in the process of being ever broadened as other fields of policy are given an innovation signature and more agents and levels of government (city, regional, national, international) are drawn into the process of building innovative capabilities. From a rather narrow focus on high technology and manufacturing industry and the private sector, attention has been widened to include social and organisational innovations and business, consumer and public services (Arbo and Benneworth, 2006).

This broadening of regional policy has wide-ranging implications for the expectations placed on higher education institutions by cities and regions. They are now expected to participate in public and private partnerships and contribute to balanced region building. Whereas previously attention was focussed on higher education institutions as a source of high technology innovations and new knowledge-based industries, these are now beginning to be regarded in a broader perspective, encompassing the whole social fabric of which higher education institutions are part. For example, the new emphasis on social innovation, tourism, the creative industries and welfare widens the academic domain from science and technology and medical faculties to the arts, humanities and social sciences.

Higher education institutions stand out as potentially important partners because they link up multiple realms of society and strands of activity. More and more aspects of the academic enterprise are thus being perceived as significant to the regeneration and transformation of cities and regions.

Evolving perspectives on higher education and the role of regions

The emergence of the Modern University

The longevity of universities as key institutions in the evolution of civil society is linked to their adaptability to changing circumstances, whilst maintaining key elements of continuity (such as the global connections which characterised the medieval foundations). The emergence of the Humboldtian university in 19th century Prussia was linked to the professionalisation of science, the requirements for specialised infrastructure to support it **and** to underpin "at a distance" the development of the state. (Wittrock, 1993; McClelland, 1998.)

The principle of "at a distance" is important because in many respects the research university that evolved in Europe during the 19th century can be described as a "denial of place" (Blender, 1998). This is because the ideal of scientific enquiry embodied in the modern university is to strive for universalism. Scientific claims to truth were deemed to be irrespective of time and place and the university had to have a mission that transcended its actual location. Indeed the notion of the university as a detached site for critical enquiry, exchange of ideas and advancement of knowledge for its own sake has been of vital importance to the creditability and legitimacy of the institution.

The nationalisation of science and education during the 20th century further enhanced the detachment of universities from places (see Crawford *et al.*, 1993). Because of their importance to nation building, universities were no longer expected to rely on the patronage of churches, town councils and local elites. They now received their core funding from national governments and in return trained the cadres for the civil service and national corporations and the professions such as law, medicine, engineering and architecture. They were to contribute to new national identities and the cultural spirit which underpinned the nation-building process. All of this was based on a compact whereby the university rendered services to the state in return for a degree of institutional autonomy in terms of internal governance. (Crawford *et al.*, 1993; Clark, 1998.)

Part of the American higher education system, however, developed in a different direction. Land Grant universities, which in the first instance promoted agricultural development, were regionally embedded "people's universities" based upon widening access to education and service to the community.[1]

Mass higher education

The second part of the 20th century witnessed a massive expansion of public investment both in research and development and higher education. This has had a profound impact on the universities that emerged in the previous century and their engagement with regions. The expansion of higher education typically took place outside the established universities which were regarded as too inflexible to meet the demands for new skills emerging in the workplace and from communities where they were not present. Thus we now speak of higher education institutions not just universities. The higher education map of most countries has been coloured in incrementally with a diverse set of institutions. Many of the new institutions have been built on previous foundations, typically with limited tradition of research (such as teaching and nurse education colleges). And many of them have a specifically regional mission.

In some countries this geographical dispersal of higher education has formed part of a conscious policy seeking to preserve the spatial distribution of the population and to achieve balanced regional development by addressing regional disparities. It has included also the objective to improve regional access to higher education. This has translated into policies to establish higher education institutions in various regions, *e.g.* in Norway, Sweden, Finland, Japan and Mexico. This objective has also led to the emergence of non-public education institutions in Poland since 1990s (OECD, 2008, forthcoming). However, in many countries dispersal of higher education has followed a simple logic of higher education expansion modified by political lobbying. This is not just a top-down phenomenon. Towns and cities have lobbied for "their" university.

The consequence is that many OECD countries have a highly diversified system of higher education with complex mixes of universities, polytechnics, regional colleges and vocational training institutions. The regional role of institutions has sometimes served to differentiate among the various types of institutions. In Finland and Portugal, for example, universities are considered to have a stronger national and international role while polytechnics are assumed to focus on their regional role (OECD, 2008, forthcoming). In Switzerland, Universities of Applied Sciences have been designated the regional role (Box 2.1).

The distribution of institutions is not necessarily structured to meet the challenge of balanced regional development in a highly competitive global economy. So while disadvantaged regions may possess locally orientated higher education institutions such as polytechnics in Finland, community colleges in Canada or universities for applied sciences in the Netherlands, these are often more geared towards upgrading the existing industry and less equipped to build new knowledge-based economy.

Science, technology and research

The expansion of public investment in science and technology inside and outside of higher education institutions has likewise had an impact on the issue of regional engagement. This expansion has largely been driven by ministries of science and technology and in many cases has taken place in public research laboratories outside higher education, characteristically in the hinterlands of capital cities. At the same time higher education institutions

---

Box 2.1. Universities of Applied Sciences in Switzerland

In Switzerland the re-organisation and merging of various community colleges has led to the creation of "Hautes Ecoles Spécialisées" (HES; Universities of Applied Sciences). Seven of these institutions have been created (one per "grandes regions"). Recently, an additional private HES has been created covering most of the German speaking part of Switzerland. Universities of Applied Sciences are designed to fill the gap between universities and tertiary type B/upper secondary schools, and between research and marketable technologies. The strategy aims to link training with local needs and helping the development of skill-based clusters. The policy aims to upgrade the educational offer and to focus on the up-skilling to support industry. Through HES, Switzerland aims to increase customer orientation of research and training and specialisation of institutions, two goals which have been difficult to achieve in traditional universities even with federal incentives.

---

were able to compete for research funding from research councils operating at arms length from government. In these councils the academic community had a major influence via peer review in a way that preserved the autonomy of their institutions and their distance from the state. This peer review process has often reinforced the position of the longest established institutions, typically in core cities, thereby reinforcing regional disparities.

From science to innovation policy

During the 1990s this model for the re-organisation of public research began to break down as governments began to demand a more immediate economic return for investment in the science base. A key challenge has been to remove barriers and bottlenecks between scientific research and industrial innovation. The institutional division of labour which implied that research was carried out in isolation from the context of application was perceived as a problem in the context when science policy was morphing into innovation policy. In this process HEIs as institutions, as well as the individual academics who work within them, have been expected to become more active players in the so-called "triple helix" of government, business and higher education institution relations (Etzkowitz and Leydesdorff, 1997).

Industrial policy and science and technology policy have thus been converging towards a common innovation policy which in some countries explicitly or implicitly embodies a strong territorial dimension. Research-intensive universities have been surrounded by science parks and a host of special purpose organisations established to support close co-operation with industry. In some instances these have served to buffer the institution from external pressures and instead of facilitating links they have operated as filters or merely served as display windows towards the universities' political environment. But increasingly universities are expected to take the lead and to rearrange the structures so that entrepreneurship and technology transfer activities form part of the academic heartland of research and teaching. Higher education institutions are now expected to contribute to economic development in four ways:

- creating new sectors and the spinning out businesses on the back of research;
- attracting to and retaining global businesses in the region through the availability of quality research links and the supply of well trained graduates;
- assisting with the diversification of established businesses in their production of new products and services;
- upgrading existing mature industry through assistance with incremental product/service and the improvement in industrial/business processes (Goldstein and Luger, 1993; Lester, 2005).

These changes in higher education are not proceeding without a struggle between different traditions and rationales regarding the purposes of higher education or at an equal pace in all types of institutions. Collaboration with industry still mainly takes place with individual academics while most research intensive universities are concerned with scientific eminence and the related academic prestige that this brings.

Moving beyond science-driven model

The science-driven model overlooks many features of regional development to which higher education institutions directly and indirectly contribute. It neglects the contribution of broad-based teaching and learning to the enhancement of regional human capital. Private and public services provide most regional jobs. The majority of graduates take up employment in financial, legal and other professional services or businesses. Some of such regionally based businesses will be trading nationally and internationally and use the skills of graduates to develop new "products", some of which will also be provided to regional high-technology-based businesses. These businesses also require non-scientific graduates, for example with a business school background to assist in activities such as marketing. Another important non-manufacturing sector recruiting graduates is the cultural industries and tourism which can serve to attract and retain creative people within the region, including those working in high technology businesses and higher education institutions themselves. And higher education institutions are creators of, and venues for, cultural and social activity.

Higher education institutions can make a considerable contribution to public services, particularly health and education, not least as regions with wide internal social disparities are less likely to be attractive to leading-edge investors in the global knowledge economy. Finally, as environmental sustainability moves up the political agenda it is becoming increasingly apparent that higher education institutions could have a key role to play through research, teaching in public education in building sustainable communities. All of these latter roles highlight the public service responsibility of higher education institutions as distinct from the more private focus of the science driven model.

Synthesis: higher educations institutions tying down the global in the local

The conceptual framework underpinning the OECD study adopted a closed model of the interface between region and higher education institution (Figure 2.1).

The left side of the diagram refers to the three conventionally identified roles of higher education institutions (teaching, research and services to the

Figure 2.1. **Closed model of HEI/region interface**

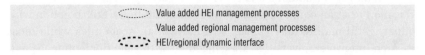

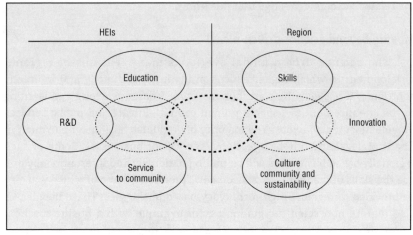

Source: adapted from Goddard and Chatterton, 2003.

community). The right side summarises the three key dimensions to regional development, namely innovation, skills and cultural and community cohesion including environmental sustainability. Just as successful regional development requires drawing together these strands so the higher education institutions' effective engagement with the region involves bringing together teaching, research and science in a coherent manner and establishing effective mechanisms for bridging the boundary between the higher education institution and the region.

If the lens is widened to the national level, it becomes apparent that many of the drivers within higher education arise due to the different priorities seen within national government. In many countries ministries of education remain as custodians of the traditional logic of higher education while ministries of science and technology espouse the logic of knowledge exploitation for business benefit and labour market ministries focus on the role of higher education in skills enhancement. Additional national drivers come from health and cultural ministries and those parts of central government with oversight of local government and territorial development (Figure 2.2).

A final influence on relationships between a higher education institution and its region is the presence of global competition. The forces of globalisation and information and communications technologies are contributing to "the

Figure 2.2. **National policies impacting on HEI/regional relations**

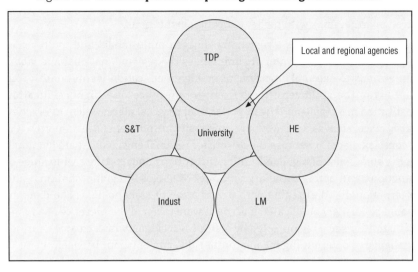

National policies impacting on university/regional relations

Key: S&T   Science and Technology
      TDP   Territorial Development
      HE   Higher Education
      LM   Labour Market
      Indust Industry Policy

Source: Goddard, 2005.

death of distance". In principle, any place with an internet connection can participate in a knowledge-based global economy (Friedman, 2005). However, innovation continues to cluster in specific regions and the tendency for innovation to coalesce is becoming more pronounced (Florida, 2005; Asheim and Gertler, 2005). Increasingly, higher education institutions need to market their education and research services across the globe and provide the supporting infrastructure that will attract and retain the best researchers, teachers and academic leaders. At the same time, regions also need to attract knowledge-based inward investment, support local companies seeking to operate on the global stage and retain within, and attract to the community the most creative people.

So just as higher education can serve the region better when at least part of the higher education institutions are globally engaged, so also higher education institutions need open regions which welcome outsiders. The rapidly increasing investment in China, India and elsewhere in terms of higher education, scientific infrastructure, skills and systems which aim to translate science into business advantage pose pressing challenges both to higher education institutions and regions across the OECD. These challenges involve both opportunities and threats and reinforce the need for regions to build strong partnerships with higher education institutions.

Figure 2.3 describes a regionally engaged multi-modal and multi-scalar higher education institution. It summarises the regional, national and global dimensions to external engagement by higher education institutions. It also highlights the spillover effects from the presence of a higher education institution in a region and the importance of physical places where interaction takes place, such as a science park, university hospital or cultural quarter. It is a complex diagram because the drivers for regional engagement are heralding in the emergence of higher education institutions undertaking a wide range of functions and acting on a large number of stages – regional, national and international and engaging with a vast array of stakeholders. The diagram would be further complicated if account were taken of the presence of a range of institutions in a region, often by historical accident, which creates a further challenge of determining the appropriate division of labour between them.

Figure 2.3. **Regionally engaged multi-modal and multi-scalar HEI**

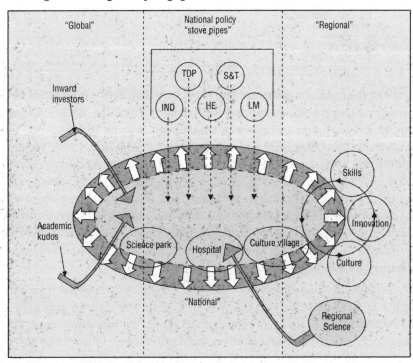

Source: Arbo and Benneworth, 2007.

Figure 2.3 is a stylised picture and implies no barriers to the effective operation of a higher education and regional development system. In practice there are many obstacles that need to be overcome. These will be considered in the next chapter.

Note

1. The granting of land to establish a Land Grant university in every state was achieved through Morill (Land Grant) Act 1862.

ISBN 978-92-64-03414-3
Higher Education and Regions:
Globally Competitive, Locally Engaged
© OECD 2007

Chapter 3

Barriers to Regional Engagement of Higher Education

This chapter examines the extent to which the external influences at the global, national and regional levels can inhibit regional engagement of higher education institutions and suggests adjustments to current policy and practice which could help to overcome these barriers. Barriers to regional engagement are addressed in a thematic manner starting with the sometimes conflicting effects of national higher education, science and technology and labour market policies. Particular attention is paid to how regional engagement is funded. The capacity of local and regional agents to engage with higher education institutions and the influence of regional governance and leadership is considered next. Finally, the chapter closes with reference to leadership at the level of the individual higher education institution.

Higher education, science and technology and labour market policy

The geography of higher education policy

In most OECD countries higher education policy does not include an explicit regional dimension. Ministries of Education characteristically act as champions of the role of higher education and research in meeting national aspirations in terms of scientific excellence and advanced education of high quality for its own sake. One of the most notable exceptions is Korea where the New University for Regional Innovation (NURI) project has been funded by the central government to strengthen the capability of higher education institutions outside Seoul metropolitan area. (See Box 3.1.)

Box 3.1. **The New University for Regional Innovation (NURI) in Korea**

The New University for Regional Innovation (NURI) project has been funded by the central government to enhance regional innovation and to ensure balanced national development outside the Seoul metropolitan area. The Ministry of Education and Human Resource Development is providing USD 13 billion in grants to selected higher education institutions during the 5-year period (2004-2008). The NURI project has 109 participating higher education institutions which are implementing more than 130 programmes aligned to the characteristics of the regional economy. As part of the NURI project Regional Innovation Systems have been established across the country.

The objectives of the NURI project is to help local higher education institutions:

- to attract and retain talent in the regions;
- to improve educational conditions and develop workforce education and development programmes to help students to acquire occupational skills that are critical for job security;
- to build productive partnership with local authorities, research institutions, and business and industry and to provide skilled workers and advanced technologies to the industrial clusters in the regions;
- to play a leadership role in developing and maintaining effective regional innovation systems (RIS).

The seemingly more mundane task of applied research and development and meeting skill needs in the local labour market may be left to lower tiers in the education system such as tertiary/community colleges. In some countries the boundaries between the levels of higher education have become blurred. Examples include the designation of polytechnics in the United Kingdom as universities, the designation of selected colleges in the Netherlands as universities of professional education (now universities of applied sciences) and the current pressure in Finland to re-label polytechnics as "universities of applied science".

Characteristically the newer institutions do not have a well established tradition in research or the infrastructure to support it and have to work hard with limited resources to build a national let alone an international profile which has traditionally been associated with university status.

An important point to note in relation to regional engagement is that longer established higher education institutions have developed and grown in locations that broadly follow the national settlement hierarchy. These locations are quintessentially larger cities with the most prestigious institutions sited in or around the capital city. In contrast the newer institutions, often with a specific remit to serve particular territories, tend to be more geographically dispersed.[1]

These are gross generalisations about very fluid national systems of higher education and many OECD countries have a complex mix of "elite" science universities, teaching based institutions and universities or polytechnics focusing on particular disciplines, *e.g.* in science and technology. As noted earlier, there has been continuous political pressure in most OECD countries to fill in the map of higher education by the creation of new higher education institutions in areas not previously "served" locally by higher education.[2] However, these policies have generally been pursued in parallel with concentration of research resources in elite institutions in the main cities. While growing the system remains high on the agenda in countries like Mexico and Brazil, in many developed countries the tide has turned due to demographic changes and/or pursuit of critical mass: there are now pressures to reduce the number of higher education institutions through mergers and other types of enhanced co-operation between institutions (*e.g.* Denmark, Finland, Korea).

In addition, social inclusion in higher education is a variable priority across the OECD countries but has emerged as a significant issue in some countries. There is variability of participation in different geographic areas (HEFCE, 2006. See also Chapter 5).

To what extent has the process of rolling out of higher education across national territories been part of conscious national policies to use higher

47

education as an instrument in regional development? The answer depends on the definition of development and the extent to which this has been a task laid upon higher education institutions by their funders in central government. It is widely accepted that the challenge of raising competitiveness via research led innovation is now at the heart of regional policy. However, it is clear that supporting excellent research in all regions has not been an objective of higher education policy. Even when engagement with business and the community has been recognised and laid upon higher education institutions as a "duty" as in all the Nordic countries, it has been very much a "third task", not explicitly linked to the core functions of research and teaching. Nor, in most instances, is this task specifically funded or linked to regional development.

Science and technology policy

There are growing pressures within national research policies to link public investment in this area to maximise its economic impact. Consequently, there is an increasing convergence between research policy and other policies designed to support business innovation.

Of the countries participating in the current OECD study, Finland probably has the most sophisticated national innovation policy composed of three pillars of business, universities and government. Even so, the Finnish national innovation system, overseen by the Ministries of Industry and Education, does not have a regional dimension. It has been left to the Ministry of the Interior with infinitely smaller resources to intervene in this domain. It has done this through the establishment of a regional network of Centres of Expertise characteristically linked to science parks and universities and polytechnics in different parts of the country (OECD, 2005a). (See also Box 5.2 in Chapter 5.)

Notwithstanding the growing recognition of the importance of organisational and social barriers to innovation most top-down science and innovation policies continue to have a high-technology and manufacturing industry focus and neglect the contribution of the arts, humanities and social sciences to new ways of working and servicing the creative industries. These dimensions arise through the interaction between producers and users of research which most readily take place at a regional level. Recent decades have witnessed the birth of the centres of expertise which have sprung up throughout the world with the focus on the same fashionable high-technology fields such as biotechnology, nanotechnology and ICT. It is, however, becoming apparent that much of innovation is neither science-based nor radical, but incremental in nature and taking place in SMEs.

National innovation policy driven by ministries of science and technology also do not pay regard to the role of teaching and learning in knowledge transfer "on legs" from the research base. Work-based learning schemes which usually involve regional links between employers and higher education institutions are designed to enhance graduate employability and not as specific tools to improve regional business competitiveness. A notable exception in this regard is the UK's Knowledge Transfer Partnership scheme under which postgraduates undertake projects in companies which are local. (See Chapter 6.)

Labour market policies

Most OECD countries have active national labour market policies by the ministries of labour or their equivalent. The focus of these policies is chiefly on intermediate and lower level skills and the unemployed, not those associated with higher education. At this level it is assumed that the market (*i.e.* demands from students and employers) will work effectively without intervention. National employer-led associations for particular professions (*e.g.* lawyers, architects, civil engineers) often play a key role in regulating supply and maintaining quality. Only in areas where the state remains a major provider of public services, most notably health, does the government undertake a planning role. While the market for intermediate and lower level skills may be **local** and therefore require a strong spatial dimension, it is assumed that the market for high level skills is national and international. There is therefore not a case for intervention at the intermediate or **regional** level.

For these reasons there appears to be little engagement by research-intensive universities in the development of human capital at the regional level, particularly as it relates to the skills required by knowledge-intensive businesses growing on the back of links with the research base. In contrast, newer and vocationally oriented institutions are usually committed to upgrading skills in the established industrial base.

Health policy

Outside of the core areas of higher education, innovation and labour market policy, a number of other domains of government bear on the capacity and responsibility of higher education institutions to engage in regional development. The previous chapter noted how the provenance of regional innovation policy was widening to embrace a range of contingent factors relating to the health and well being of local populations, cultural vitality and environmental sustainability. Each of these areas is characteristically the responsibility of separate departments of national government; these departments have a varying commitment to a regional dimension to their policies and to engagement with higher education regionally as well as nationally.

The area where higher education has been most directly interwoven with national policy and where there is a strong regional dimension is health. University hospitals linked to medical schools play a key role in health research and development and contribute to the training of doctors and nurses as well as the health of the local population. Indeed, university medical schools and hospitals best epitomise all the facets of the multi-scalar and multi-modal higher education institution outlined in the last chapter (Figure 2.3). As the scientific base underpinning medicine advances and new technologies based on these advances are developed in the private sector major consequences for the organisation and delivery of health case can arise. As the relationship between government, higher education institutions and the private sector in the health domain has developed over the last fifty years, a strong territorial dimension has emerged. It is therefore not surprising that university medical schools and hospitals now find themselves at the heart of the higher education/regional engagement agenda. Significantly this agenda does not only embrace the promotion of biotechnology and business but also business process re-engineering necessary to embed new technologies in health service delivery. Medical Science is also an area where the region can quite literally be the "laboratory" (Chapter 7.)

Notwithstanding its success story, health policy is seldom viewed as part of the higher education/regional development nexus. This is particularly worrying in the light of policy changes in the health domain being introduced by OECD countries in response to the need to control the spiralling demands on the public purse arising in the health domain from technological advance and an ageing population. For example, the consequences of replacing untraded dependencies between medical schools and university hospitals – a model which is prevalent in much of Europe – by market mechanisms could undermine the symbiotic relationship which underpins many successful regional partnerships. (See *e.g.* Smith and Whitchurch, 2002.)

Cultural policy

The cultural domain is another area where the role of higher education institutions in contributing to city and regional development is not widely acknowledged in national policy. Higher education institutions are often owners of or custodians of cultural assets displayed in their own museums and galleries. Their music, arts and drama departments directly and indirectly contribute to the vibrancy of their cities through performance and related activities. In some counties support for the arts and heritage does have a regional dimension which embraces higher education, but this is an exception rather than a general rule. Increasingly higher education institutions are finding it difficult to support such activities out of their core teaching and research budgets and are seeking support from regional sources to maintain expensive facilities and activities (OECD, 2001b). At the same time, the fast growth of the creative industries is shifting the focus to new enterprise formation by graduates of creative arts, design and media (see Chapter 7).

Environmental policy

The last area where national policy has impacts on regional engagement by higher education institutions is the area of environmental sustainability. Unlike medicine and the arts, policy in this area is very new. Yet there is a realisation that the research base of higher education, especially when linked to the region as a laboratory, can play an important role in the development of energy technologies and their implementation. Through their education programmes and alumni higher education institutions can also play a key role in opinion forming on sustainability issues.

As a major land user and trip generator in their local communities, higher education institutions can contribute to more sustainable ways of working. However, there is only limited evidence that this regional contribution is widely understood in national ministries responsible for sustainability policy and practice or within the higher education institutions themselves. (See Chapter 7.)

Funding regional engagement

OECD *Thematic Review of Tertiary Education* (2008, forthcoming) suggests that there are two guiding principles to allocation of higher education funding: first, designing the funding approach to meet the policy goals and, second, allocating public funds in relations to the relevance to society.

Attitudes of higher education institutions towards regional engagement are sensitive to the way they are funded. In centralised systems, core funding of public higher education institutions is generally based on criteria that do not reward regional engagement. In the absence of incentives, higher education institutions, particularly research-intensive universities are more inclined to prioritise their national and international role. While emphasis on regional engagement seems more likely when the funding of higher education is regionalised or responsibilities transferred to regional government with related taxation power, the decentralisation of higher education funding is by no means a guarantee that higher education institutions will move towards this direction if this activity is not otherwise incentivised and outcomes monitored. In Spain, the decentralisation first took place in the "old" regions including Catalonia and the Basque country but has been extended to all regions where higher education is now taking steps to engage in regional R&D and services to business community. In Germany, financial and administrative responsibility for higher education rests with the 16 Länder rather than the federal government but there are few requirements for the Länder to engage with the region.

Regional engagement of higher education institutions is better grounded when factors beyond funding are acting jointly. In the United States, the localised nature of the funding base derived from sources such as state taxation, tuition fees and regional alumni have been reinforced by the land grant tradition and the existence of many state universities. As a result, many institutions are strongly integrated in the community economy. Their missions emphasise not only the intellectual or academic dimension, but also the commitment of the institution to the state or region.

Research funding

All of the areas of national policy that have been reviewed and that encompass higher education, *i.e.* science and technology, labour markets, health, culture and the environment have public funding streams associated with them. How can these resources be mobilised to support regional engagement by higher education institutions?

In the case of support for research in higher education institutions, funding regimes are often geographically neutral or work against goals of balanced regional development. In unitary countries with a centralised higher education system the capital city and some big metropolitan areas generally have the largest universities and a considerable share of HEI research. Many countries are concentrating their research capacity to create world-class centres of excellence. For example in the United Kingdom the system for determining research funding on the basis of peer review of academic research output results in over one-third of the resources for research in higher education institutions being allocated to four institutions in London and the South East of England. Indeed, the UK government research policy to fund the best wherever it occurs, is part of the government's policy to maintain a leading position in the global league table of universities – geographical concentration is simply an incidental consequence of this policy. While this concentration of funds applies to many unitary countries in Europe, there are also exceptions. In countries like Sweden and the Netherlands a more balanced distribution of university research funding has been reached. In Spain, decentralisation has widened the distribution of resources but the dominance of the capital region remains.

Allocation systems for research that favour central regions may impose a particular limitation on less advanced regions. In many countries smaller/ newer higher education institutions in less developed regions simply lack the infrastructure to contribute to the development of a new economic base or renew old and declining ones. In peripheral regions while higher education institutions are well placed to shape the regional agenda in the absence of other research institutions (public laboratories, business with strong R&D departments), the low absorption capacity of local and regional firms further limits the development of research for local needs.

Higher education institutions receive also income from other sources such as business and communities. In the last decade, the decrease or slow increase in public R&D funding has encouraged higher education institutions to look to external sources to maintain or expand activities. The proportion of higher education R&D financed by industry has grown in every G7 country over the period 1981 and 2001 (OECD, 2003a). A certain trade-off has taken place between external and internal funding. It is nevertheless often difficult to expand the regional share of external funding. Usually industry contracts involve larger firms which operate on a national basis. Such relations are often developed with higher education institutions with a particular specialisation, regardless of regions (Goddard *et al.*, 1994). This seems the case in the United States where the share of university research funded by industry has grown in the most entrepreneurial universities exceeding the growth rate of the university total budget for research and development, but where the extent to which research is contracted by regional firms is less important (with some exceptions such as Pennstate university).

The nature of project funding also places constraints on greater engagement. In Finland where external funding of universities witnessed a rapid growth in the 1990s, the bodies providing funds – ministries, communities, private business, foundations and international organisations such as the European Union – only financed direct project costs *i.e.* marginal cost. When core funding is linked to teaching via graduate output numbers there is not enough leeway to invest in translational research facilities and knowledge transfer supporting regional and national innovation systems. In some instances, this gap has been partially filled by municipalities and city councils (OECD, 2005a).

There are a number of consequences that flow from the above. First, there is a simple direct impact on the local economy of large research-intensive universities competing successfully on the global stage for research contracts, well-paid staff and well-qualified students regardless of the extent of its dynamic engagement with local businesses and the community. Second, if the role of science-driven innovation in economic development particularly through the creation and attraction of new businesses is accepted, then those regions which lack a research intensive university would be at a disadvantage. Smaller higher education institutions without a substantial research capacity will not be able to develop a new economic base for their regions. Nevertheless, science-driven innovation is not the only route to economic development. Alternative endogenous development models based on the upgrading of the existing core competencies may be more appropriate for smaller regions and their higher education institutions.

A further characteristic of the financing of research is that it is generally underfunded. Full economic costing of research to enable the institution to reinvest in the research infrastructure is seldom undertaken. This is particularly problematic in terms of the limited ability of institutions to create financial headroom to invest in capacity to translate research into goods and services that are ready to be marketed to investors.

Funding for teaching

OECD Thematic Review of Tertiary Education (2008, forthcoming) suggests that the basis for allocating core funding to the institutions, in particular to education, should, to some extent, be output oriented with that the performance-based funding mechanisms should be carefully implemented. The experience from a number of countries, e.g. Denmark, The Netherlands, Norway, and Sweden, suggests that tying funding to results can facilitate enhancement of institutional performance. Indicators used in performance-based funding system should reflect public policy objectives and relate to aspects to be enhanced in institutions. In practice, however, funding for teaching in most countries relates to agreed numbers of students or graduates, usually in specified discipline areas linked to student demand and/ or national need (e.g. IT and Medicine). Limited regard is paid to where graduates are finally employed geographically.[3]

In terms of student recruitment, federal funding is available for example in the United States to recruit able students from disadvantaged backgrounds. In the United Kingdom, there is national encouragement for recruitment of students from disadvantaged backgrounds which may have an implicit local dimension to it (AimHigher[4]). This is, however, an incidental consequence of aspirations to raise participation in higher education in recognition of the fact that students from disadvantaged backgrounds often need greater academic support, since the school system has not prepared them as well as others. Australia and China have recently added a regional dimension to student recruitment policies. In Australia, allocations to institutions under Higher Education Equity Support Program (ESP, launched in 2005) are driven by enrolments, retention and success of students from low socio-economic status, with a weighting to the students from rural and isolated backgrounds. In China, a specific initiative (Decision on Deepening the Reform of Minority Education and Speeding-up Its Development) was launched in 2002. It gives incentives to Chinese institutions to provide special conditions for the access of ethnical minorities. Graduates who have entered higher education through the special arrangements are required to return to their areas of origin for entering the labour market. See OECD Thematic Review of Tertiary Education (OECD, 2008, forthcoming).

In general, however, there is limited evidence that recruitment incentives targeted at disadvantaged groups form part of national support for regional human capital development strategies which enable local students to progress into higher education and then into local employment. In some countries barriers to progression between further and higher education arise from the lack of transferability of pre-entry qualifications and different funding and regulatory regimes under which the two levels operate.

Funding for third task

Many countries have tried to reinforce the higher education apparatus in relation to firms and regional economies as well as their willingness to engage in the region. Some have embarked on large regional projects associating a wide spectrum of stakeholders to lay the foundations of regional innovation systems such as the NURI project in Korea (Box 3.1) or the Regional Growth Programme VINNVÄXT in Sweden. However, in most cases, they have developed temporary incentives under the form of grants, call for projects or joint programmes to facilitate collaborative research at regional level but seldom through fiscal advantages. The third task is characteristically not directly funded by national governments and funds for regional engagement remain underdeveloped.

In the United Kingdom where the regional dimension of higher education is among the most accentuated within unitary countries, the Higher Education Innovation Fund (HEIF) and its predecessor, Higher Education Reachout to Business and the Community (HEROBAC)[5] which is supported by the Higher Education Funding Council in England (HEFCE) finances a number of business-friendly schemes for universities but it does not seem to provide more than some percents of the total resources of higher education institutions. HEIF is not explicitly a regional fund even though many of the initiatives supported under it are regional in character. Like funding for teaching, HEIF now has a formulaic component based on past performance. This inevitably rewards the already successful institutions and there is no attempt to weight the fund according to regional needs. In other words higher education institutions facing more adverse innovative environments receive no more than institutions in more dynamic regions.

National higher education and innovation policies have generally not provided the necessary resources to underpin regional engagement by higher education institutions. In this situation it is hardly surprising that higher education institutions in parts of the European Union have seized the opportunity provided by European Structural Funds to initiate a host of projects to support their contribution to regional development. The Self-Evaluation Reports of the 14 regions in the current OECD study document numerous EU-funded projects to support knowledge transfer and skills development in less favoured regions. However, few of these projects have been embedded into mainstream research and teaching programmes, and are in danger of foundering as these funds wind down.[6]

Measuring outcomes of the third task and regional engagement

Mainstreaming funding for third strand activities is not without its problems. While the output from investment in research can be measured in terms of publications and from teaching in terms of numbers of students graduating, the appropriate metrics in the regional domain are far from clear. Many countries, for example the Netherlands, Australia and the Nordic countries are in the process of identifying adequate indicators to underpin funding allocation. This has proved a challenging task.[7]

A problem with most indicators is that they are essentially retrospective rewarding past performance rather than development work that may lead to future income or services in the public interest and the outputs of which are not reflected in the bottom line of university accounts. Indeed, the benefits of the regional public service role of higher education institutions are likely to accrue in the performance indicators of explicitly regional public agencies such as local authorities, where they take the form of measures such as job generation. This is not a benchmark against which higher education institutions would expect to be judged.

Outside of higher education, publicly funded development agencies have been required to adopt stricter accountability regimes. For example, the Atlantic Innovation Fund administered on behalf of the Federal Government of Canada by its Atlantic Canada Opportunities Agency (ACOA) has developed a "Results-based Management Accountability Framework" to assess the regional impact of its assistance with collaborative research projects between business and higher education institution. (See Chapter 5, Box 5.7.)

Regional structures and governance

Higher education and territory

Although many regions across the OECD area are looking to business and higher education institutions to contribute to their economic, social, cultural and environmental development, the capacity of the regions to "reach into" higher education is often constrained by a wide range of factors. At the most general level, the public governance of territory operates within closed boundaries. Local and regional governments are responsible for administratively defined areas and these are usually linked to unambiguous political mandates. By contrast research-intensive universities cannot have a mandatory geographical sphere of influence; indeed such institutions operate at the local, regional, national and international scales. Some vocationally oriented higher education institutions have a specific regional mandate but it is increasingly less likely to be enforced by national, regional and local governments as the institutions compete for students and contracts wherever these can be obtained. So the delimitation of its "region" is a challenge for many higher educations institutions.

Local government

OECD *Thematic Review of Tertiary Education* (2008, forthcoming) indicates that decentralisation policies can promote the collaboration between higher education institutions and regions. In some counties, devolution of powers in higher education has been carried out so that regional governments can actively contribute to the establishment of higher education institutions and better respond to the needs of the local community. In Japan, for example, this trend was strengthened by the parliamentary resolution on decentralisation in 1993. Some countries have set up coordination bodies to manage higher education planning at the regional level, *e.g.* In Mexico the State Commissions for Higher Education Planning (COEPES) are playing this role.

However, the evidence from the current OECD study on the implications of different national territorial governance systems in terms of the capacity of the higher education institutions to engage for their regions is not clear and requires further investigation.

In some countries, municipalities pool resources across several units and/or establish joint development agencies that have a capacity to work with the higher education institutions in the combined area. At the next level of aggregation (or disaggregation of the national governance system) some countries have regional authorities with a specific mandate to support higher education in their region. This is the case in the Spanish autonomous regions, the Provinces of Canada, and the States of Australia.

In highly centralised countries like the UK the national government has devolved powers to the countries of Scotland and Wales including some aspects of higher education. Within England, regional development agencies in each of the 9 regions have been established by the central government. These agencies have some autonomy and are increasingly seeking to mobilise higher education in support of economic development even though it remains a central function.

In many countries local government is fragmented and has limited powers to engage in economic development let alone to support higher education. Rolling programmes of reform are, however, underway, notably in the Nordic countries with strong local government traditions where individual municipalities are being merged. In other circumstances local authorities are coming together to support special purpose economic development organisations from the bottom-up which are beginning to work with local higher education institutions.

In attempting to engage with some level of government between the national and local and even when there is a specific regional administrative structure in place, higher education institutions often face challenges of intra-regional competition for their attention. Relating to the specific municipality in which they are located is one thing – serving a multitude of locations across the broader region with several centres of population is another. Multi-campus solutions raise questions of dilution of resource and partnerships between several higher education institutions across a region can be very demanding in terms of senior management time and energy as well as staff and student mobility.

The private sector

The third stakeholder with an interest in mobilising higher education in support of regional development is the private sector. Identifying who speaks for the private sector in relation to what higher education has to offer can be challenging, especially in regions without a strong private sector R&D base. In strong and dynamic regions there are often well developed private sector networks that are plugged into higher education and articulated through Chambers of Commerce. But in weaker regions the small and medium-sized enterprise (SME) sector is often inchoate and there are not well developed industrial clusters. In such regions branches of national and international companies can lack the autonomy to engage with higher education for the development of new products and services and provide placements for students and jobs for graduates. In addition, higher education institutions and firms, particularly SMEs, experience significant gaps in their collaborative relations (see Chapter 5).

In summary, the environment for higher education to engage in regional development across the OECD countries is highly variable. Where the governance and industrial structure is poorly developed and where there is no strong regional leadership, it is often necessary for higher education institutions to not simply respond to regional needs but to set the development agenda. Whether the higher education institutions are able to do this depends on their own governance, leadership and management.

Governance, leadership and management of higher education

Transversal, cross-cutting mechanisms

Regional engagement is a challenge for higher education institutions, particularly for longer established institutions organised around academic disciplines and along a supply-driven agenda. The framework set out in Chapter 2 highlights the transversal mechanisms for managing teaching and research and their integration with one another. Most higher education institutions recognise the importance of teaching quality and research excellence and link these qualities to the cross-cutting roles of vice rectors (as distinct from the disciplinary roles of deans and heads of department). However, the integration of teaching and research within the disciplines to deliver regional impact is seldom recognised.

Third task activities may be the responsibility of a member of the senior management team but quite often this is passed on to parts of the central administration, e.g. to those responsible for legal aspects of technology transfer. Support for knowledge transfer via teaching and learning will reside somewhere else in the administration. In both domains specialised intermediate units such as science parks or centres of continuing education with their own staff can play a pivotal role – either bridging between the region and the academic heartland or keeping the messy world of business and the community at bay. Which of these alternative modes of operation is adopted depends very much on leadership from the top of the institution.

Higher education institutions in regional decision making: the role of academic leaders

The role of higher education institutions in regional development is closely linked to their role in regional decision making. In many OECD countries, higher education leaders or other representatives are playing a more visible role in regional economic policy making. There is enhanced participation of academic staff in regional bodies and increased networking with regional governance institutions, such as regional agencies, regional development organisations, city and municipal development offices, planning commissions and local science councils. In some public programmes and countries, the participation of higher education institutions is mandatory on the boards or in partnerships that manage economic development agencies. In most cases, the identification of regional needs by higher education institutions takes place through supervisory and advisory boards which involve regional stakeholders and particular business representatives. However, many institutions remain passive and prioritise their national and international role. In certain cases academic leaders advise against closer regional engagement in fear of provincial and narrow image. Some communities and cities may also be reluctant to draw on the expertise of higher education institutions in policy formulation.

Whatever approach the higher education institution adopts, the all embracing nature of regional engagement implies that it is a task for the head of the higher education institution. He/she can integrate the function and disciplinary areas and represent the corporate view of the institution externally. In many cities and regions rectors and vice chancellors are key members of local elites, participating in many forums. At the same time, individual academics or other staff members may be active as business or social entrepreneurs in projects supported by the city and region. But in many instances there is little connection between the high level engagement of the senior management and the actions of individual academics. Indeed, the customs and practices of the institution may act as a barrier to more systematic engagement across the institution.

Institutional barriers within higher education institutions

There are numerous institutional barriers. First and foremost is the lack of incentives to individuals. Few institutions recognise regional engagement as one of the grounds for academic promotion; this is characteristically based around research excellence as reflected in peer reviewed publications with an occasional nod towards innovative teaching or academic management.

Second, resources to support the development of ideas (proof of concept) into products or services are often not available let alone translational research facilities to build prototypes or test drugs. Third, intellectual property can also be a major source of conflict between the academic and his/her institution even where the national legislative environment is favourable.

Fourth, continuing professional development for small businesses and the community does not easily fit into conventional full time teaching programmes and can require evening and weekend teaching, eating into time for research and scholarship. Finally, also problem-solving R&D for local SMEs (who may have difficulty in formulating their needs) can be very time consuming and diversionary from what are regarded as core activities.

Governance and management

How far are these barriers to institutional mobilisation, in support of regional development, a function of traditional forms of institutional governance and how far are they a matter of the underfunding of the third task? The evidence from the OECD countries suggests that it is a combination of both factors.

Enhancing the development of more entrepreneurial universities is thus an objective of the new higher education policies in many countries (Clark, 1998).[8] Some OECD member states, for example the Netherlands, Austria, the United Kingdom and Denmark, which have embraced New Public Management approach, have replaced collegial forms of governance and management (i.e. elected rectors, deans and heads of departments) by a system of stronger and more overt managerial roles by appointed vice chancellors or rectors and the heads of the faculty. However while it is recognised that more leeway need to be granted to higher education managers, reducing the burden of regulation does not necessarily proceed at a fast pace. Governments which have legislated to reform institutional

HIGHER EDUCATION AND REGIONS: GLOBALLY COMPETITIVE, LOCALLY ENGAGED – ISBN 978-92-64-03414-3 – © OECD 2007

governance and management are often not in a position to cede full autonomy to institutions until the changes are bedded down.

Over the last twenty years the policy objective of the Dutch authorities has been to decrease rules and regulations governing higher education institutions. The plan for a new law on higher education and research shows a further stage in this development to loosen control over specific programmes. However the autonomy has not increased in all fields. New policy issues have sometimes brought about new regulation. In addition, the power to decide on research priorities resides in national organisations.

In Denmark, higher education institutions have been granted more autonomy to handle their business while the ministry and its agencies steer the system vertically through setting explicit targets, performance contracts and monitoring the results. The Danish reform has thus introduced a wider scope for decentralised decision making and reduction of detailed regulation, but maintained a strong element of central steering and monitoring. The wish to ensure that the universities are capable of administering the extended degree of autonomy has resulted in re-regulation.[9]

Since 2004, Japanese national universities were transformed into National University Corporations with the authority to own land and buildings and hire staff. Faculty are no longer civil servants which has facilitated more flexible forms of employment and salaries. The change has also facilitated channelling funds to university-industry cooperation rather than individual companies. Over the last five years, university-industry collaborations have become more widely diffused into small start-up firms. It is expected that the smaller firms will gradually reduce the dependence on in-house R&D conducted within larger corporations. About 70% of firms which have R&D activities are involved in some forms of R&D collaborations with universities. The reform has also favoured mobility and permitted to offer part-time positions for university professors at research institutes to lead research there.

In some OECD countries, higher education institutions have limited autonomy (in contrast to the autonomy of the academic staff) in terms of their mission, academic profile, programme offer and management of human resources and infrastructure. The ability to exercise control over the higher education estate can be a key asset in city and regional development and as a significant financial resource it is often retained by the central government.

Where governance of universities has not been changed to a greater degree, the national government has often looked to new institutions, notably polytechnics, to address the regional development task. Such institutions characteristically are strongly managed. The external mechanisms which mobilise the institutions to support the region are well tuned using a variety of performance measures. However, these institutions characteristically lack a strong research base capable of transforming a regional economy as distinct from improving the existing industrial base. In these instances, delivering the higher education capacity that has both global reach and local engagement requires strong inter-institutional collaboration – a further challenge for the leadership. (See Chapter 8.)

Reference to the entrepreneurial approach is not to imply that this is the appropriate model to ensure all higher education institutions are able to actively engage in regional development. An institution with greater freedom of action may well pursue the achievement of international status rather than local utility. The challenge for academic leaders is to manage the tensions arising from the different rationalities embedded within higher education and engagement with business and the community. The role of the leadership is to produce a synthesis through which the institution not only responds to regional needs but also becomes a motor for regional development and which has its mainspring in a strongly independent academic heartland.

These tensions and their resolution are summarised in matrix form in Table 3.1 (Vestergaard, 2006). First, in terms of the role of government and other external agencies, there is a higher education rationality which focuses on academic independence and a business rationality which focuses on closer links between science, business and society. The synthesis is one where there is interaction but in which an academic heartland for long term creativity in basic science is preserved. Second, in terms of the division of tasks between the higher education institutions and the world outside, the higher education rationality leaves the translation of research and teaching into products, services and public policies to others while in the science and business driven logic there is no distinction between what is undertaken in higher education and elsewhere. The synthesis involves inter-digitation both physically (e.g. on campus) and functionally (e.g. student enterprise) but with a careful regulation of the boundaries. Third, in terms of activities undertaken, the higher education rationality requires the academy to stand aloof while the business logic turns the higher education institutions into an "innovation factory" driven by the needs of business, society and government. The synthesis involves the higher education institution acting as a cradle for new knowledge which it translates into application in partnership with users. Finally, in terms of roles and responsibilities, the higher education institution is both a guardian of truth and a facilitator of innovation. In practice, however, higher education institutions have a portfolio of activities and staff operating under all three rationalities.

Table 3.1. **External engagement of higher education institutions**

	Higher education rationality	Science and business rationality	Synthesis
Role of government	At a distance	Close interaction	Close interaction but carefully managed
Division of tasks	R&T: higher education institutions C: Other actors	R&T: higher education institutions C: higher education institutions	R&T: researchers C: students and private sector partners (on campus)
Activities undertaken	Guardian of truth	Innovation factory, key agent in the innovation supply chain	Innovation cradle
Roles and responsibilities	Independent academics	Responsive academics	Guardians of truth and innovation facilitators

R: Research; T: Teaching; C: Commercialisation; Adapted from Vestergaard, 2006.

Conclusions

It is appropriate to conclude the review of barriers to regional engagement by returning to higher education policy and considering the tools that governments could use to steer higher education institutions in ways that can enhance their contribution to regional development. In this regard it is clear that higher education has not been exempt from a general rolling back of the role of the state in delivering public services. Of the countries participating in the current OECD study this has been most pronounced in Australia, the Netherlands and the United Kingdom.

For higher education institutions the rolling back of the role of the state has meant a pressure for stronger management and the adoption of performance targets in return for greater institutional autonomy from government. Equally important has been the emergence of publicly supported single-purpose delivery organisations with their own performance targets laid down by government. Many of these organisations operating in fields as diverse as labour markets, economic development, cultural and health provision have territorial structures and responsibilities and seek contributions from higher education institutions towards delivery of their own targets. These emerging structures have created many local and regional networks and partnerships in which higher education institutions are expected to participate. These partnerships have been lubricated by short-term project funding designed to deliver regionally specific outputs from higher education. The consequence has been a reduction of the capacity and willingness of central governments to directly steer the development of regional higher education systems "in the public interest". While government may seek to hold the ring between these different agencies, as far as higher education is concerned it is often unclear who is the ringmaster at successive levels of territorial governance (national/regional/local).

Not all countries have moved in this direction of marketisation of public services, new public management and networked governance and/or applied it to steering the role of higher education institutions in civil society. France and Germany have maintained a strong civil service and elaborate body of administrative laws whilst Spain and many Latin American countries emerging from the influence of military regimes have sought to democratise institutions like higher education institutions and emphasise their social obligations rather than their position in the market place.

This chapter has highlighted the challenge of regional engagement by higher education institutions arising from within national policy, the regions themselves and at the institutional level. It is clearly a difficult agenda for actors at all levels and there is no single key that could unlock all of the doors and create at a turn a well-tuned regional development and higher education system. Rather policy and practice is being and has to be forged by a process of trial and error, of learning by doing.

Notes

1. In this respect the United Kingdom with Oxford and Cambridge and the United States with Harvard and MIT are exceptions.

2. Examples include: *a)* the establishment of new universities in northern and eastern Finland during the 1950s-1970s and the establishment of Finnish polytechnics in the 1990s which doubled the higher education sector; *b)* a network of upgraded colleges to university status in Sweden; *c)* the current plans for new universities in the largely rural areas of England, like Cumbria, Cornwall and Suffolk, and the recent establishment of the University of Lincoln. In Australia new institutions have recently been designated in areas of high residential amenity witnessing rapid population growth through inward migration such as the University of the Sunshine Coast in Queensland.

3. Countries which have implemented performance-based allocation mechanisms use a wide range of indicators. Indicators associated with study completion include student graduation/completion rates, number of credits accumulated by students, average study duration, ration of graduates to beginners, or number of degrees awarded. Other indicators focus on the labour market outcomes of students: employment rates of graduates, extent to which employment is in a field related to the area of studies or student performance in professional examinations. Some countries use stakeholders' views (*e.g.* employers, students, government, social partners) of programmes' effectiveness, including assessments of the quality of graduates and about the extent to which a range of needs are being met and a degree of student satisfaction.

4. Aimhigher is a national programme in England which aims to enhance the widening participation in higher education. It is run by the Higher Education Funding Council for England (HEFCE) with support from the Department for Education and Skills.

5. The recent change of name indicates a shift from a broader to narrower definition of the third task.

6. Exceptions in the current OECD review include some of the masters' degree programmes which have been established with the help of the European funding and have now been mainstreamed in the higher education institutions. This is the case e.g. in the Faculty of Information Sciences of the University of Jyväskylä in Central Finland which launched a number of master's programmes in the 1990s to combat the recession and to build up the knowledge-based economy.

7. In England, HEFCE has established a Higher Education and Business and Community Interaction Survey (HEBCIS) covering a large number of indicators but in the end the Council decided to use gross institutional income measures to determine allocations under its HEIF scheme.

8. According to Burton Clark, "entrepreneurial" universities are seen to be able to determine their own destinies within a Government regulated system. "Expanded developmental periphery, strengthened management core and independent academic heartland" belong to the key characteristics of such institutions.

9. The Peer Review of Jutland-Funen in Denmark notes that "while the new governance system has been put in place enhancing the development of more entrepreneurial universities… the government at the same time continued to practise strong control over them. Matters such as the launch of the new study programmes, course assessment, setting up activities abroad, ownership of buildings and human resource development are controlled by the ministry".

ISBN 978-92-64-03414-3
Higher Education and Regions:
Globally Competitive, Locally Engaged
© OECD 2007

Chapter 4

The Regions and their Higher Education Institutions

This chapter presents the empirical part of the OECD study: an intensive case-study analysis of higher education institutions' engagement at the regional level. Self evaluations and external reviews of 14 regions and their higher education institutions were carried out in order to provide insight as to the causal connections and processes underlying regional engagement (OECD, 2007a).[1] The case study descriptions address the following issues: national policy towards territorial development and the role of higher education in this agenda; the characteristics of the region itself; higher education in the region; and the development trajectory and maturity of the relationship between higher education and the region. Case studies reveal considerable diversity across regions in terms of their population and physical size, numbers and types of higher education institutions and the extent to which they are engaged in regional development.

Australia

Territorial development and higher education

Australia is one of the wealthier OECD countries with high GDP growth, low unemployment and steadily improving living standards. Wide ranging reforms bolstered the economy's resilience to a series of major shocks such as the Asian crisis in the late 1990s, and the global downturn at the turn of the millennium. Over the long term, its key challenge is to sustain growth in the face of population of 20.6 million which is ageing and in need of up-skilling. (OECD, 2006b)

Australia has a federal system of government with legislative powers shared or distributed between Commonwealth and the States and Territories. The term "region" is used to describe those recognised geographic areas with a common community of interest that are smaller in size than states and larger than local government areas. There are no universally designated regions in Australia, these varying according to administrative and planning requirements of various institutions and governments.

The Australian higher education system is unitary with 37 public and two private universities, one approved branch of an overseas university, four other autonomous and self-accrediting higher education providers. There are over 957 000 students including a considerable number of overseas students. There are 119 university campuses across the country, with 42 located in metropolitan areas and the remainder spread throughout rural and non-metropolitan urban centres. State Governments have legislative responsibility for most universities, therefore prescribing university governance arrangements. The Federal Government has funding and policy responsibility for higher education, and over the past ten years it has driven an agenda for universities to become more financially independent of the public purse. As a result, universities have adopted a more entrepreneurial approach to their funding and the proportion of funding derived from student fees has increased.

There is a concentration of higher education in the main cities reflecting the high proportion of urban-based population in Australia. Non-metropolitan higher education institutions have distinct territories; some of them also have a campus presence in the cities, cross-subsidising their rural campuses by attracting overseas students and Australian students who prefer an urban setting. Funding is provided to cover for increased costs of non-metropolitan location. The so-called regional loading supports higher education providers that offer places at eligible regional campuses in recognition of the unique contribution these campuses make to their communities in regional and rural areas, and of the higher costs faced by providers due to their location, size and history. Regional campuses may also have a limited potential to diversify revenue sources, a smaller capacity to compete for fee-paying students and a narrower industrial base providing fewer opportunities for commercial partnerships. In 2007, the Australian Government is providing AUD 29.9 million in regional loading.

Between 2005 and 2010, the Australian Government is providing over AUD 51 million through the Collaboration and Structural Reform Fund (CASR) to promote structural reform in the higher education sector and collaborative activity between universities, business, other tertiary education providers and the wider community, particularly in regional areas. In its two years of operation, CASR has funded several projects that promote collaboration between regional universities and engagement with their local communities. Funding has been provided, for example, to enable the University of the Sunshine Coast, the University of Tasmania, the University of New England and Charles Darwin University, to pool Indonesian teaching and curriculum-development resources. Funding has been provided to Griffith University's Gold Coast campus to address, in collaboration with the Gold Coast Institute of technical and further education (TAFE), local skills shortages. The University of Southern Queensland, has received CASR funding for the development and delivery, with Charles Sturt University, of a joint Bachelor's degree in wine science, and the University of Tasmania, with local government in the Cradle Coast region of north-west Tasmania, has been funded to establish an Institute for Enterprise and Regional Development.

Regional engagement has been further strengthened through initiatives such as the Australian Universities Community Engagement Alliance (AUCEA) project for which the Australian Government has provided establishment funding through CASR. AUCEA is providing leadership in community engagement and regional development, creating opportunities for peer and community discussion and benchmarking, and promoting social, environmental, economic and cultural development in communities across Australia.

The region: Sunshine-Fraser Coast

The Sunshine-Fraser Coast is a rapidly growing coastal region located to the North of Brisbane in South-East Queensland, one of the six States and two Territories that comprise the Commonwealth of Australia. The population of Queensland is more than four million. It is a loosely established region in terms of identity; it lacks a single structure of governance and is fragmented with multiple local authorities. An aggregate regional vision and leadership is provided in the main by the regional organizations of local government, of which the individual local authorities are a member of.

The Sunshine and Fraser Coast consists of a rapidly growing north-south coastal plain settlement, a central transport corridor and an inland hinterland with a modest and declining agricultural base. The total population of 400 000 is expected to increase to about 650 000 over the next 20 years. The attractiveness of the region arises from its quality of life with high amenity value in terms of climate, leisure facilities and access to natural environment coupled with relatively low housing and living costs. The region is experiencing a rapidly ageing population profile as there is significant in-migration of older people seeking lifestyle change. Around 29% of the population of the region is 55 years and over. The situation is exacerbated by the outflow of productive young adults.

There is limited economic diversification. Micro businesses, SMEs and the public sector dominate. The dependence on new arrivals supports an economic structure that is limited to household and commercial construction, tourism and personal services. The region has little manufacturing or agriculture activity. There are local planning initiatives underway in the region to diversify its economic base to embrace sectors where there is a comparative advantage such as in leisure and sports, design for living, and food and nutrition as well as in tourism. Tourism is the primary form of export industry although not as strongly developed as on the Gold Coast to the South or in North Queensland. Hervey Bay has a strong international orientation but mainly attracts backpackers.

Higher education in Sunshine-Fraser Coast

Sunshine-Fraser Coast has two relatively young campus-based universities, both small and with a limited programme range: the University of the Sunshine Coast and the Wide Bay campus of the University of Southern Queensland in Hervey Bay. Collaboration between the two universities is still evolving but is seen in positive terms.

Development trajectory and maturity of the relationship between higher education and the region

The universities' core contribution to region building is through its local labour market course offerings. The universities have a strong culture of responsiveness and entrepreneurialism. Processes, including staff reward system, and organisational structures such as the Regional Engagement Committee have been developed to support their responsiveness. Universities are also developing a regional research focus but from a low base. The development of local partnerships and cultural contributions is limited by lack of resources. Contribution to the formation of knowledge-intensive jobs would enable graduates to remain in the community. There is, however, limited funding available for regional universities to undertake this role.

Brazil

Territorial development and higher education

Brazil belongs to the world's ten biggest economies with its nominal GDP of about USD 900 billion. It is the second largest economy not only in the Americas after the United States, but also in the developing world after China. With a population of more than 185 million people and an annual per capita income of around USD 4 000, Brazil has the largest domestic market in Latin America. Since the mid-1990s considerable progress has been made in achieving macroeconomic stability and restructuring the economy. Brazil's GDP growth (about 2.5% per year on average since 1995) needs to improve to close a widening gap relative to the OECD area. Faster growth requires boosting innovation in the business sector, stepping up formal labour market utilisation and narrowing the attainment gap at all levels of education. R&D density is comparatively low by OECD standards and carried out predominantly by the government and public universities. (OECD, 2006c.)

The population is spread out over the vast area of 8.5 million km^2. In recent years Brazil has witnessed a high degree of devolution of powers to the state and local government levels. The Federal Constitution guarantees a relative autonomy at all levels of political-administrative organisation of the Brazilian Federative Republic. Economic growth in future is seen as waiting on significant macro-economic policy liberalisations, and a new model of social and economic development built on competitive transformation, social equity and sustainability.

Brazil is made up of three levels of government: federal, state and municipal. The 27 states have a fair level of autonomy which is in practice narrowed down because the right to levy taxes rests with the federal government. Two thirds of the 5 562 municipalities are small in size and in practice dependent on transfers from the state and federal government. They lack the capacity to invest in knowledge-based economy and higher education or R&D.

There are five natural regions and concentration of population (42.6%) and economic activities (55% of GDP) in the southeast region. There are regional imbalances and the GDP per capita in the north-east is under 40% of that of the south-east, the most developed region.

To improve innovation outcomes widening access to education is important at all levels. This is particularly important at the higher education level, where the performance shortfall is worsening: only 7.6% of the 18-22 year-old youth enter higher education. The diverse higher education system is dominated by profit-seeking private institutions, which have accounted for the recent expansion in the supply of higher education. There are 1 859 institutions of which 1 652 are private and 207 are public. Federally run institutions represent 40% of the total, state institutions 31% and municipal institutions 28%. There are only 163 universities which represent less than 9% of all higher education institutions. The students in private institutions generally perform less well in the standardised tests than those enrolled in public universities. Private institutions also specialise in low-cost provision in management and humanities which does not improve the skill imbalance in terms of science and engineering. (OECD, 2006c.)

The Ministry of Education is responsible for education, ensuring the quality and the fulfilment of the governing law. In carrying out its responsibilities, it relies on collaboration from the National Council of Education. The states and the Federal District can however authorise, recognise, provide credentials for, supervise and evaluate the programmes conducted by the higher education institutions that they maintain. The federal, state and municipal levels are expected collaborate in the organisation of the educational systems.

The region: Northern Paraná

Paraná is a state located in the southern part of Brazil. It represents 6% of the Brazilian GNP and with its 9.6 million inhabitants 5.6% of the total population. The main city is Curitiba with a greater metropolitan population of close to 2 million. It is rapidly becoming the site of new investments in the Brazilian automobile industry.

The State of Paraná, like all Brazilian states, is divided into municipalities. For analytical purposes the state has been divided into ten regions which however do not have any formal government authority. One of these "regions" is central northern Paraná. With 20% of Paraná's population it is the State's second most important region after the Curitiba metropolitan region. It is composed of 71 municipalities which include Maringá and Londrina, the two biggest cities after Curitiba, each hosting one of the two main state universities in Paraná and each building their individual efforts to develop their micro regions.

There is no clear consensus as to what exactly constitutes the northern Paraná. Nonetheless, it is generally understood to refer to the area that is dynamically located along the Londrina-Maringá axis, covering a vast area that extends over at least three meso-regions: northwestern Paraná, North Central Paraná and the Northern Pioneer Meso-region. Thus, the region of

North Paraná has a fuzzy identity with no formal political or administrative structure. In addition, its integration in the state of Paraná is limited as a consequence of distinct migratory settlement patterns. The region's settlement and development around the 1950s was driven by coffee bean plantations which have declined since the mid-1970s. Since the 1980s, Northern Paraná has seen growing economic prosperity based in the value chain of agribusinesses, along with diversification into services and other fields of industrial production such as clothing, fabrics, furniture, food, alcohol, plastics and mechanical parts.

Northern Paraná has one of the highest living standards in Brazil. While it is performing positively in economic and social terms, since the 1970s, it has witnessed a loss of relative position within the State of Paraná, across all sectors. The regional economy, however, has significant potential for technology-driven growth at a faster rate than the state economy and even the national economy, especially in the areas of biotechnology, bio-energy, consumer goods and agro-industrial food production.

Higher education in northern Paraná

Paraná is one of the few states where the state system of higher education is larger than the federal system. The state educational system comprises 151 higher education institutions of which 22 are public and 129 private. Together, they represent almost 50% of the total of higher education institutions in the southern region of the country. There is a federally funded university located in the capital of the state, five state funded universities and a variety of privately owned institutions. Two of the state funded institutions are located in the Northern region: the State University of Londrina and the State University of Maringá. Together, they represent 50% of the total student population enrolled in state universities in Paraná. In addition, there is a variety of private higher education institutions which complement the academic offerings of the state universities.

Widening access remains an important challenge in the region where only 4.7% of the 18-22 year-old youth enter higher education, a figure well below the Brazilian average of 7.6%, which, in turn, is rather low when compared with other Latin American countries.

Development trajectory and maturity of the relationship between higher education and the region

The objectives for the future of the region are geared towards knowledge-based development which cannot be implemented without higher education institutions in the region. Systematic channels of communication between higher education and society and industry, and among higher education institutions, remain limited with lack of coordination and collaboration among them. There is also limited organisational flexibility in higher education institutions, a lack of institutionalised system of financial incentives for engagement in regional innovation, limited vision and capacity in SMEs in the region; outdated research infrastructure; and a lack of regional innovation policy. The relevance of a closer collaboration between the two major cities Maringá and Londrina remains important in order to achieve economies of scale.

Canada

Territorial development and higher education

Canada is one of the wealthier OECD countries with high GDP growth and low unemployment. Its population of 32.6 million enjoys one of the highest living standards in the OECD. As the proportion of the population of working age will soon start to diminish, enhanced productivity growth and more dynamic business environment will be needed, coupled with a clearly articulated and integrated national science and technology policy, and a lift in the skills level. (OECD, 2006d.)

The population is spread out over the vast area of 9 million km^2, with an average of 3.3 people per km^2. There are big regional differences and a concentration in larger cities such as Vancouver, Montreal and Toronto with diverse knowledge-rich environment and international connectiveness. There has been a steady increase in population, averaging slightly less than 1% per annum since 1971.

Canada has two levels of independent government: the federal government (Government of Canada) and 10 provincial governments. In addition, there are three territorial governments which have some of the powers of provincial governments, and thousands of municipal governments. There are no separate independent regional government structures. The federal and provincial governments are assigned separate constitutional powers, some exclusively federal, others provincial, and a few shared. The Canadian Parliament and the provincial legislatures, together with the government of Canada and the provincial governments, are committed to promoting equal opportunities for the well-being of Canadians, furthering the economic development to reduce disparity in opportunities and providing essential public services of reasonable quality to all Canadians. Furthermore, Parliament and the government of Canada are committed to the principle of making equalisation payments to ensure that provincial governments have sufficient revenues to provide reasonably comparable levels of public services at reasonably comparable levels of taxation.

Education is the responsibility of each province and territory. An intergovernmental body founded in 1967 by ministers of education, the Council of Ministers of Education, Canada (CMEC), serves as a forum to discuss policy issues across provinces and territories. The federal government plays an important role in terms of funding research, providing financial support for students and via indirect funding of post-secondary education. The binary system of higher education encompasses 157 public universities and 175 recognised public community colleges and technical institutes. There are 1.5 million higher education students, out of which 1 million attend universities. Universities are largely autonomous whereas colleges are more closely managed by government, with boards that include a range of community stakeholders. The educational system is marked by high mobility of human capital and competition, particularly for research funds. The governance structures, organisational structures, pay scales, hiring practices and promotion criteria vary from institution to institution. Higher education staff are not considered civil servants. Universities are highly averse to top-down planning and resist direct government interference in their affairs.

The region: Atlantic Canada

Atlantic Canada comprises the three Maritime Provinces, Nova Scotia, Prince Edward Island and New Brunswick along with Newfoundland and Labrador, which joined Canada only in 1949. Of Canada's 32.6 million people, 2.3 million (7.1%) live in the Atlantic Canada region. While the Canadian population has increased steadily since 1971, that of Atlantic Canada has been more changeable. The region's population was increasing up to mid-1990s, but stagnated and began to decline thereafter. The biggest decline has been in Newfoundland and Labrador due to loss of economic opportunities, but both Nova Scotia and New Brunswick have also lost population. There is brain drain, the most mobile being the most educated. The region has a significantly lower proportion of foreign-born residents than the national average. There is also a lower proportion of Aboriginals who nevertheless represent a significant group in the region (2.4%).

For most of the past 100 years, the Atlantic Provinces have been poorer than the rest of Canada, although the gap has closed in recent decades. While there are significant differences in the economic performance of the individual Atlantic provinces, overall the region has had difficulty sustaining economic growth, per capita income, employment rates and R&D investments. A higher share of income in Atlantic Canada comes from government transfers than it does in the rest of Canada. The service industry represents the dominant source of employment. Employment in the resources sector and health and education is relatively more important in the Atlantic provinces than for Canada as a whole while manufacturing and business services are less significant. Although the region has a small internal market, consumer spending, investment, and government revenues are sustained by relatively large exports that amount to almost 30% of GDP and are increasing steadily.

R&D performed by the business sector is more likely to be commercialised and translate into new products and processes that will generate innovation and improve productivity. Firms engage in incremental on-the-floor improvements and the adoption and adaptation of new technologies and techniques. Business expenditures on R&D as a share of total R&D are, however, significantly lower than in Canada. While higher education research expenditure is closer to the Canadian average, it is still below it, with the exception of Nova Scotia where Halifax is the region's centre of research and higher education. Emerging high-tech manufacturing industries are concentrated in the Halifax-Moncton-Fredericton corridor with Halifax capturing the lion's share. Research-based activities are often linked to the natural resource base or coastal geography[2] drawing from the endogenous knowledge advantage. There are clusters of health science activity in Halifax, bioscience in Prince Edward Island, and information technology scattered throughout the region.

Despite reference to Atlantic Canada as a region, it is still "more of a conception than a distinct constitutional entity" (Locke *et al.*, 2006). There is no constitutional or legislative basis for the region, nor separate elections, legislative assembly or capital city: it is recognised as a convenience for some government purposes. As a loose association with sometimes conflicting interests of the provinces its capacity to operate as a region is limited. There are very few voices – among them the Atlantic Canada Opportunities Agency (ACOA) – speaking for Atlantic Canada on intergovernmental issues with the federal government or with other provincial governments. The Council of Atlantic Premiers exists to explore areas of joint action between the provinces, for example in harmonising regulatory regimes, but can not act independently of the provinces.

Higher education in Atlantic Canada

Educational attainment across the region is low by Canadian standards. All four provinces register net out migration of university graduates, with Newfoundland and Labrador showing the greatest losses.

The Atlantic Canada post-secondary education system has 17 universities and 4 community college systems (with about 50 campuses in total) enrolling 153 000 students: 96 000 in universities and 57 000 in community colleges.[3] The higher education institutions range from full-service universities with a significant graduate component (*e.g.* Dalhousie

University, Memorial University of Newfoundland, and the University of New Brunswick) to small liberal arts institutions (*e.g.* Mount Allison University) and community colleges. Despite the quality and size of the major universities they are mostly minor players from a Canada-wide perspective.

For most higher education institutions, there is a clear and explicit recognition of the importance of service to the community and commitment to local/provincial/regional engagement. This engagement is however more voluntary than imposed, at least for universities. The economic impacts of universities located in smaller communities are substantial. For example Acadia University is estimated to generate 43% of the employment and 62% of the income in the community of Wolfville, N.S. Even in larger communities universities have an impressive economic impact, *e.g.* Memorial University is associated with 7% of the employment and 6% of the income in St. John's, N.L. Community colleges are estimated to generate nearly 100 000 direct and indirect jobs with Atlantic Canada. In addition they have an economic output effect of CAD 1.7 billion within the region and have been responsible for CAD 30 million in R&D expenditures. The have demonstrated considerable capacity in applied sciences.

In addition to investments made by ACOA through programmes like the Atlantic Innovation Fund which have promoted entrepreneurship and business skills in community colleges and universities (see Chapters 5 and 8), the federal government is an important player through its impact on research funding and the installations and institutions it administers on the ground.[4] The four National Research Council laboratories, plus the Canada Foundation for Innovation and granting bodies such as the Natural Sciences and Engineering Research Council or the Canadian Institutes of Health Research, are other chief sources of research funding, and as such influence the research agenda and academic priorities of higher education institutions. The Federal Government is not obliged to co-ordinate its actions with provincial or local authorities, although it often does.

Development trajectory and maturity of the relationship between higher education and the region

In numerous communities local university campuses and community colleges are the loci of community action and of economic development initiatives. Many smaller communities have had population decline, with continued decline likely, threatening the existence of essential infrastructure and institutions for local economic development. Competition for scarce resources and differing priorities within the region constrain partnerships that are essential for regional success. The complexity of the higher education system in a vast geographic area has mobilised several coordinating bodies and lobbies across four provinces, but mainly for the different sectors of higher education.

Denmark

Territorial development and higher education

Denmark is a small Nordic country with a population of 5.3 million. Its economy is in good shape, reaping the benefits of 25 years of well-managed economic reform that have produced sound macro-economic policies and a flexible labour market. After some years of slow growth, the economy has recovered to a GDP growth of 3% in 2005. Unemployment is historically low. In the longer term, a declining work force and increases in the ageing-related expenditure make the current public welfare system difficult to sustain. Although the Danish economy is buoyant, it has a key weakness of slow progress in human capital formation. Among the 25-34 year olds, only 86% have at least upper secondary education. In order to take full advantage of globalisation, Denmark needs to reinvigorate its education system and develop greater interaction between higher education and firms on R&D. (OECD, 2006e.)

Denmark has experienced a rapid shift to service and information economy which has been accompanied by a concentration of the population in the metropolitan area and the main university cities which now have the vast majority of the highly educated people and the R&D activities. Hence, in skills and knowledge-based development, there are regional imbalances. About two thirds of total public and private R&D expenditure is spent in the Copenhagen area. According to labour market projections for 2015 the demand for labour will increase by approximately 80 000 people in the Copenhagen area and the County of Aarhus, while the rest of the county will witness a reduction of 40 000 people.

The degree of regional disparity is among the lowest in Europe and the regional policy is focused on improving competitiveness rather than equalisation between regions. In addition, essential parts of the Danish regional policy have been determined by the European Union and the various Structural Funds. Since the 1970s inequality between the regions, earlier marked by disparities between rural and urban areas has been reduced due to structural changes in industry and the growth of public services. As a result, in 1991 the core of the pre-existing regional policies were dismantled and the focus was turned to employment. A system of *ad hoc* interventions was put in place, encouraging foreign inward investment and enterprise creation in order to link economic development to local assets rather than to increase transfers from central government. In 1995 the improvement of framework conditions for enterprise development in regions became the primary objective and the specific strengths of each region needed to be identified. In 2001, another explicit goal in strategy was introduced: regional balance. Thus, an equilibrated redistribution of Structural Funds has been maintained: funds have been channelled to Öresund's less developed areas help to rebalance the development within the entire region while the remaining part of the funds has gone to regions in Jutland and Funen. (OECD, 2003b.)

Recently, the focus has moved to spurring knowledge-based growth; the regional action plan (2004) aims *a)* to put research, technology and innovation on the regional agenda; *b)* to promote close regional interaction between knowledge institutions and industry; *c)* to provide regional lift of competence; and *d)* to foster knowledge-based entrepreneurship throughout the country.

The Europeanisation of regional policy has been met by a corresponding regionalisation: the counties and their social partners have taken an active role in industrial development and the creation of new employment opportunities by developing regional strategies and partnerships. Local and regional governance has recently undergone a structural reform which came into effect in January 2007 after a one-year period of transition. The number of municipalities was reduced by half and 14 counties were abolished and replaced by 5 new regions with new responsibilities. Regions will continue to work on regional development but they have lost of authority of levying taxes that the counties had. The reform has created larger regions and adopted the principle of public-private partnerships through the establishment of permanent growth forums with representation from municipalities, local trade and industry, institutions of education and research and the labour market parties. The regional councils and the regional growth forums will give a voice to their regions and make co-ordinated efforts to set priorities, apply for state funding and lobby for policies. The financial resources that the regions will have at their disposal and the extent to which they will be able to influence the policy-making of municipalities and national government remain uncertain.

Unlike most OECD countries, in Denmark the responsibility for tertiary education is divided between three ministries: the Ministry of Science, Technology and Innovation is responsible for 12 research universities, the Ministry of Education for tertiary education outside the universities (55 institutions) and the Ministry of Culture for tertiary institutions specialising in different fields of culture. The SME-based economy is competitive, and there is well-developed life long learning provision and on-the-job training. There are pressures for rationalising the higher education system through a process of mergers which will lead to a reduction in the number of institutions in order to enhance the global competitiveness of the sector.

The vision is to make Denmark a leading knowledge society through capitalisation of the opportunities provided by globalisation. This includes the development of world class system of education and research, enhancing the interplay between research and industry, creating a strong entrepreneurial culture and ensuring rapid spread and implementation of ICT and telecommunications. Focus is on framework conditions and interaction between the different parts of the knowledge system. In the university sector the reforms have introduced a wider scope of decentralised decision-making, while at the same time maintaining a strong element of central steering and monitoring. Danish universities have become public self-governing bodies led by a Board with external majority and managed by appointed leaders at all levels. All universities enter into a Development and Performance Contract with the Ministry specifying goals and deliverables in the fields of research, education and knowledge dissemination and interaction with industry and society.

The Danish University Act has designated a third task for universities but with no significant income stream to support this work. The current reward systems favour concentration in the Copenhagen area. Competitive funding is used for the distribution of a substantial proportion of funds (40%) which may result in substantial costs and lead to an excessive burden on institutions.

The region: Jutland-Funen

Jutland-Funen is the western part of Denmark, comprising the Jutland peninsula, the island of Funen and several smaller islands west of the Great Belt. The area makes up 77% of Denmark's territory and, with just under 3 million people, 55% of the population. There are three major cities, Aarhus, Odense and Aalborg; the largest city, Aarhus, is less than 300 000 strong. The region has no administrative governance standing, being brought together by Jutland-Funen business development cooperation in 1998. Jutland-Funen is thus a loose configuration originally comprising eight counties and 173 municipalities with their own decision-making capacity. As of January 2007 three new regions have replaced the eight counties. The new regions each have Regional Growth Forums which can prove a key to development and cooperation.

Jutland-Funen has a diversified industrial structure. It has for a long time been the stronghold of Danish agriculture, based on livestock farming, cereal production and horticulture. During the last decades the number of farms has been reduced and the highly specialised farming sector now employs only a small share of the workforce. One out of four is employed in manufacturing industries, construction and building. There are salient clusters in agro-business, furniture, textile and clothing, shipbuilding and engineering, ICT

4. THE REGIONS AND THEIR HIGHER EDUCATION INSTITUTIONS

and energy and environment technology. The bulk of the companies are SMEs. In spite of the increasing population, the proportion of active population is becoming smaller. In 1994-2001, 90 000 new jobs were created which brought unemployment down to 3%.

There has been a rapid shift to service and information economy. Today the service sector occupies 68% in the Jutland-Funen (83% in the Copenhagen area). About two thirds of total public and private R&D expenditure is spent in the Copenhagen area. The County of Aarhus comes next with 10% of private R&D and 15% of public R&D. The western part of the country has a lower level of formal education. In the Copenhagen area 28% of the population has post-secondary education while in Jutland-Funen the equivalent number is 19%. Furthermore, Jutland-Funen is experiencing brain drain and the relative number of knowledge-intensive companies is smaller than in the Copenhagen area.

Similar disparities are evident also within the Jutland-Funen region. During the last ten years, the fastest growing Danish counties were the counties of Vejle and Aarhus in Mid-Jutland. The southern and the northern parts of Jutland have lagged behind. These areas are marked with out-migration, ageing population, a lower level of labour market participation and a higher level of unemployment. Thus the east-west polarization in the development of Denmark is paralleled with by an even more pronounced polarization within Jutland-Funen.

Higher education in Jutland-Funen

Jutland-Funen has four universities. The non-research-intensive higher education institutions with close local linkages were not brought within the scope of the review. Among the universities, regional orientation is strongest at the younger of the four universities, Aalborg, established in 1974, now with 13 000 students, and Southern Denmark established in 1966, now with 16 000 students. Aarhus, with 22 000 students, dates from 1928, and the Aarhus School of Business from 1939. There are also a number of vocationally oriented centres for higher education. The regional efforts of the universities are geared towards their sub-regions and remain project-based and diversely funded from different sources, without systematic planning and development.

Development trajectory and maturity of the relationship between higher education and the region

The challenge for Jutland-Funen is to strengthen its position in the global knowledge economy, counter-balancing the pull of metropolitan Copenhagen, now a part of the Öresund region, where most of the highly educated human resources and the national R&D are concentrated. Although the Danish economy is buoyant, with flexible labour markets and low unemployment, the western part is clearly more vulnerable than the Copenhagen region. Talent is draining to the capital city region. Despite the rapid shift to a service and information economy there is greater dependence on traditional agriculture and manufacturing industries. The national disparity is reflected within Jutland-Funen, where city regions having universities are growing and the more rural north and west lag behind.

The OECD review coincided with a time of organisational, managerial and constitutional change affecting Danish higher education and their regions. The changes included the implementation of the new University Act including appointed heads and boards with external members, changes in the local and regional government in terms of boundaries and responsibility and the possible merger of institutions. The three new regions and Regional Growth Forums with representation from higher education can prove a key to development and cooperation.

Finland

Territorial development and higher education

Finland is a Nordic country with a population of 5.3 million, half of whom live in eight city regions. It has a low population density (15 people per km^2), low proportion of foreign-born residents and an ageing population with one of the fastest-rising old-age dependency ratios in the OECD. Its growth performance over the past decade has been among the best in the OECD, underpinned by a strong innovation performance and high educational attainment. Public sector services are strongly developed as in other Nordic countries. The unemployment rate has dropped below the euro average. Economy has been spurred by the success in high growth mobile telecommunications but dependency on a single sector has left the economy fragile in the context of globalisation. There has been a marked weakening in growth performance since the turn of the millennium: the contribution from the ICT sector to aggregate productivity has been smaller and increases in the employment rate have been meagre. A comprehensive reform is needed in order to sustain the growth (OECD 2005a; OECD, 2006f).

The two-tier system of local government comprises 20 regions and 416 municipalities. Municipalities are major employers and suppliers of health, social and education services. As a result of a rapid demographic change the local and regional government is undergoing reorganisation. This is likely to result in the transfer of responsibilities and changes in the distribution of competences between national, regional and local authorities.

Regional development (Acts 1994 and 2003) has focused on knowledge- and programme-based policy including enhancement of knowledge infrastructure and innovation diffusion across regions and firms. Today, regional policy is geared towards enhancing cities competitiveness and maintaining a balanced urban network of cities of different sizes, rather than providing support for distressed urban areas. The Centres of Expertise programme, launched in 1994, is one of the main tools of the regional innovation policy. It aims to increase cooperation between higher education institutions and enterprises, develop top-level expertise, attract investments and talents to the region and improve region's ability to raise R&D funding. As an integral part of regional policy, key ministries have defined their regional development plans. The plan of the Ministry of Education (2004) defines and strengthens the role of higher education institutions in regional development.[5] See also Chapter 5.

Finland has a binary system of higher education marked by extensive enrolments, robust public funding and generous student support, with no student fees. It represents a planned system of higher education where individual institutions have limited autonomy, universities are state accounting offices and their staff civil servants and the system of resource allocation for teaching is driven according to the forecast labour market demand rather than by student demand. (Davies *et al.*, 2006) The system is stable in terms of its size but in flux in terms of its structure, distribution and governance. There are currently 20 universities – 10 multi-faculty and 10 specialist – and 26 polytechnics. The differentiation between the two sectors is weakening. The Ministry of Education has recently launched a structural development programme to reform the higher education system including mergers of and enhanced collaboration between HEIs.

Improved geographical accessibility to tertiary education has been achieved by regional expansion of the university sector and the establishment of polytechnics throughout the country. In total, 80 out of 431 Finnish municipalities are university and polytechnic towns. Open University studies can be pursued in a variety of units within a widely dispersed network throughout the country. With the demographic decline in several regions and concentration in larger city regions, the dense network of institutions is likely to become looser with new institutional configurations. The universities have a third task – to interact with society and promote the social impact of their scientific and cultural activities – whereas the recently created polytechnics were created to support the development in their regions. The Ministry of Education has required higher education institutions to prepare joint regional strategies but has not provided adequate machinery to implement the strategies, for coordination and joint regional projects.

In research and innovation the national agenda aims to establish Finland as a world leader in science and technological research and to deploy R&D base for economic development, especially in the regional context. The total funding for R&D is among the highest among OECD countries with higher education, mainly universities, receiving 20% of the total expenditure. About half of the support for higher education goes to the Helsinki area, while only 35% of the support from TEKES funding mainly for applied research ends up there. This implies that higher education institutions outside the capital support local technological and economic development (Davies *et al.*, 2006).

The region: The Jyväskylä region

Central Finland has six sub-regions covering 30 municipalities. It has a population of 267 000, of which over 60% (163 000) are in the Jyväskylä sub-region. The sub-region is growing at the expense of the rest of Central Finland. As elsewhere in Finland, there are marked intra-regional disparities with rapid growth in the centre and a decline in prosperity in the periphery characterised by ageing and depopulation.

The Jyväskylä region is one of the key urban areas in Finland. From the 1980s affluence it plunged into recession in the 1990s with unemployment reaching 25% followed by a rapid structural change. Since the end of the 1990s combined efforts from the local authorities, the higher education institutions and the business sector generated a new knowledge economy with a series of steps, including a science park, EU funded university master's programmes, high technology companies, and a multidisciplinary polytechnic.

Today, the Jyväskylä region is one of the fastest growing city regions in the country but lags behind the national average on critical performance measures. For example, the unemployment rate remains higher than the national average including a hard core of long-term unemployed. Social inclusion remains problematic. Central Finland as a whole suffers from low productivity within the existing business base which is predominantly SMEs with low levels of R&D investment.

Higher education in the Jyväskylä region

Central Finland has two higher education institutions, the University of Jyväskylä and Jyväskylä University of Applied Sciences with a total employment of nearly 3 000 staff and more than 20 000 students accounting for 7% of the total population of Central Finland and one-third of the population of the city of Jyväskylä. Reflecting the Finnish binary system of higher education the two institutions are very different with distinct history, missions, governance structures and funding systems.

The University of Jyväskylä is a multi-faculty institution which produces the second largest number of Master level graduates in the country. The output of graduates exceeds the absorptive capacity of the region and two-thirds of its graduates leave for employment elsewhere. It strives to become internationally important research institution. As befits its mission, the 1990s foundation

Jyväskylä University of Applied Sciences (*i.e.* the polytechnic) is, however, more embedded in the region and its economy. It offers bachelor degree programmes and is building its masters level provision and R&D base. More than 30% of polytechnic's students are from Central Finland and 60% of its graduates find employment in the region.

Development trajectory and maturity of the relationship between higher education and the region

The expansion of higher education has been a key factor in the growth of the regional economy in Jyväskylä. The recovery from the early 1990s recession was made possible by the collaboration between the local authorities, the higher education institutions and the business sector. The region led by the City of Jyväskylä was able to take full advantage of the opportunity provided by the EU structural funds. There was a decision to invest in the knowledge economy *e.g.* master's programmes many of which have later been mainstreamed in the university work and have helped it to build an entire IT faculty.

The Finnish regional development system is complex with multi-faceted aspects and wide sharing of responsibilities between different actors. Overlapping mandates, multiplication of strategies, initiatives, programmes and projects characterise regional development in the Jyväskylä region. At the same time the cooperation between the higher education institutions is taking its first steps. Incentives for regional engagement and the lack of institutional autonomy remain a challenge for of higher education institutions.

Korea

Territorial development and higher education

Korea's rapid economic development has lifted its per capita income from one-third to two-thirds of the OECD average during the past two decades. Its economy is changing profoundly as a result of the structural reform programme launched in 1997. It is experiencing exceptionally rapid population ageing, the fastest in the OECD area. A key to faster productivity growth is in upgrading the innovation framework through enhanced R&D system; strengthened competition in the service sector and restructuring of the tertiary education sector. (OECD, 2005b.)

The capital region surrounding Seoul is the largest agglomeration in the OECD countries after the Tokyo region. Achieving balanced regional development by limiting the concentration of population and economic activity in the capital region has been on the Government agenda since the 1960s which has resulted in a set of top-down regulatory policies. In 2004 a special law on balanced national development was enacted. It led to a set of policy initiatives, such as the building of a new administrative city and the creation of innovation cities and enterprise cities. The policy of encouraging regions to develop their distinctive excellence in the new knowledge economy is aimed to equip Korea for the global competition.

There are also attempts to raise the quality and relevance of Korean higher education to serve competitive regional (and thus national) development, by creating greater specialisation and diversification, making higher education teaching and research relevant to the economic needs and potential of each region. The decentralisation includes a key role for a reformed university system with less preponderance of R&D effort in the capital region, through a national New University for Regional Innovation (NURI) project. NURI aims to develop curricula in terms of specialised areas which are closely aligned to characteristics of the regional economy, to promote regional development by training high quality manpower. (See Box 3.1 in Chapter 3.)

Korea has an extraordinarily high age participation rate generally exceeding 80% in an integrated higher education system that is largely (about 80%) private and comprises two/three-year vocationally oriented colleges, four-year universities and specialised universities (i.e. polytechnics, education colleges, technical colleges). Higher education is under the supervision of the Ministry of Education and Human Resources Development which regulates the national institutions directly and private institutions indirectly. Lack of autonomy in terms of budgetary flexibility and organisational affairs are constraints to greater engagement in national institutions. Inter-institutional relationships in the form of joint education programmes and research collaboration are relatively recent phenomena. After a long period of expansion in higher education, Korea is now facing the challenge of reducing the sector as the demographic balance is rapidly changing to an older population.

The region: Metropolitan Busan

Metropolitan Busan, with a population of 3.75 million, is the second economic centre in Korea after the capital area of Seoul and one of the regional poles in Northeast Asia. It represents a case of urban development within one of the fastest growing countries in the OECD and fastest urbanising regions in the world. Busan has experienced a rapid demographic expansion and has a high population density. The growth has however stagnated; the birth rate is low and population ageing. There is also net outward migration.

Busan is the second largest urban contributor to the national GDP but its share has been falling reflecting the gradual decline of the region's economy.

It demonstrates greater vulnerability to external shocks and slower and weaker pace of recovery. Labour market conditions are somewhat weaker than the national average with lower activity rates and higher employment. Although Korea has one of the highest levels of R&D expenditure in the OECD area, Busan ranks only ninth in its share of the national expenditure. It is characterised by small scale research bodies in various industrial sectors.

During Korea's economic take-off phase, Busan was a leading manufacturing centre and powerful driver of national growth with export oriented industries such as shipbuilding, logistics, footwear and textile. The spearhead of the local economy was the port, which is now the largest international port in the country and the top five container ports in the world. After significant investments in long-established industries, Busan faces the challenge of restructuring and revitalising it economy.

Taking advantage of the two interlinked national policies: balanced regional development and decentralisation, Busan seeks to reinvent itself as "dynamic Busan" through an identified set of key economic growth areas and as a revived cultural centre that will attract inward investment, human resources and tourists. (OECD, 2004.)

Higher education in Busan

Busan has 13 universities and 11 junior vocational colleges. The universities include 4 national and 9 private institutions.[6] Participation in higher education is high: 85% of high school graduates progress to higher education against the national average of 81.3%.

Management of higher education policy is highly centralised and the role of the local government weak. Recently the Government has established Regional Innovation Committees in each metropolitan city and province to encourage dialogue among local governments, higher education institutions and civil society. This is expected to boost regional interest in the operation of higher education institutions and regional demands for local universities and colleges. Within the framework of its 2004-2008 five-year regional innovation plan Busan has launched a Regional Innovation Agency which is composed of 56 representatives for government, business community, universities, research institutes and civil society and is anticipated to play the role of a coordinator and networking facilitator.

Development trajectory and maturity of the relationship between higher education and the region

There is limited tradition for higher education institution's regional engagement in Busan as elsewhere in Korea. The high participation rates in higher education are not matched by adult and lifelong learning or community engagement programmes, although the private institutions display a strong sense of community service and civil obligation. The national NURI project may provide a leading edge for higher education institutions and regions to develop knowledge-based industries as a basis for wider engagement. Korea's policy instruments for balanced regional development and regional engagement of higher education institutions are impressive policy initiatives. Regions and cities like Busan need to establish how to make best use of their higher education institutions which have hitherto looked for all purposes to the Ministry of Education and Human Resources Development in the capital. A number of OECD countries have shifted away from policies aimed at greater equity between regions and instead focused on granting greater autonomy to sub-national governments to implementing regional development strategies. Mobilisation of higher education to support regional development will require greater autonomy not only to local governments (for providing services), but also to higher education institutions.

Mexico

Territorial development and higher education

Mexico is a democratic federal republic with 31 states and a federal district which is the political and administrative capital. It is the 11th most populous country in the world (103 million inhabitants) and a multicultural nation with more than 60 different ethnic groups. 75% of the population lives in urban areas dominated by mega agglomerations of Mexico City, Guadalajara and Monterrey: over the last decade also medium-sized and satellite cities have been growing strongly. Rural areas are highly fragmented with 75% of ca. 150 000 rural localities with less than 100 inhabitants.

Mexico has been pursuing sound macroeconomic policies and making progress with structural reforms to open the economy. It is the world's 10th largest economy but 68th in terms of per capita income. It has a young and expanding labour force and increasing participation at all levels of civil society. Despite innovative anti-poverty transfer programmes social disparities remain. Living standards are lagging far behind the OECD average and although decreasing, poverty is still widespread. Potential GDP growth is too slow to narrow the income gap. Human capital is the lowest in the OECD and the education system does not perform well enough to reduce the lag. Improving the performance of the education system remains high on the agenda along with improving conditions for business and investment and reforming the powers and responsibilities between the levels of government (OECD, 2005c; Brunner et al., 2006).

There has been an explosive growth in higher education in terms of student numbers and the number and variety of institutions.[7] The higher education system is marked by heterogeneity: there are 11 subsystems that are different in terms of size, nature and composition. The growth continues in a context of tight budgets and rapid growth of the school age population. However, participation in tertiary education is among the lowest in OECD countries.[8]

Higher education is seen as an important way by which Mexico is to be modernised. The proactive equity strategy and revitalised federalism have been reflected in the growth of education in regions.[9] In the 1990s, policy was specifically aimed at mitigating regional imbalance, boosting growth and regional distribution of higher education. The creation of new institutions, new technological universities, technological institutes, polytechnic universities has taken place mostly in regions less engaged with higher education.[10] (Brunner et al., 2006.)

Higher education governance, co-ordination and regulation take place at the federal and state levels through the Ministry of Public Education and the respective state ministries. In addition, the State Commission for Higher Education Planning (COEPES) manages public higher education planning at the regional level and is expected to reflect community needs and those of the local productive sector. There is weak interaction between higher education and the productive sector, challenges to link higher education system to labour market and under-developed lifelong learning offerings.[11] (Brunner et al., 2006)

The region: Nuevo León

The State of Nuevo León is located in a strategic position in north-east Mexico next to the US border. It has 4.2 million people, about 4% of the total Mexican population. It is the third largest of the Mexican state economies. The average per capita income is significantly above the national average. Its capital Monterrey, only 200 km from the border, is Mexico's third largest city, one of the mega cities in Mexico and a key transaction point between the region and the US and the industrial and financial centre of Mexico. The population has a young age profile and high life expectancy. About 85% of the population lives in the Monterrey metropolitan area.

Nuevo León has an entrepreneurial culture that spans generations. Manufacturing is the most important part of the economy but has a limited technological base. In the situation with enhanced US-Mexican links created by NAFTA, the state is moving towards the knowledge-based economy, developing new high technology sectors and specialised medical services. It is advancing technology-driven economic development through multiple strategic initiatives such as INVITE, an agency dedicated to promoting cross border regional integration between North East Mexico and Texas, and Monterrey International Knowledge City which is a new Triple Helix framework linking the scientific research of academia, the private sector and government. Other technology innovation plans have followed for Monterrey since then, involving the three leading universities, and including the creation of 16 new research centres.

Higher education in Nuevo León

The state of Nuevo León has a higher proportion of higher education students than the Mexican average. There are 44 institutions with more than 111 000 undergraduate and 10 000 graduate level students. In addition, there are 8 000 students in other categories (vocational technical studies and teacher training).

The three key higher education institutions which were in the scope of the OECD review include: the Autonomous University of Nuevo León, a public research comprehensive university with 61 000 students; the Monterrey Institute of Technology (ITESM), a private comprehensive university with the tradition of offering programmes in engineering and business; and the University of Monterrey, a private undergraduate and master's degree teaching oriented institution.

The higher education institutions contribute to the development of the region by means of human capital development, R&D and technology and knowledge transfer, and a range of educational endeavours including social and community programmes. They have multiple campuses and virtual delivery systems. They collaborate in the government-initiated Monterrey International Knowledge City and 16 new research centres sponsored by the national science agency. There is a wide variety of programmes implemented by the higher education institutions to foster social and cultural development in the region. These include mandatory social service to all students in public (and some private) institutions for 480 hours (see Chapter 7).

Development trajectory and maturity of the relationship between higher education and the region

There has been significant progress in growing the student numbers in higher education system. Despite various co-ordinating bodies there are limited links between the educational and economic systems. As a consequence there is also limited effectiveness of policies to promote equity regarding gender and socio-economic status and limited mechanisms to develop, obtain and disseminate measures and indicators that allow for the evaluation and benchmarking of the higher education in the region. The recent strategic initiatives such as INVITE, and Monterrey International Knowledge City (MICK) represent an opportunity for greater engagement and collaboration.

The Netherlands

Territorial development and higher education

The Netherlands has experienced a rapid growth in population which tripled in the 20th century and is now more than 16 million and still growing. After having stagnated since the mid-1990s, the Dutch economy is making a recovery. Major labour market, social benefit and health care reforms are underway to enhance labour utilisation and productivity. One key to the perceived lack of resilience and faster growth lies in enhancing the diffusion of innovation. (OECD, 2005d.)

The Netherlands is a decentralised unitary state with central government, 12 provinces and hundreds of municipalities. South and North Holland are still dominant but Brabant with its (international) industries and strategic location is a developing economic factor in the country. Local governments have a certain degree of discretionary power on local matters, but they are subordinated to the national and provincial government. The higher administrative levels also supervise the lower ones and can demand cooperation from them. Central government has the responsibility in matters macro-economic and social-distributional policies while the local governments have the responsibility of the provision and allocation of local amenities.

The Dutch higher education system is binary with 13 research universities and 45 HBOs i.e. institutions of higher professional education and the open university. The two sectors differ in focus, entry requirements, length of studies and funding arrangements. HBOs have recently embarked on R&D with the help of Government funded programme such as Knowledge circles and Lectors programme which is considered key element of the Dutch innovation policy. Dutch higher education sector include both public and private institutions and students pay tuition fees. While research universities are stable in terms of student numbers, the HBO sector is growing. Policy for the higher education sector is set by the Ministry of Education, Culture and Science. Over the last 20 years, the policy objective of the central government has been to decrease its steering and regulatory role and increase institutional autonomy. The Ministry retains the power to cancel programmes and to prohibit the launch of new ones.

The Netherlands has a long history of decentralisation of higher education. There is a legal requirement for higher education institutions to engage regionally, but no serious efforts to resource or reinforce this with major incentives, funding streams or monitoring of outcomes. There is no direct regional education or scientific policy in the sense of a regionally-sensitive policy to meet different needs.

The importance of innovation to the knowledge economy is widely acknowledged and the government initiatives include the launch of Innovation Platform based on triple helix cooperation including public authorities, business and higher education. The Ministry of Economic Affairs is shaping regional policy for higher education, particularly around research application and innovation. The policy framework involves concentrating resources on excellent research to be applied into innovation and removing barriers to commercialisation process through a range of instruments, such as Knowledge Vouchers.[12] The Peaks in the Delta is a policy strategy which designated R&D Hot Spots in order to strengthen the Dutch economy through targeting resources into key measures to strengthen the overall national economy. Higher education institutions are important to the strategy, particularly in the north and east of the country where there are few other innovation stimulating institutions with research excellence.

The region: Twente

Twente, on the Netherlands' eastern border, is a part of the Euregio trans-regional co-operation between Germany and the Netherlands. It is the eastern part of Overijssel Province, not recognised in the national administrative system. There are, however, clear regional boundaries, and a strong sense of identity and of industrial heritage. Three main cities, Enschede, Hengelo and Almelo, account for half of the 600 000 population.

The region has an affluent past based on textile production and machinery. The Twente economy has experienced a roller-coaster ride, with massive de-industrialisation between 1955 and 1980 leading to the disappearance of 80% of the jobs in the textile industry. In 1980s and 1990s a regional knowledge economy emerged through a series of steps, with a science park and high tech spin off companies. At the end of the 1990s the knowledge economy surge and an IT-driven boom was followed by the bursting of the IT bubble which brought along a number of business closures.

Today, the economy lags behind the rest of the country. Endogenous growth capacity is weak despite the Twente university's record in spinning out high-tech companies. The level of R&D expenditure per capita is higher than the national average but concentrated on a small group of knowledge intensive firms. As a whole, the region suffers from low productivity within the existing business base which is predominantly low tech SMEs. The overall absorptive capacity of the region is therefore limited. Major weaknesses of the region include worklessness, in particular among the young, brain drain and low skills.

The lack of an administrative base has hampered regional development and the capacity of the Twente region to create a decision-making structure and express a will for planned development. In the past 40 years Twente has not been able to mobilise a strong political will to produce a collective response to the economic problems in the region. Past efforts have failed because of intra-regional conflicts between the main cities undermining local and national efforts to enforce regional co-operation. Recently an Innovation Platform Twente, following the national and international examples and including the higher education institutions, has been established to bring together different stakeholders in the interest of regional development.

Higher education in Twente

The Twente region has a diverse set of higher and further education institutions. Participation in the current OECD study was initiated by the Saxion Universities of Applied Sciences (formerly Enschede Hogeschool), with 18 000 students, the largest and only multidisciplinary of the four HBOs, and co-funded by the University of Twente, the only "scientific institution, undertaking research". While all institutions articulate – to a greater or lesser extent – regional engagement strategies, there is inter-institutional diversity in focus and emphasis. HBOs have closer links with the community while Twente University demonstrates tension between orientation towards international excellence and regional engagement.

Development trajectory and maturity of the relationship between higher education and the region

There is a long history of supporting business innovation built around the University of Twente and Saxion. Recently, despite its traditional industrial base and the peripheral location, Twente was identified as one of the R&D hot spots in the country in recognition of the contribution the higher education institutions have made to the regional and national endeavour to promote innovation. The commitment and action towards innovation and entrepreneurship have not been reflected in regional development parameters which lag behind the national aggregates.

Despite long-standing co-operation in technology-based initiatives there is limited mechanism of co-ordination between higher education institutions for engaging with projects of strategic regional interest. The key challenge in Twente is to bring together an effective decision making structure for the whole region in order to address fragmentation, opacity and informality. The Innovation Platform Twente, initially established between firms and higher education institutions, now involves local government. It has led to an agreement between the traditionally antipathetic cities of Hengelo and Enschede and may prove crucial in mobilising the region and their higher education institutions.

Norway

Territorial development and higher education

Norway is one of the wealthier countries in the OECD with robust growth, low unemployment, a small population of 4.6 million and a low population density (14 people per km^2). Norway's economy and society have benefited from its oil and gas resources underpinning a higher per capita income and an extensive welfare system. There is a strong national emphasis on equity and regionalisation. The two-tier system of local government comprises 19 counties at regional level and 431 municipalities at the local level.

The two core public service activities of education and health both have high expenditure by OECD standards. Higher education has high levels of participation and attainment, and emphasis upon wide and equitable access. The public higher education sector comprises 6 universities, 5 specialised university institutes and 25 university colleges which were formed in 1994 through mergers of 98 colleges and now account for 43% of all students. Additionally, there are 2 national academies of arts. There are also 24 private colleges receiving state funding (and a small number which do not). A vocational college sector offers short courses of up to two years. Lifelong learning is well developed. Higher education is almost entirely funded by public funds. There are no tuition fees in public institutions, student grants are generous and student-teacher ratio is low. Despite recent changes, higher education remains regulated and institutional autonomy limited.

Higher education policy has a regional dimension in the sense that it aims to preserve the geographical distribution pattern of the population; increase tertiary participation in the non-urban, especially northern regions of Norway; and reduce the brain drain towards the three biggest cities.[13] This has been reinforced through an emphasis on the needs of higher education to meet the education and research needs of regional economic development. Recent changes in higher education have emphasised the universities' responsibility for national and international excellence, and on the other hand university colleges' responsiveness to local and regional needs. Universities may thus play a regional role but are not expected to. Regional engagement of universities is not incentivised: research performance funding is based on publications.

Norway has a lower rate of R&D spending than the OECD average and a smaller share of the R&D efforts takes place in the private sector than in many OECD countries. The government has, however, set ambitious goals to promote innovation, hoping to raise the rate of R&D spending, especially in the private sector. There has been a late shift from science and technology policy to innovation policy. The region-driven innovation policy stresses redistribution rather than knowledge-building. While most European countries suffer from the so-called Innovation Paradox, Norway witnesses the opposite situation: despite relatively low investments in R&D and innovation, it has a favourable macroeconomic situation and strong economic performance. Norway faces a major challenge to develop new sources of growth and added value other than the resource-based industries.

The region: The Mid-Norwegian Region Trøndelag

The Trøndelag region of Mid-Norway has a population of 400 000 centred on Norway's third largest city, Trondheim with 39% of the total population. It is a prosperous region with virtually full employment and no evidence of industrial decline. As in Norway generally, educational attainment and living standards are high. The region is a major centre for higher education and it is over-represented nationally in terms of R&D activities. More than 11% of R&D is carried out in the region while it has only about 9% of the population.

The Trøndelag region is not recognised in the national governing structures. It comprises two counties, Sør- and Nord-Trøndelag which share a common history and identity. In anticipation of a change in regional governance, Trøndelag Council consisting of representatives of the two counties was established as a co-ordinating body. It has drafted a Regional Development Plan for 2005-2008 identifying creativity, competence and interaction as the three key drivers of development. There are intra-regional differences: while the northern part Nord-Trøndelag is mainly rural with an ageing population, Sør-Trøndelag with the city of Trondheim dominates in terms of economic performance, the level of disposable incomes, the share of the employed workforce, the level of educational attainment, the presence of high tech industries and service and larger companies, the intensity of R&D activities and patenting.

The economic structure in the region is not fully geared towards knowledge-economy. Employment in high technology manufacturing is below the national average, while employment in services – based on education, health and social work – equals the national average. The export value from the region is lower than the national average, the predominant sectors being farmed fish, processed wood and other processed goods. The industrial specialisation is skewed towards primary production. The region has many small firms and only a few companies with more than 100 employees. The fastest growing sector is the service sector. Oil and gas provide a major contribution to the regional employment and growth. A knowledge economy is emerging with the help of university research and graduate production. For example, Trondheim has emerged as "Europe's search capital" when Yahoo, Google and FAST established their research centres there.

Higher education in Trøndelag

In the absence of strong regional government, the Norwegian University of Science and Technology (NTNU) and the largest independent research foundation in Scandinavia, the Foundation for Scientific and Industrial Research at the Norwegian Institute of Technology (SINTEF) are key players in the region but also have a national role with international aspirations. The NTNU was established in 1996 through a merger of several specialised higher education institutions. It is the second largest university in Norway and holds a strong position in terms of competitive research funding. The two university colleges, Sør-Trøndelag and Nord-Trøndelag, are vocationally oriented institutions with widespread regional presence due to the merger of earlier institutions. They are building their R&D capacity from a low base. There are altogether more than 33 000 higher education students, 29 000 of them in Trondheim.

Development trajectory and maturity of the relationship between higher education and the region

Trøndelag is a small region "in construction". It has a relatively weak identity and fragmented governance due to limited regional powers. There is a lack of immediate problems and thus limited collective vision for the future of regional development. The innovation system is fragmented. Awareness of globalisation is not yet translated into concrete action and the links between the city of Trondheim and the university are limited. Inter-institutional collaboration has increased and innovative outreach activities have been developed in recent years but the region's absorptive capacity remains low. Incentive structure appears not to be sufficiently conducive to integration of all higher education institutions into region building. The great advantages which Norway enjoys as a result of oil and gas wealth have masked the need for reforms.

Spain

Territorial development and higher education

Spain's economy has witnessed a remarkable performance in terms of growth, employment and public finances over more than a decade. Productivity gains are still modest, risking a substantial weakening in output and per capita income growth. Spain has adopted measures to make up for its shortfall in innovation and the use of technologies, to strengthen entrepreneurship and to bolster the education system. It is important to implement the reform of tertiary education based on greater independence of universities, more rigorous evaluation procedures and diffusion of research results. Reforms are also needed in order to prepare for the ageing of the population, now 40 million strong and growing because of immigration. (OECD, 2007b.)

Spain has 17 autonomous regions which are divided into provinces. The regions each have a Regional Office of the Central Government. Legislative power is exercised by the parliament, while the government has the executive power. Local administration is structured around municipal and provincial councils. Three different levels of administration – central, regional and local – co-exist and interact in the regions, and the way the responsibilities are shared between them is not always clear.

Regional governments are responsible for funding and administering higher education. The central government is, however, responsible for ensuring university quality standards in higher education: it determines the core curriculum for each programme of study,[14] degree programmes on offer, salary levels and general staff policies (basic structure, teaching load) in all public universities.[15] In recent years, regions have established their own mechanism to provide discretionary increments on the basis of individual merit. Academic staff retain the status of civil servants and must obtain national authorisation. In practice, three levels, *i.e.* higher education institution, regional government and central government can influence the universities' human resources.

Spain has about 1.5 million students in a unitary higher education system. It comprises 48 state-funded universities including one distance learning university (UNED) and 23 private universities, one of which is a distance learning institution based in Catalonia.[16] There is almost no non-university higher education. Although more than a third of the universities are private, they produce only 8% of graduates in a system that has grown rapidly since the 1970s, with growth flattening in the last decade. There are delayed completion rates and limited student mobility. Spain's expenditure in higher education stands at 1.2% GDP, slightly below the OECD average; significant resources have been spent recently on infrastructure. Private funding has increased considerably during the 1990s (over 25%). Financial support for students is modest. Recently a student loan system was launched.

The rapid growth has been achieved by means of geographic expansion of higher education throughout the country. Universities have been located in the main cities of the regions with the implicit aim of playing an important role in the region's economic, social and cultural development, but without financial or political incentives to support this aim. In practice, the university system is not yet fully connected with the regions and the productive environment. They are not seen as relevant or effective by employers. Few companies look to universities for research, and they rank low as suppliers of labour market training (Fundación CYD, 2005). The need for universities to promote economic and social development is coming to be recognised; regional planning is required to expedite this.

Following the restoration of democracy in 1978, the reforms of university governance have led to strengthened collegialism and academic autonomy. Elected rectors are appointed by the university senate. Different types of commissions overseeing various administrative levels decide on the hiring of deans, heads of centres and departments. The Social Council has been established as an external body to represent the interests of the society. Also governing councils have people from outside the university. The impact of external members, however, remains limited.

The Spanish policy on science and technology has two lines of action: The national plan for scientific research and technological innovation and projects for the Ministry of Industry, Tourism and Trade. Spain has seen relatively high economic growth in the last decade. Loss of competitiveness with falling productivity and exports, however, give cause for concern. The national government's *Ingenio 2010* programme, with its focus on technological innovation and R&D and increased investment in research generally, is a response to these challenges.

The region: The Canary Islands

The seven islands making up the Canary Islands region of Spain comprise two provinces: Las Palmas de Gran Canaria and Santa Cruz de Tenerife. The region with a population of close to 2 million enjoys special fiscal status within the European Union as an ultra-peripheral region. Its historic status as a staging post to the Americas has been added to more recently as a link to West Africa and in 2006 as a main landfall for illegal immigrants to Europe. The Canary Islands aim to become a logistics platform for South-South trade between Africa and America and North-South-North trade between America, Europe and Asia. For this purpose, the Canarian ports are in the process of adapting to the new requirements of large scale container transport.

A massive rise in tourism and related construction industry in the late 20th century transformed the economy from primary to flourishing but fragile tertiary economy. The engine for regional development is tourism and related business, currently representing 37% of GDP. There is a dependency on external demand and concerns about protecting the economic tourism base by enhancing quality and, related to this, containing environmental degradation, while seeking to diversify. Another motor of growth during the last 25 years has been the regional public sector.

Considerable convergence in per capita GDP has been achieved with respect to other European countries but intraregional differences remain: there are marked differences between the economic growth of the seven islands ranging from the mature industries (Gran Canaria and Tenerife) to mass tourism driven growth (Lanzarote and Fuerteventura) and to traditional and agriculture-based structures (La Palma, La Gomera, El Hiero). Economic growth has not been able to integrate the different island economies and the domestic market. Transport infrastructure problems and inter- intra-island mobility difficulties continue to be permanent constraints on development.

The Canary Islands enjoy low indirect taxation and substantial fiscal incentives for business activities. As elsewhere in Spain, the existing business base is dominated by SMEs. Almost half of the firms have no employees, while 94% employ 10 or less staff. The economic base where the activities are generating most employment are low skilled. The high share of low skilled and low per capita productivity jobs is coupled with salary levels which are lower than the national average. The high number of temporary contracts remains a major problem. Since 1993 the unemployment rate has fallen rapidly from 28% to 11%.

Higher education in the Canary Islands

The Canary Islands has over 50 000 higher education students and some 3 000 academic staff in all. Higher education in the region has a lower performance than the rest of Spain and important issues remain to be addressed in terms of access, quality and relevance of higher education to the region.[17] There are two universities, Universidad de La Laguna and Universidad de Las Palmas de Gran Canarias and a low profile branch of the national Distance Education University. The Univesidad de la Laguna is an old institution. The Universidad de Las Palmas de Gran Canaria was created recently by merging a small and new technical university with a La Laguna campus on Gran Canaria. It leans more to engineering than to sciences and humanities. Tensions to do with the founding of Universidad de Las Palmas de Gran Canaria amplified the divisions between the island and the universities display competitive rivalry, rather than co-operating in support of regional planning and development.

Development trajectory and maturity of the relationship between higher education and the region

The Canary Islands show intra-regional disparities and competition between the islands and the two provinces as well as between the universities. Government centres for the region in both Tenerife and Gran Canaria involve costly duplication of activities. There is great scope as well as need for partnership for regional development, given the increasing autonomy of the Spanish regions and the special status of the region. The current economic structure has a relatively modest skills requirement. Consequently, there is limited collaboration between the sectors employing the great majority of the region's labour force and its universities. Some in the Canaries private sector already hope for more university partnership, but for the large number of small enterprises the universities seem largely irrelevant.

The Autonomous Region of Valencia

The Autonomous Region of Valencia has over 4.5 million people or 10.5% of the total Spanish population. It is situated on the Mediterranean coast between the regions of Catalonia and Murcia and has an area which corresponds to 4.6% of the whole country. Its high population density (195 inhabitants per km^2) exceeds the national average (85 inhabitants per km^2). Its demographic weight increased considerable in 1950-2004 when the population almost doubled. Recently, the growth in population has been attributed to immigration mainly from abroad.[18]

The region is divided into the provinces of Castellon, Valencia and Alicante. The population is unevenly distributed within the region with the largest concentration in five urban centres.[19] The largest city of Valencia has 17.3% of the population in the region. The region has a slightly lower GDP per capita than the national average while the unemployment rate (11%) is at the national average.

The economic growth of Valencia is somewhat below the national average but well above the European. Of the three provinces comprising the Valencia Community, Alicante has the lowest income per capita at 91% of the Spanish average. The economic structure has moved towards tertiary economy although industrial sector and construction continue to play a stronger role than in the rest of the country. SMEs with less than 50 employees represent 99% of all businesses. Industry in the region is declining while construction, tourism and related industries are growing. Services sector has traditional sub-sectors (shopkeeping, hotel and catering, transport and communications) which account for 50% of net added value and employment in the sector. Innovation intensity is relatively low. In 2003, the total R&D expenditure was low at 0.87% of GDP; altogether 35% of this was covered by the private sector. High technology companies generate only 8% of industrial net added value, whereas low technology businesses generate 65%.

Higher education in the Region of Valencia

The participation rate in higher education increased considerably between 1992 and 2002 (18% to 30%), but still lags behind the Spanish average. Valencia has seven higher education institutions: five public and two private universities.[20] Four of the universities are located in Valencia, one in Castellon and the other in Elche. Some have satellites in other towns. Together they account for 146 000 students (13 000 in the private sector) or 10% of Spain's student population, along with 11.5% of its university staff. The Universidad de Valencia dates from 1 499, Technical University of Valencia and University of Alicante from the 1970s, while the rest were established in the 1990s and 2000s. About 80% of students come from province in which the university is situated. The funding system, which is based on student numbers, contributes to enhanced competition between the universities.

The Regional Government of Valencia is responsible for funding the public universities by means of direct subsidies and by regulation of the level of student fees. It is also responsible for endorsing new degree programmes and for some issues related to non-academic staff. The Valencian Public University System is one of the best funded in Spain. According to education indicators (drop outs and completed courses) it is also one of the most efficient. The Regional Government of Valencia was the first government to introduce a funding model for public universities in 1994 with clearly stated objectives of the universities and funding linked to performance. The regional government aims to establish a policy linking regional development and universities. The Region's Strategic Plan considers the universities key players in the development of the region.

Development trajectory and maturity of the relationship between higher education and the region

As in the Canaries, the university system is not yet fully connected with the region and the productive environment. There has been progress in the generation of knowledge, but limited success in its dissemination. Although universities' own R&D is vigorous, there appears to be falling cooperation with industry in line with the national trend. There is also limited co-operation between the higher education institutions in the region.

Sweden

Territorial development and higher education

Sweden is a Nordic country with a population of 9 million. It has the highest rate of R&D spending (4%) in the OECD countries, high levels of educational attainment and well-developed public sector as elsewhere in the Scandinavian countries. There has been a remarkable surge in productivity since the mid-1990s and the country enjoys excellent macroeconomic performance with high rates of growth, low unemployment and stable inflation expectations. In order to sustain the welfare state, the labour market needs to be made more inclusive and flexible. (OECD 2007c.)

Swedish regional policy, in place since the 1960s, has traditionally focused on the northern counties, where the main challenge results from a combination of peripheral location, population decline and unemployment. During the late 1970s and 1980s, when industrial restructuring brought high levels of unemployment to southern Sweden, the policy emphasis shifted from making convergence in the northern regions towards ensuring regional equality in the whole of the country. In 1998 Regional Growth Agreements were introduced to achieve greater integration between policy areas and to adopt a regional outlook on the use of the sector-specific public support that regions already receive. Integration between Regional Growth Agreements and EU Structural Fund Programmes was encouraged in order to achieve better leverage on financial resources and co-ordination between policies. This policy aimed to stimulate sustainable economic development by encouraging enterprise formation and business development. The county administrative boards and regional councils are responsible for pursuing and co-ordinating the agreements. As the idea was to co-ordinate the use of the already existing resources within industrial, regional and labour market policy, no additional financial resources were provided. In 2004 Regional Growth Agreements were replaced by Regional Growth Programmes (VINVÄXT), so as to make the policy more proactive and to increase the focus on achievements. Reflecting the shift from a regional cohesion focus to an economic growth focus, the name of the regional policy had been earlier changed to regional development policy. Experimental decentralisation is being pursued and new regional self-governing bodies have been established notably in the pilot region of Skåne (OECD, 2003b). In 2004, Sweden launched a metropolitan policy to promote a holistic approach of aiming to end social ethnic and discriminatory segregation in the metropolitan areas and to work for equal and comparable living conditions for people living in urban areas.

Sweden has a unitary system of higher education since 1977. It comprises 14 state universities, 22 state university colleges and 3 private institutions. There are also 10 small university colleges or independent programme providers, who have the right to provide undergraduate education and are partly financed by the state. Extensive advanced vocational education, which is not part of the higher education system, is designed and carried out in close co-operation between enterprises and course providers. The number of students in undergraduate higher education, converted into full-time equivalents, was 302 000 in 2004. Higher education and research policy is nationally led and financed mainly by public funds. State institutions are government agencies subject to management by objectives and results. Decision making is decentralised with a relatively high degree of responsibility being delegated to the institutions. Autonomy does not however apply to the ownership of the facilities.[21]

Higher education policy has a regional dimension and there are higher education institutions in each county. Enrolment has increased considerably but regional differences remain at the municipality level and between rural and urban areas. Higher education institutions are expected to contribute to regional growth and are key actors in the development of society. The Ministry of Education has, however, not incentivised this activity nor does it monitor the results. Higher education funding is based on output, not on regional engagement. Institutions can, however, apply for project-based funding.[22] Sweden invests 4% of its GDP in research.[23] Resources in higher education research are thinly spread due to the establishment of new university colleges which are getting a considerable share of the funding. For the commercialisation of research results certain higher education institutions have holding companies. In addition there is a number of programmes operated by public agencies – among them VINNOVA (the Swedish Governmental Agency for Innovation Systems). Sweden is highly dependent on high technology industries and has during the past 30 years developed a full scale innovation system. The Innovation Bridge of Sweden consists of a nation-wide system responsible for the transfer of inventions to innovations. The financing of the system is mainly public.

The region: Värmland

The Värmland county is a central Swedish region bordering Norway. It is a border region with pull to different centres – Gothenburg and Stockholm in Sweden, and Oslo in Norway. There is active commuting between Norway and the region which seeks to reform itself through a growth corridor between Oslo and Stockholm (regional Growth Programme in Värmland 2004-2007).

Värmland has some 274 000 people, half of them in the labour region of the main city, Karlstad and a third in Karlstad itself. There are intraregional differences with a centralisation within Karlstad and rural decline and low population density elsewhere.[24] Most municipalities have 10 000-15 000 inhabitants. It is a region of slow economic growth and development, higher than average unemployment and low educational attainment. The demographic development of the region shows a long term negative trend. The birth rate is low and population older than the national average. There is also a net out-migration.

The economic structure of the region is dominated by a strong public sector and the capital intensive pulp and paper industry and steel industry. There are few big companies with high productivity and jobless growth. Originally locally owned, the companies which draw from natural resources are now part of global firms. The number of business start ups is lower than the national average and there is a lack of growth promoting SMEs. There is some evidence of growth in services including tourism and information technology. The region's economic success depends on its ability to create growth supporting companies and attract and retain inward investment.

There is evidence that without purposeful effort the region could slip into decline.

The region is a target of special support from the central government to compensate for the loss of an army regiment in 2004: a number of central boards and agencies have been to the region; there is also a commitment to invest into growth promoting activities. The university is directly involved in the preparation of these plans.

The Regional Growth Programme, in which higher education is one of the key players, is one of the main policy instruments of the Swedish regional development in Swedish counties such as Värmland. It offers a joint context for the many actors involved in the sustainable development of the region and provides direction for their plans and actions. It is based on Triple Helix cooperation and focused on paper technology. Funds are mainly directed to efforts to stimulate cooperation and development in regional business and industry and to raise the educational competences in the region.

Higher education in Värmland

In a small city and region the only university is a major employer and focus for inward migration. From university college origins in teacher education in the 1970s Karlstad became a full university in 1999. It has 10 500 students and a thousand staff. Almost two-thirds of the student intake is female influenced by teaching and nurse training. The gender problem here is one of low participation of young males from outlying areas.

The university sees itself as a major regional development partner. It emphasises the importance of the social, ecological and economic development of the society as well as the university's high quality and social relevance. The university has modernised management and governance structures including appointed Vice Rectors and high institutional capacity to collaborate with external stakeholders. It plays an important role as an education facility and more and more as a research centre. Part of the university's educational and R&D portfolio has been geared to support the local forest industry including master of science in engineering programme. It has, however a fragmented research portfolio and a physical separation of campus from the city.

Development trajectory and maturity of the relationship between higher education and the region

The Regional Growth Programme is the major policy instrument for the regional development in Värmland. It offers a structured context for university-stakeholder collaboration. As the only higher education institution in the region the university has a key role to play in region building which is widely recognised. The regional governance is undergoing change and the arrangement called Partnership Värmland, of which the university is a part, has no formal authority. There may be a significant transfer of responsibilities and changes in the distribution of competences between national agencies and regional authorities.

United Kingdom: England

Territorial development and higher education

The United Kingdom has a population of more than 60 million, out of which 50 million reside in England. The population is increasing due to substantial immigration especially from the new EU countries which is providing additional labour market flexibility. The stability and the resilience of the UK economy has been impressive and product markets are among the most flexible in the OECD. There is, however, a need to raise the general skill level of the workforce, address the mediocre innovation performance and to increase labour utilisation. (OECD, 2005e).

Regionalism in the United Kingdom is marked by uncertainty, ambiguity and change. In the late 1990s a Parliament and Executive were established in Scotland and Assemblies in London, Northern Ireland and Wales. They all have an elected tier of government. The central government led an agenda for greater devolution also to the English regions. The North East, which was chosen for the referendum in 2004, however, voted against an elected assembly, and plans to hold further referendums in other English regions were cancelled. With no elected bodies there is a regional democratic deficit. Instead there is a fragmented system of regional governance surrounding elected local authorities highly dependent on central government transfer payments (CURDS, 2005; OECD, 2006g).

The London metropolitan region dominates the English economy which results in a regional imbalance in the UK. In some respects, the UK has one of the most centralised systems of government in the OECD. Key decisions affecting regional competitiveness are taken by the central government. The levers available to local government are weak. Matters relating to economic development, such as major transport, investments, skills and training, and further education are outside the scope of their powers. There is limited adaptation of policy to meet regionally specific needs. This practice differs from that of most OECD countries, and flies in the face of evidence which shows that the most successful regions are those with their own strategic decision making powers. (OECD, 2006g.)

The two national pillars of regional governance – Regional Development Agencies, and Government Offices – are a focus of policy coordination and have become stable features of the regional governance landscape but lack a bottom-up mandate. Regional Development Agencies aim to "co-ordinate regional economic development and regeneration, enable regions to improve their relative competitiveness and reduce imbalance which exist within and between regions". They draw up Regional Economic Strategies. Government Offices seek to co-ordinate national policy within the region but have limited opportunity to initiate or amend those policies. From the bottom up there is a Regional Assembly of Local Authorities which does have a minor statutory responsibility in relation to spatial planning. Higher education's contribution to regional development has been incentivised through the Higher Education Fund (HEIF) administered centrally by Higher Education Funding Council (HEFCE). (See Chapter 3.)

Higher education in the UK is highly diverse and differentiated but without formal dividing lines since 1992 when the distinction between the universities and polytechnics was abolished. Higher education is provided mainly in universities and higher education colleges, but about 10% is provided by further education colleges where the degrees are ratified by a university.[25] There are now more than 100 universities and the number is growing as more colleges achieve the specified criteria of size and quality. There are also specialised single subject higher education institutions. (Clark, 2006.) The age participation rate has rapidly expanded exceeding 40%. The target of 50% has been reached in Scotland and Northern Ireland, but not in England. Universities are encouraged to compete and to be entrepreneurial. Tuition fees for UK and EU undergraduate students were introduced in England and Northern Ireland in 2006 and in Wales in 2007. These were capped at GBP 3 000 and linked to bursaries for students from disadvantaged background. For non-EU students institutions are free to charge market rates.

Higher education is a national responsibility, funded by the home country – England, Wales, Scotland and Northern Ireland. In England it is supported through HEFCE which has regional consultants. HEFCE respects institutional autonomy while steering the system through policy and funding initiatives including third stream and widening participation. It thus influences the sector by indirect means within the broad policy steer of government provided by the Department of Education and Skills (DfES). DfES has limited interest in regionalism. Regional engagement is not a formal requirement of universities in the UK, although it is seen as a key element of third strand activity.

Higher education institutions have considerable autonomy, subject to the same constraints as businesses in the private sector: if they have no customers, they risk failure. Indeed the UK Treasury classifies universities as falling in the private sector.[26] The Government and funding bodies have powers through conditions of funding to deliver their policies for higher education even though in the larger research intensive universities the HEFCE block grant covers less than one third of the institutional income. Allocation of research funding is related to a Research Assessment Exercise which emphasises excellence and has no regard to regional impact.

The region: The North East of England

The North East is the smallest and geographically most peripheral of the nine English regions. It is a region of deep diversities next to the Scottish border. It has extensive rural areas and three river-based conurbations. The population of 2.5 million, is ageing and was until recently declining.

During the 18th and 19th century the region was a centre of leading edge innovation: it was a major industrial wealth producer based on coal mining, shipbuilding, heavy engineering and steel production. The 20th century, however, saw relative economic decline compared with other UK regions and absolute decline of the traditional industries. In 1934 Government reacted to the decline of traditional industries by designating the North East as one of the first "depressed areas" in the country. Measures to counterbalance the depression were aimed at attracting inward investment. In 1979 government aid was cut back. Many previous US manufacturing investors closed sites and transferred production to newly industrialised countries. The result was a massive de-industrialisation and a widening economic gap from the rest of England. With the decline of traditional industries the North East lost its economic control. There was a marked over-representation of externally controlled branch plants, under-representation of innovative SMEs and a limited network economy. The early 1990s were a period of renewed investment from the Far East but many of these plants have also closed in the last five years.

Today, the region's economy has started to recover but lags behind in most socio-economic and innovation indicators, such as gross value added per person, employment, proportion of self-employed, business start-ups, employment growth, qualification level and R&D expenditure. There is virtual elimination of heavy engineering, low productivity in the mainly SME business base, few clusters and difficulties in generating endogenous growth. Chronic unemployment and service-led growth in the bigger cities exacerbate intra-regional disparities. R&D investment and business start-ups are at a low level. Recent growth has been mainly public sector driven and education, health and social sector remain dominant in the employment profile. Pockets of dynamic growth have emerged in limited locations based on cultural regeneration, knowledge-intensive business services and creative industries with strong links to higher education. The Regional Economic Strategy focuses on building a new economy based around science-led innovation and the attraction and retention of talent to regenerated cities.

Higher education in the North East of England

The region is marked by lower age participation rate and proportion of graduates in employment than the national average. There are 90 000 students in five universities – Durham, Newcastle, Northumbria, Sunderland and Teesside. In addition, there is a regional office of the national Open University and 17 further education (FE) colleges offering higher education programmes to 6 000 students. Durham and Newcastle are pre-1992 universities, and Newcastle is a member of the research-led Russell group of universities with Medical Schools. The other three new universities were polytechnics until 1992. Northumbria has the largest student population in the region and a large share of overseas students (10%). Sunderland and Teesside have a strong local network and further education partnerships. 60% of the universities' combined total income is from sources other than the HEFCE. They employ 14 000 people and represent some 2.3% of regional GDP. Universities dominate the public R&D expenditure. The North East has a strong and long-lived higher education regional association – Universities of the North East (Unis4NE). (See Chapter 8.)

Development trajectory and maturity of the relationship between higher education and the region

Despite pressure to compete, there are a number of examples of cooperation between the universities and a commitment to regional development. This commenced with co-ordinated R&D advisory services for SMEs. More recently the universities have adopted a broad social and cultural role although these activities remain poorly funded (see Chapter 7). Widening participation in higher education is an agenda shared by the universities given the region's low educational attainment and low skills base. Regional governance is characterised by a complex mix of organisations with overlapping strategies. The fragmentation of regional structure and limited horizontal co-ordination among local authorities poses challenges for higher education.

The dominance of the higher education R&D, as a result of low investment by government and business, has lead to an approach in which university centres are seen as opportunities to establish new high technology industries for which there are no recent industrial precursors within the region. At the same time incremental development strategy aiming to increase the efficiency of existing businesses remains important (Boxes 5.5 and 5.6 in Chapter 5).

Cross-border co-operation between Denmark and Sweden

The earlier sections presented the different trajectories of the Danish and Swedish regional development and higher education policies. In Denmark most regional policies were discontinued from 1991 except for limited *ad hoc* interventions. The bulk of regional development policies were linked to

European Structural Funds. In Sweden, the regional policy evolved from focusing on the north to a more balanced approach towards socio-economic and environmental issues throughout the country. Within the framework of Regional Growth Agreements introduced in late 1990s, co-ordinating responsibilities were passed to counties (OECD, 2003b).

The development of the Öresund region is a regional project, indirectly supported by the national regional policies in Sweden and Denmark. This is in line with the general trend followed by the majority of industrialised countries which are limiting their direct involvement in regional development and are focusing instead on creating framework conditions. Öresund is a focus of the regional strategies of the two countries and is the object of support through external and specialised programmes. The decisions are made as a result of informal co-ordination between ministries involved in the Öresund strategy. Öresund Committee is a political cross-border co-operation of local and regional authorities in both sides of Öresund (OECD, 2003b).

The region: Öresund region

Öresund region spans two countries, in a cross-border partnership between Sweden and Denmark, reflecting the wider regional development aspirations of the European Union. It centres on and is symbolised by the 16km bridge opened in 2000. It is the only region in the current OECD study encompassing a national capital (Copenhagen). The goal of the Öresund regionalisation is to achieve economies of scale and economies of scope through regional integration. Öresund region has a strong urban emphasis; the main urban centres are Copenhagen and Malmö. The population of more than 3.5 million represents a quarter of the whole combined Swedish and Danish population and is growing faster than all the other regions of these two countries. In the last 10 year the number of foreign citizens has increased considerably.[27] The region includes some of the most advanced and some of the most depressed areas in the two countries. The economic gap within the region has tended to increase due to the negative backwash effect of growth i.e. cities draining the peripheral areas in terms of population, industry and services, which outweigh the positive effects (see OECD, 2003b).

There is considerable long term investment in large scale urban development and restructuring. One of the largest ongoing new town development projects in Europe is taking place in the heart of the region; within 30 years the Science City Ørestad within the Greater Copenhagen Region will become a living lab for the testing of new technologies with tens of thousands people working there.

The region ranks third behind London and Paris in biotechnological and medical research. It also has strengths in ICT, food processing and environmental technologies. Both parts of the region are heavily dependent on the knowledge-extensive service sector. A large part of the economy is, however, based on traditional and low-technology-based activities. While over three quarters of employers have no graduates on the payroll, low-technology companies remain competitive because of massive on-the-job training. There is evidence of existence of two different labour markets, with different arrangements each side of the bridge.

Higher education in the region: Öresund region

Öresund University is a voluntary organisation – a network consortium – of 14 universities. On the Danish side, the university colleges (71 at the time of the review) and a number of art schools were outside the consortium. Öresund University has 150 000 students and 11 000 researchers. It is based on regional collaboration between higher education institutions despite the dominant ethos which favours competition. The nine different triple helix platforms of the Öresund Science Region provide a coordinating link between the higher education institutions and the community.

The two national higher education systems differ, the Danish being currently a three-part system (research-based universities, university colleges and schools of art) whereas the Swedish system is unitary, including both universities and university colleges. Sweden has a stronger tradition of community links, including private sector linkages for R&D and knowledge transfer while the Danish universities have chosen to retain their tradition of pursuing excellence in teaching and research without significantly developing their links with the society and the economy (OECD, 2005f).

Development trajectory and maturity of the relationship between higher education and the region

The ambition is to make Öresund a leading world science region, building on its status as third after London and Paris in biotechnical and medical research, while increasing cross-border integration. The main involvement of government in the Öresund region and Öresund Science Region is at the local and municipal level. As of January 2007, two new regions were formed in the Danish side of the Öresund region. In the Swedish part, Region Skåne remains the main player in the regionalisation process of the Öresund region. The Öresund University has a valuable role in representing the higher education institutions collectively to regional stakeholders. A key challenge is to develop linkages between regions in two countries with different education systems, labour markets, and politico-administrative arrangements. Cross-border collaboration has been built up through the use of technology platforms. Core areas of teaching and research where the institutions often compete, however, remain "off limits". The new developments tend to be viewed as top-down, with limited civil society involvement.

Conclusions

The discussion of drivers behind and barriers to regional engagement in Chapters 2 and 3 touched upon differences within and between countries, regions and higher education institutions. Every region is unique, however, and in building towards high level conclusions applicable at an international level it is important to understand the diversity of higher education institutions and context within which they are operating. This chapter has discussed this diversity in terms of the case studies which lie at the core of the current OECD study. It has highlighted a number of the dimensions along which diversity can be assessed.

First, are the characteristics of the region itself – the history and level of economic development and location within the national territory. Higher education institutions situated in older heavy industrial areas that have experienced major restructuring (e.g. the North East England and Twente), are in a very different situation to those in cities surrounded by rural areas and/ or an industrial base built around agriculture and forestry (e.g. Värmland). The organisation of the private sector, for example the balance between large enterprises and SMEs with low investment in R&D and limited graduate job opportunities will have a bearing on the possibilities for knowledge transfer. Equally important is the structure of local governance, for example the powers and responsibilities of local and regional governments in relation to economic development generally and higher education specifically.

Second, and moving to the national and supranational level, there is a need to see to what extent there is an ongoing commitment to regional development – and what shape this commitment takes – and the extent to which higher education is considered a tool in achieving greater equity between regions and improving regional competitiveness. For example, European higher education institutions situated in regions which have benefited from assistance from the European Structural Funds have had stronger incentives for regional engagement than those elsewhere in Europe even when there has not been a specific national regional policy for higher education. With the challenges of globalisation some countries are now focussing on their strongest regions and the support of the leading higher education institutions within them. However, the extent to which higher education and industrial policy are fully co-ordinated to support territorial development varies significantly between countries.

The third dimension of diversity relates to national systems of higher education. Most national systems embrace a wide range of institutions from multi-faculty research intensive universities (with and without medical schools), technological universities, specialist single discipline institutes through to vocational and community orientated colleges. The state of development of higher education (growing, stable, shrinking), the balance between the public and private sector and the nature and extent of public steerage of the system also varies. All of these factors have a bearing on the incentives and capacity of higher education institutions to engage with their region.

The final dimension relates to the development trajectory of both the higher education institutions and of the region and the evolution of the partnership between the two. All higher education institutions have a history which can have a heavy bearing on their current academic profile. Likewise regions have an industrial and socio-political history. Taken together these histories can result in varying degrees of mismatch between the needs and aspirations of the two parties.

In the regions involved in the OECD study, partnerships are being developed between higher education institutions and the public and private sector to mobilise higher education in support of regional development. Most OECD countries have attempted to reinforce higher education institutions in relation to firms and regional economies. The case for engagement is also becoming acknowledged across a wide range of institutions in most regions. The partnerships, which are in most cases at early stages, are usually bottom-up initiatives with limited engagement and support from national governments (apart from the Korean case). The early stages are characterised by numerous small scale and short term projects championed by key individuals. For such partnerships to progress to maturity a number of conditions have to be met:

● embedding engagement and partnership working in the heartland of higher education institutions and in the practices of regional agencies **and** related adjustments to national policy;

● clear leadership at every level (national, regional, local) and across all agencies (government, higher education institutions, business and the community);

● commitment to long term partnerships;

● effective co-ordination within all the partners – whether it is the integration of policies between Finance, Education and Science ministries, the development of a single voice for business within a region or the coordination of a response from the diverse elements within a higher education institutions;

● appropriate incentives for all concerned – explicit long term core funding for higher education institutions to enable sustainable activity, whilst for governments and other stakeholders it means explicit measurement and reporting of the returns that this investment generates;

● a supportive environment – with appropriate fiscal structures, proper accountability regimes that do not place an undue burden on the higher education institutions and businesses, mechanisms to spread good practice and effective systems of communication;

● a wide agenda to ensure that the partners consider the whole range of opportunities for engagement whether economic, social or cultural and then continuous evaluation and monitoring of results.

The next three chapters illustrate this diversity with reference to how regions and higher education institutions are working together in different domains to overcome barriers to effective engagement.

Notes

1. Full accounts of the 14 regions are available in the self-evaluation and peer review reports on the OECD website *www.oecd.org/edu/higher/regionaldevelopment*.

2. Key fields in Atlantic Canada include marine and ocean sciences, aquaculture; potato genomes; offshore drilling; biotechnologies and biochemistry as related to ocean resources, etc.

3. These higher education institutions belong either to the Association of Atlantic Universities or the Atlantic Provinces Community College Consortium.

4. Agriculture and Agri-food Canada runs experimental stations in all four provinces, and the Canadian Forest Service operates the Atlantic Forestry Centre attached to the University of New Brunswick in Fredericton, with another centre at Corner Brook, Newfoundland. The Department of National Defence is a huge presence in Nova Scotia and elsewhere in the region. The Department of Fisheries and Oceans runs the Canadian Coast Guard College, located in Cape Breton. The National Research Council has four laboratories in the region; one in each province. The federal government via four departments – finances the Bedford Institute of Oceanography, the largest of its kind in Canada, located in Dartmouth.

5. The overarching vision is that "Finland's welfare and international competitiveness rests on the vitality and international innovativeness of the regions, which is promoted by a regionally comprehensive provision of education and research".

6. In Korea, the private higher education institutions are not-for-profit institutions often with strong religious or other charitable foundations and significant income streams from often church-based sponsors and donors. Community engagement and service tends to feature strongly in mission statements, and these and the value base of service are up-front in student recruitment publicity.

7. In Mexico, the number of higher education students has grown from less than 1 million in 1950 to more than 30 million students in 2000.

8. In Mexico, in 2003, 16% of the population aged 25-34 had tertiary education. The average number of years in formal education was 8.7, the next to last figure among the 30 OECD countries reflecting the low rates of completion of upper secondary education.

9. Until the 1970s about 80% of students in Mexico were enrolled in the capital district: today the metropolitan and mid-south regions have about 40% of the total enrolment.

10. In Mexico, the new institutions, such as technological, polytechnic and intercultural universities, still represent markedly low proportion of enrolment. Although the regionally based institutions had the highest enrolment rates in the period 2001-2006 their total enrolment was only 15.5% of the total national enrolment.

11. In Mexico, a significant proportion of graduates, 46%, appears not to have found employment in and area matching the competencies and skills acquired in higher education suggesting a mismatch between the supply and demand.

12. The Netherlands has launched Knowledge Vouchers. They are an incentive to enterprise that purchases services from knowledge institutes in order to improve its innovation processes, products and services.

13. Norway has nurtured the idea that everybody should have access to employment opportunities, community services and a healthy environment no matter where they lived. The expansion of the public sector was instrumental to this notion of regional balance when this sector was growing, although it was ultimately to become part of the problem when the public sector began to diminish in size.

14. In Spain, the decision about the core curriculum will be granted to the individual universities as a consequence of the New University Law in 2007.

15. In Spain, tenured academic staff account for over half of the staff in publicly funded universities and are governed by state regulation. National pay scales apply for academic staff and the criteria for obtaining research-related discretionary increments are also agreed centrally.

16. Spanish state funded universities may also have affiliated institutions with no degree awarding powers. They can be private or publicly funded but do not form part of the university as such.

17. In the Canary Islands, the pass rates for admission examination are substantially lower than those for Spain as a whole, and the region is among the lowest ranked in the country. In addition, non-completion rates are almost five points above the Spanish average in the case of one university and slightly lower than the national average in the case of the other university.

18. In 1994-2003 the Autonomous Region of Valencia had a positive migration of almost 450 000 people, of whom 23% came from other regions in Spain and 77% from abroad.

19. The Autonomous Region of Valencia has a population density ranging from 272 inhabitants per km^2 in Valencia to 77 in Castellon.

20. Public universities in the Autonomous Region of Valencia are University of Valencia (established in 1499), Technical University of Valencia (1971), University of Alicante (1979), Jaume I University of Castellon (1991) and Miguel Hernandez University in Elche (1997). Private universities are Cardenal Herrera University (2000) and Catholic University of Valencia (2004).

21. University autonomy in Sweden covers the following aspects: how the operations are organised, the division into organisational units, the organisation of studies, structure and content of educational programmes, the undergraduate programmes and courses to be offered, the number of places in each programme, research profile, contract education, the award of degrees, resource allocation, the establishment of new professorship and the appointment of professors,

postgraduate programmes, overall salary level apart from the vice chancellor/president, and equipment.

22. At the end of the 1990s, some Swedish foundations offered extensive funding for the development of the regional role of higher education institutions.

23. In Sweden, most research and innovation activities take place in the industry but nearly all of the publicly funded research goes on in the higher education institutions.

24. Värmland has an average population density of 16 inhabitants per km^2 while in some municipalities it is as low as 3 inhabitants per km^2.

25. In the UK, there is also a very small number of private colleges, not publicly funded.

26. In the UK, universities have their own legal identity; they appoint their governing bodies and staff including the Vice-Chancellor who is the chief accounting officer; they are responsible for their financial affairs; they set their own salaries, missions and objectives; they determine their profile of academic programmes; set their own research priorities; own their own estates and plan their own capital programmes. They are accountable to their own governing bodies, students, and quality assurance authorities.

27. Within the Öresund region in the metropolitan area, the share of foreign citizens is approximately 7%, peaking in Copenhagen at 13% and Malmö at 22%.

ISBN 978-92-64-03414-3
Higher Education and Regions:
Globally Competitive, Locally Engaged
© OECD 2007

Chapter 5

Contribution of Higher Education to Regional Business Innovation: Overcoming the Barriers

This chapter discusses the relationships between higher education institutions and business and industry and the interlinked policy implications. It analyses mainly top-down policy approaches which aim to improve the link between higher education institutions and regional innovation systems and clusters. Finally it highlights policy practices and instruments as examples of overcoming some of the barriers to regional business innovation.

Innovation is a key catalyst for productivity and economic growth in the knowledge-based economies (Aghion and Howitt, 1998; Scott and Storper, 2002). Between 1970 and 1995 more than half of all total growth in output across the developed world resulted from innovation; as economies become more knowledge-intensive, the proportion is likely to grow (Simmie *et al.*, 2002). As a consequence OECD countries are increasingly investing in the science base. The countries finance a large proportion of gross expenditure on R&D, often ranging from 40% to 60%. A considerable part of this investment finds its way into higher education institutions which are expected to contribute not only to knowledge creation, but also knowledge exploitation, supporting the overall innovation efforts directly and indirectly. Higher education institutions, like airports, have become "magic bullets" in many regional development strategies, symbolising the significance of the global/ local nexus.

Collaboration with firms underpins the contribution of higher education institutions to business innovation. This collaboration may face a number of challenges. These can be cultural, *e.g.* firms and higher education institutions are managed with different logics and objectives (while market efficiency is the key driver for firms, higher education institutions have a focus on the provision of knowledge and training). The challenges may also be linked to the weak absorption capacity of the business sector (particularly in the SMEs), firms' insufficient knowledge of what higher education institutions can offer and their inability to formulate demand for innovation. They may be inherent to the commercialisation process of new ideas in the research sector.

Challenges may also be intrinsic to policy design. First, national science and technology policy can reinforce established hierarchies of higher education institutions and regions; it can also unintentionally lead to global, as distinct from national, knowledge exploitation. Second, the linkage between science and technology policy and innovation policy is often poorly articulated at the national and regional levels, being based on linear models of innovation. Third, science policy tends to emphasise a technology-push approach to innovation, focusing on manufacturing and high technology and overlooking the contribution the social sciences and humanities can make to innovation, *e.g.* in the delivery of services. Finally, the link to higher education policy generally and the role of students, particularly in contributing to the social basis on which the exploitation of technology depends, is often poorly developed. All of these challenges come together at the level of the individual higher education institution and its interaction with its region.

As implied above, innovation policy initiatives which attempt to reinforce the interface between higher education and business are driven by a number of ministries, for example ministries of science and technology, industry and enterprise, education and research. Innovation programmes are also linked to regional policy which aims to capitalise on local assets in regions, including geographically peripheral regions and/or those undergoing industrial restructuring.

In order to address the various issues, this chapter reviews not only co-operation between higher education institutions and business and industry and the policy strategies that encourage this co-operation but also a number of bottom-up mechanisms and practices in order to reflect the diversity of initiatives that national and local governments use to better tap the HEI resource for innovation.

Co-operation between higher education institutions and business and industry

While higher education institutions have emerged as engines for regional economic growth, their role is primarily indirect. To contribute to business innovation, they need to undertake research contracted out by firms, sell licenses or create start-ups that will market research results. While most HE research is basic research, their R&D work is becoming more industry-relevant, notably in the fields of high technology. At the same time, very few firms can independently master the innovation process from the initial idea to the introduction of a new product or process. These trends tend to enhance the interface between firms and higher education institutions.

Three main types of relationship between higher education institutions and industry are often distinguished:

● Relations between multinational enterprises and world-class universities. Multinational enterprises externalise part of their research and development activities and are looking for laboratories, scientists and students.

● Relations between higher education institutions and small high technology firms (spin-offs and knowledge-intensive business services).

● Relations developing in a regional context between firms, often SMEs, and the local higher education institutions. Here firms are looking for short term, problem-solving capabilities. These services are often promoted by means of regional clusters around higher education institutions.

While the technology, knowledge and research outputs of higher education institutions are available not only regionally, but also nationally and globally, physical proximity remains important in HEI-industry relationships. For example, a patenting decay effect has been identified whereby beyond fifty miles of home base, the citations of academic papers decline sharply, suggesting strong interaction among patenting entrepreneurs and regionally-based academics (Cook, 2004). Proximity also affects consulting work and the recruitment of students which are both important channels for industry-university relationships and often more appreciated than patenting and licensing (Table 5.1). Universities in different countries show different patterns with regard to these activities (see Table 5.2).

Physical proximity is however not enough. Many studies show that higher education institutions are a relatively minor source of information and knowledge for creating new products and processes in firms, apart from a small number of high technology fields including biotechnology and Information Technologies (See Table 5.3 for information on the UK situation). Higher education institutions and firms, especially small businesses, continue to experience significant gaps in their collaborative relationships. First, they may have divergent objectives and priorities, as well as difficulties in identifying partners. Second, universities are not always interested in research topics proposed by firms whereas firms may favour a more

Table 5.1. **Perceived importance of alternative channels of knowledge transfer from university to industry**
%

Consulting	Publications	Recruit graduates	Collaborative research	Patents and licenses	Co-supervising	Others
26	18	17	12	7	9	11

Source: Agarval and Henderson "putting patents in context: exploring knowledge transfer from MIT". Management science. January 2002.

Table 5.2. **Research and innovative activities performed by universities in selected European countries**

% of active universities in the following field:	Finland	Ireland	Portugal	Spain	Sweden	UK
Contract Research	50	69	45	70	45	57
Consulting	44	68	54	61	51	53
Scientific Projects	42	68	42	82	44	48
External Training	37	73	37	67	40	36
Testing/Trialling	25	40	25	22	15	30
Patenting/Licensing	20	26	20	7	12	16
Spinout firms	11	19	11	7	12	10
Research Marketing	6	6	6	5	6	6

Source: EU-TSER project, Universities, Technology Transfer and Spinoffs (UNITTS) adaptation of table 4.6, Andersson and Klofsten, 1997, quoted in Cook (2004).

Table 5.3. **Sources of information and knowledge for innovation activities in UK manufacturing (year 2000)**

Type	Knowledge source	Not used %	Low %	Medium %	High %
Internal	Within the enterprise	32	14	27	28
Market	Suppliers of equipment, materials, components and software	32	20	32	16
	Clients or customers	34	22	28	16
	Competitors	46	27	20	6
	Consultants	62	22	13	3
Institutional	Universities and other HEI	73	17	9	2
	Government Research Organisations	82	14	4	0
	Private research institutes	82	14	4	1
Average		54	22	18	7

Source: Laursen and Salter (Danish Research Units for Industrial Dynamics).

professional approach than the one followed by academia. Third, restrictions on publishing research results may act as a disincentive for HEIs. However, these gaps can be bridged or reduced if the key drivers of academia and industry (the need to find new resources for the former and access to new technologies for the latter) are clarified. In the case of market failure, partnership structures and incentives can help both parties to come to an agreement.

Implications for government innovation strategies

OECD countries have taken steps to improve industry/science collaboration, reduce or remove the obstacles to co-operation and tackle market and systemic failures such as institutional rigidities in the research system. Better matching the university supply of skills and services with the demand of local and regional firms is becoming an increasingly important part of regional policy, given its growing orientation towards regional competitiveness, innovation capacity and skill enhancement. Improving the ability of business to exploit higher education outputs belongs to the top agenda of regional policy makers. The challenges that the OECD countries face in this domain are linked to:

● the capacity of higher education institutions and academia to respond to the needs of business and society (i.e. the need to improve framework conditions and remove regulatory barriers);

● the incentives and rewards to encourage higher education institutions to better link research and innovation, to undertake joint research with firms and public sector employers, to provide services to SMEs and to promote enterprise formation (i.e. the need for HEIs to embark on new tasks and play their role in regional innovation systems);

● the improvement of the mobility between higher education institutions and the private sector and the enhancement of the absorptive capacity of the private sector (i.e. the need to create more interest among firms, particularly SMEs and clusters, in higher education activities).

The response to these challenges often rests upon a hybrid of education initiatives and innovation and cluster policy schemes. It also focuses on efforts to promote mobility between the academic sector and the private sector, and to encourage cooperation between higher education institutions and regional development organisations. Recent trends in the four policy areas – regional policy, education policy, science and technology policy, and the industrial and enterprise policy – are described in Table 5.4. How this policy mix is organised depends on the national and regional policy characteristics of the country. For example, where regulatory barriers in the education systems remain significant, more attention is needed with regard to the removal of cultural barriers. In peripheral regions there is often a need to target SMEs to improve their absorptive capacity. In cross-border regions networks between higher education institutions may be prioritised.

Emphasis at the level of an innovation platform is nevertheless generally on the co-operation between higher education institutions and firms, regardless of their regional location. A limited number of programmes, particularly in federal states or countries with a strong regional level, have focused on regional firms and local development. For example, in Canada where education is a provincial responsibility, different regional needs are answered by the specific policies and programmes conducted by the four regional agencies of the federal government and the provinces.

Enhancing the engagement potential of higher education institutions

Deregulation of research and knowledge activities within higher education institutions is the first step – and maybe a necessary condition – for higher education institutions to gain a greater margin of manoeuvre for regional engagement. Many countries have reformed their education laws in order to grant higher education institutions more decision-making authority and flexibility to respond to the demands of the changing environment. New legislation has opened the way to regional co-operation with firms and made it possible for universities and polytechnics to align their research portfolio to regional demand, especially in advanced regions. OECD countries have improved framework conditions by passing specific acts[1] and launching profound reforms which allow higher education institutions to become nodes in regional innovation systems and to strengthen the links with the SME sector.[2] Enhancing the development of more entrepreneurial higher education sector is the objective in many countries, but in practice the progress in reducing the burden of regulation has been slow. (See Chapter 3.)

Stronger autonomy does not guarantee a regionally-engaged higher education sector if incentive structures and monitoring of outcomes are not in place. While most OECD countries have aimed to improve the HEI apparatus in relation to firms and regional economies, most incentives have been temporary and seldom through fiscal advantages. (See Chapter 3.)

The deregulation of higher education reduces limitations and disincentives for higher education staff to work on joint projects with firms. Where deregulation has taken place and collaboration is incentivised, higher education institutions have better ability to develop their interface with business and find new opportunities to enhance research and co-operation.

Table 5.4. **Policy trends supporting clusters and regional innovation systems**

Policy stream	Old approach	New approach	Innovation focus
Regional policy	Redistribution from leading to lagging regions	Building competitive regions by bringing local actors and assets together	• Include or target lagging regions • Focus on smaller firms as opposed to larger firms, if not explicitly then *de facto* • Broad approach to sector and innovation targets • Emphasis on engagement of actors
Science and technology policy	Financing of individual, Single-sector projects in basic research	Financing collaborative research involving networks with industry and links with commercialisation	• Usually high technology focus • Take advantage of and reinforce the spatial impacts of R&D investment • Promote collaborative R&D instruments to support commercialisation • Include both large and small firms; can emphasise support for spin-offs
Education policy	Focus on teaching role of HEIs and on "pure" research	Promoting closer links with industry and joint research; Enhancing greater specialisation among HEIs	• Usually high technology focus (following research budgets) • Increasing emphasis on commercialisation (*e.g.* support for spin-offs in some HEIs) • Joint work with large firms; increasing HEI-SME links is a new goal • Regional HEIs perceived as core partners in regional policy-led innovation programmes
Industrial and enterprise policy	Subsidies to firms; national champions	Addressing the shared needs of firm groups and supporting technology absorption (especially SMEs)	Programmes often adopt one of the following approaches: • Target the "drivers" of national growth • Support industries undergoing transition • Help small firms overcome obstacles to technology absorption and growth • Create competitive advantage to attract inward investment and brand for exports

Source: OECD (GOV).

The objective of regional innovation policies is to unlock the potential of the enhanced interface between higher education institutions and business, to establish new institutional links and to facilitate the use of HEI creativity. Two prominent ways are 1) integrating higher education into regional innovation systems and 2) targeting clusters.

Integrating higher education into regional innovation systems

Regional innovation systems are scaled down versions of national innovation systems. They emphasise the region as the most appropriate environment for knowledge creation and diffusion. The regional innovation system requires the creation of the necessary nodes of the system as well as a continuous flow of ideas and facilitation of linkages. These interactions may be user-producer interactions but also shared knowledge among potential competitors or between those who generate knowledge and those who adopt it.

In regional innovation systems factors which affect the ability of the higher education institution to transfer and commercialise its research include the strength and focus of the HE research base, leadership, entrepreneurial climate, incentives and rewards, the strength of corporate relations with the HEI and research units and the availability of funding. The most successful US universities draw on a combination of well-developed entrepreneurial culture, extensive networks, a strong and focused research base, federal R&D funding and support from private corporations and foundations. They also have access to early stage capital for launching start-ups (Innovation Associates Inc., 2005).

Many OECD governments have sought to improve the quality of linkages and interactions among the various actors in regional innovation systems. This has been achieved, for example, by setting up institutional frameworks for common university-industry programmes. More formalised public-private partnerships have been established in a number of countries to facilitate longer term interaction among public and private sector research organisations. In the last decade the number of existing public-private partnerships have been increased considerably.

A stronger focus on the contribution to commercial output has also been encouraged. Policy mechanisms which increase benefits from intellectual property help to enhance the contribution of higher education institutions to innovation and knowledge transfer. In the United States, the Bayh-Dole Act (1980) which permitted US universities to own inventions developed with federal funding, has given a new thrust to technology transfer, commercialisation efforts and university spin-offs. The record in this area is, however, mixed. While university propensity to patent has doubled in the United States in the last decade and increased in many other OECD countries, few universities worldwide have been able to generate revenues from commercial exploitation of research. The economic benefits of university-based research are often uncertain, at least in the short term.

In general, the position of higher education institutions and their instruments to collaborate with firms are often weak. The complex process of commercial exploitation of inventions and patents requires specialised expertise that universities can themselves develop by setting up liaison offices (See Box 5.1). In some countries, only a limited number of higher education institutions have liaison offices or centres of entrepreneurship (see a selection of main programmes in Annex B). For example, in France, only one-fourth of universities have a commercial service department. The liaison offices often lack resources in terms of staff and budget (*e.g.* Denmark, Norway, Spain or Italy) and have excessive emphasis on obtaining patents and too little on exploiting them through licenses.

Box 5.1. Examples of industrial liaison programmes in OECD countries

The industrial relations offices of higher education institutions are highly diversified in terms of resources and programme offer. They range from technology transfer offices (TTO) or technology licensing offices (TLO) to ambitious initiatives with a wide portfolio of industry-research partnership, technology transfer, industrial extension and technical assistance or industry education and training partnerships. The US research universities provide some of the most innovative and successful examples in this area, often based on the entrepreneurial drive and initiative of the university leadership backed up by federal funding and support from the private sector. Universities in the US but also elsewhere are increasingly employing professionals and entrepreneurs from the corporate world to lead their institutes.

The MIT Industrial Liaison Office is one of the best known models of linkages between universities and companies. For a membership fee, companies gain unlimited access to specialised information services.* Other universities have developed "community clubs" for companies. In the UK, for example, *Cambridge University's Computer Laboratory* and *Newcastle University's Centre for Software Reliability* have both created a club that invites companies to seminars and symposia or distribute copies of technical reports and organise exchanges of material. In some countries, higher education institutions have formed companies which receive government support to handle technology transfer (*e.g.* in Finland or Sweden).

Box 5.1. **Examples of industrial liaison programmes
in OECD countries** (cont.)

Some higher education institutions provide bespoke services to their region. In the US *Purdue University*, originally a land grant university, has had a central role in agricultural and industrial extension in Indiana. In recent years, it has played an increasing role in generating technology start-ups and new licenses to advance technology firms. It has an Office of Technology Commercialization and a research park with more than 100 companies and 2 500 employees. Purdue Research Park, which is one of the most successful in the United States, is located in a remote area where the university is the primary economic activity. Purdue University has also developed a virtual "Discovery Park" that is home to interdisciplinary research centres. These structures identify technologies with potential for commercialisation in the state. The university also runs a Technical Assistance Program which provides technology extension services to Indiana companies and a Gateways Program for entrepreneurs in incubating phase. The Office of Engagement and the Centre for Regional Development complement the university's regional strategy.

In some countries, direct support has been provided by the Ministry of Education's programmes. In Korea, *Divisions of Industry/University Cooperation* (DIUC) has been established in universities on a contract basis. DIUCs are building relations with companies or group of companies that have been able to formulate their development and training needs. Universities with a focus on industry collaboration have been identified on a basis of national competition and designated as regional hubs which receive subsidies over 5 years. Part of the funding (5%) comes from local governments and business.

* The MIT Industrial Liaison Office services include access to information services and seminar series, a monthly newsletter, the directory of MIT research organised by area of expertise and faculty visits and expert meetings that often result in consultancy or research sponsorship. The programme is managed by a panel of Industrial Liaison Officers, each responsible for a focused portfolio of companies with the responsibility to serve their interests.

Targeting clusters

Another way to involve higher education institutions in the regional economies has been to target clusters. As illustrated by Porter (1990, 1998, 2003), clusters, especially in non-high technology fields, account in many countries for a significant part of domestic GDP and of employment. Cluster theory highlights the complex system of value chains linking together the different steps in the economic process, so that each step adds new value to the whole process. Higher education institutions can play a catalysing role in this context in helping to diversify the local economy and allow clusters to expand their range of products and R&D base (Paytas *et al.*, 2004). To that end, higher education institutions can offer not only their "traditional" services, *i.e.* technology and knowledge transfer, licensing, consulting and problem-solving services, but also public space for open-ended dialogue on technological perspectives and market opportunities for industry. For example, Aalborg University's Network Centre is running 24 cluster-based networks with a total of 2 800 members from the industry, public sector and the university.

Major programmes have been launched in a number of countries to strengthen clusters through the activation of linkages between business and industry and knowledge-creating organisations. These include the Finnish Centres of Expertise which has been the origin of a family of programmes particularly in other Nordic countries, the French poles of competitiveness with 66 poles and the Japanese dual programme on clusters. The programmes show varying focus on the role higher education institutions and have limitations deriving from their lack of autonomy. Different approaches have been followed – broker-based, entrepreneurial and thematic/sectoral – which have their merits and drawbacks. All three programmes have involved a large number of stakeholders which has resulted not only in high transaction costs, but also in increased opportunities for innovation. In the long run, the costs do not, however, seem sustainable which may lead central governments to gradually phase out their contributions.

More specific conclusions can be made on each of these programmes (see also Table 5.2):

● The Finnish Centre of Expertise Programme is noteworthy not only for its long-standing nature, but also for its capacity to regenerate regional expertise and attract foreign direct investment. The Finnish experience underlines the importance of leadership and governance. First, the division of labour between universities and polytechnics has not always been clear and there has been unhealthy competition. Second, the centres of expertise involve a large number of intermediary organisations which make them complex. It has been argued that if universities with polytechnics were assigned a leading role in the centres, they would become better anchored in national innovation systems and regional programmes (OECD, 2005a). Third, while the centres have drawn universities closer to their cities, the funding system has limited this tendency.

● In France, the weakness of higher education poses major challenges for the knowledge-based economy. The role of the universities in the poles of competitiveness and in the economic life in general could be enhanced through changes in higher education funding, governance and system structure. France invests less in tertiary education than other OECD countries engaged in the knowledge economy. Increased funding would strengthen the position of universities. The universities also suffer from a lack of autonomy and are dependent on the Government for the appointment of faculty and remuneration policy. Governance reform would enhance the universities' position in the knowledge economy. In addition, institutional fragmentation could be reduced through the creation of university consortiums. The government has taken steps in this direction by introducing new legislation which has supported the creation of poles of research and higher education (PRES). A PRES agreement which is concluded with the authorities set forth the objectives of the new structure, the resource level and the system of performance assessment.

- The Japanese dual cluster programme underlines the importance of co-ordination and the use of resources. The two separate programmes, one focusing on universities and public institutes developing new technologies, and the other supporting commercialisation, had a common network approach. To reduce the risk of duplication of tasks and under-optimal use of resources better co-ordination has been introduced.

Box 5.2. **Three cluster model programmes**

The Finnish Centre of Expertise Programme sponsored by the Ministry of Interior is the most explicit regional element in the national innovation policy. These centres focus on key industries in many different sectors including culture, media and digital content where there is a degree of regional specialisation in the private sector and research competence in universities and polytechnics. Successive round of centres have been designated following national competitions. In 2003-2006 there were 18 different regional centres in Finland. The Centres were expected to network nationally as well as regionally so as to develop their core competencies and to create a mutually supportive framework all over the country. Besides the 18 regional clusters of competences, 4 centres had a specific national vocation, comprising regionally based sub-centres. Three of these centres were relevant to the industrial development of rural or peripheral regions. Most universities and polytechnics have been involved in the programme. Companies, the Finnish Funding Agency for Technology and Innovation TEKES and the EU have accounted nearly for two-thirds of the funding of the projects. The Centre of Expertise organisation was transformed early 2007 designating national co-ordinating bodies for specific competence clusters. The decision was based on the expertise and achieved track record in innovation and internationalisation and support from business and industry. There are now 13 nationally co-ordinated clusters that comprise 4 to 7 regional centres of expertise. Although the investment in the centres has been small compared to mainstream science and technology policy initiatives, the programme has been considered a highly successful component of Finnish regional policy. According to the 2006 evaluation, the investment of

---

Box 5.2. **Three cluster model programmes** (cont.)

EUR 52.5 million in 1999-2006 has levered in EUR 578 million of total funding. In addition, the programme has created more than 13 000 new knowledge-intensive jobs, preserved 29 000 jobs and led to the formation of 1 300 companies.

The French Poles of Competitiveness Programme is an ambitious industry-led programme which involves numerous stakeholders and is endowed with a significant budget. Poles are made up of businesses, research and testing centres, basic and further training organisations which, through their activities, help to ensure that there is a satisfactory range of products and services available on the market. The goal is to achieve a critical economic, scientific and technological mass in regions in order to maintain and enhance their dynamism. Partners benefit from various incentives including public subsidies, tax exemptions and reduced social contributions, financing schemes and specific guarantees. Businesses located within one of the pole's R&D zones benefit from exemptions from social contributions and lower payroll taxes (50% for SMEs, 25% for others) when they take part in the pole's projects in key industries. In 2005, 67 poles were designated on the basis of national competition, 6 of which were worldwide poles, 9 with high international visibility and 52 regional or national poles. In 2005-2007, the government supported the launch and development of the poles with EUR 1.5 billion. The programme is now entering its second phase.

The Japanese approach. The METI Industrial Cluster Programme (2001-2005) was launched by the Ministry of Technology and Industry (METI) to capitalise on the existing endogenous capabilities of 19 major regions and their R&D and industry base. The programme aimed to support exchanges and co-operation between the university, industry and the government, the development of technologies for local application and training for entrepreneurs. The 500 civil servants of the regional METI offices cooperated with 5 800 SMEs and researchers from more than 220 universities. METI invested USD 350 million into the programme over a 5-year period. The programme entered the Phase 2 in 2006-2010. While METI approach has a focus on existing industrial strengths, the MEXT Education Cluster Programme (2001-2005) developed by the Ministry of Education, Culture, Sports, Science and Technology (MEXT) targeted the universities with the aim to bring new technologies to the market. The programme aimed to reform the R&D centres and improve the flow of knowledge by setting up networks and granting start-up subsidies for joint activities. For each knowledge cluster, activities were managed by a lead organisation (usually a R&D centre). A team of science and technology co-ordinators and experts led the clusters mainly by organising forums and seminars. MEXT invested USD 410 million in a 5-year period spread over 18 designated clusters and 5 exploratory clusters, each cluster receiving on average an annual subsidy of EUR 3.9 million.

Policy practices and instruments

In many regions, local areas and cities, higher education institutions are working with regional development authorities to focus part of their technology transfer and commercialisation activities on the local as well as the global arena. The case studies of generally bottom-up initiatives are building upon a growing recognition in national governments that regional engagement by higher education institutions is a way of establishing better bridges between investment in science and technological research and business innovation.

In the following sections, initiatives drawn from the OECD countries are discussed as examples of overcoming some of the barriers to business innovation at the regional, local and city/city region level. The specific initiatives or bounded programmes of action that are introduced usually involve several actors or agencies. They seek to add value to the normal operations of the stakeholders with the ultimate objective of bringing about new ways of working in both higher education institutions and business. Most cases have been built from a project base and now form a part of the core functions of the higher education institutions concerned.

The examples illustrate specific areas where higher education institutions can significantly increase their contribution to regions and business innovation. These areas include new enterprise formation, support and services to established business and industry, the attraction and retention of external investments and the promotion of new arrangements between higher education institutions and industry within the city region framework.[3]

New enterprise formation

A widely used mechanism of knowledge exploitation is new enterprise formation by higher education institutions, their academic staff and graduates. Based on the experience of Silicon Valley, the Boston area and Cambridge, England, this is regarded as one way to build a new economy on the back of scientific research. Higher education institutions and regional development authorities across the OECD have invested heavily in support for spin-off activity. Nevertheless, the evidence regarding the scale of new business formation based upon the exploitation of university science and technology suggests that even in the United States, where there are fewer barriers to this type of activity than elsewhere, spin-offs represent less than 3% of the annual rate of new business starts.

In general, governments and their agencies have mainly invested in science parks, financed incubators and granted venture capital funds to accelerate higher education spin-off although with different emphasis and budget. Apart from specific cases (*e.g.* TETRA Flemish programmes, see Annex B) most initiatives prioritise the uptake and development of high technology industries. Mechanisms to support social entrepreneurship and developing innovation for wider needs of excluded groups in rural or inner cities areas are limited. There is also less emphasis on services, which account for 70% of the workforce in the OECD countries, as well as employment-intensive sectors such as health.

Spin-off activity has often involved a physical separation between research and commercial activity. The experience of higher education institutions and regions suggests a shift towards embedding business innovation and new enterprise formation in the heart of the academic endeavour – within the research of individual departments and generic and subject-specific education programmes (see also Chapter 6). Likewise the historic regulatory role of the technology transfer operations of HEI central administration are being revised to become more pro-active and collaborative, building bridges with external agencies, business and the academic community.

Supporting established business and industry

While the creation of new enterprises is a way of diversifying a regional economy by far the greatest gain can arise from improving the competitiveness of existing businesses, especially SMEs that dominate, at

---

Box 5.3. **Twente TOP programme**

Launched in 1984 by the University of Twente, the TOP (Temporary entrepreneurship position) programme assists university graduates, staff and people from trade and business to start their own companies. Since 1984 about 370 individuals have received TOP support and some 320 companies have been created. The survival rate of all companies is 76% (data from 2000) and after 5 years 89%. TOP companies are usually SMEs with 5 to 6 employees. They generate about 150 new jobs every year.

Annually there are about 20 TOP participants. TOP participants must a) have a concrete idea of a knowledge-intensive or technology-oriented company that can be linked to the fields of expertise of the university; b) be available for a minimum of 40 hours a week; and c) have a business plan that meets a number of set requirements. During the one-year support period the TOP entrepreneur receives office space and facilities, access to networks, a scientific and a business manager, and an interest-free loan of EUR 14 500. The loan has to be repaid within four years starting in the year after leaving the TOP programme.

---

least in numeric terms, most regional economies. However, SMEs face great difficulties working with higher education institutions (see Table 5.5). An incremental approach is often required with the higher education institutions first assisting with a solution to relatively minor business or technology problem and subsequently moving the enterprise into more innovative product/process/service development.

As noted early in this chapter, barriers to collaborative working exists on both sides. To overcome these problems, public/private organisations are sometimes created to mediate in the matchmaking process; however, in certain circumstances the business support environment can become a jungle which both SMEs and higher education institutions find themselves enmeshed.

The following are examples of practices in building bridges between SMEs and higher education institutions at the regional/state level. Establishing a single entry point for SMEs has proved successful in many regions. In the North East of England, the support for established enterprises through Knowledge House by five universities in the region counterbalances the focus of Science City on the research intensive universities and technologically based business. In the United States, Georgia Tech's Economic Development Institute is the oldest component of the university's outreach arm which serves more than 1 000 enterprises every year through 13 regional offices (see Box 5.4).

Attraction and retention of external investments

Higher education institutions can provide regions with gateway to the global knowledge base, and links to international businesses which have a potential for investing anywhere. This will include not only enterprises that

Table 5.5. **Co-operation of firms with research institutions in connection with product innovation according to the size of firms: in percentage**

	10-19	20-99	100+	All
Denmark				
Universities and research institutions	9	16	31	17
Norway				
Universities	17	23	34	28
Research Institutions	32	41	56	48
Austria				
Universities	9	22	48	33
Contract research organisations	18	20	29	24

Note: These calculations do not make differences between regional and national cooperation. However in the case of small firms, links are quasi local and regional.

Source: Christensen, Gregersen and Rogaczewska quoted in B-A Lundvall: The University in the Learning Economy, DRUID 2002.

Box 5.4. **Entry points for SMEs to the university knowledge base**

Established in 1995 *Knowledge House* is a joint effort of the five universities in the North East of England (Durham, Newcastle, Northumbria, Sunderland and Teesside) along with the Open University in the North through the universities regional association, Unis4NE. It helps companies access university skills, expertise and specialist resources. It offers expert solutions for developing ideas and solving problems through collaboration, consultancy, training and research. Knowledge House has a central Headquarters and staff distributed at the partner sites. The network and its operations are supported by a web-based enquiry handling/project management and client relationship management system. Knowledge House receives over a thousand enquiries from client companies and delivers around 200 client contracts on an annual basis. Business growth averages 25%. The cumulative economic impact of the Knowledge House activity has been estimated as being in excess of GBP 35 million (a six fold return on the investment). In contrast to networks providing only signposting services, Knowledge House offers a cradle-to-grave service, stretching from the receipt and circulation of enquiries through project management and delivery to post-completion evaluation. It is also playing its part in the integration and consolidation of the business support services in the North East through formal agreements and joint appointments with other, non-university, business support agencies such as the Business Links service and the Regional Development Agency.

Started in 1940s, *Georgia Tech's Economic Development Institute (EDI)* is one of the strongest university-based economic development programmes in the United States. EDI serves businesses with a staff of more than 100 professionals and 13 regional offices located throughout the State. Most staff in the regional offices hold engineering degrees and have worked in the private sector and lived in the communities that they serve. EDI provides a comprehensive set of services designed to help Georgia companies become more productive and competitive. It provides technology-driven solutions in quality and international standards, energy and environmental management, lean enterprise transformation, information technology, government contracting, trade adjustment assistance, and marketing and new product development. Its service portfolio includes workshops and seminars, short courses, certifications, information dissemination and extension services. In future, EDI aims to focus more on product development, marketing and attracting financing. After the initial period, firms are charged fees for services. In 2004, EDI served 1 889 customers through projects, technical assistance, counselling sessions and information requests; Companies assisted by the Procurement Assistance Center gained contracts worth USD 500 million; EDI helped attract or retain USD 112.5 million

Box 5.4. **Entry points for SMEs
to the university knowledge base** (cont.)

investment and create or save 450 jobs; 11 778 jobs were created or saved in companies. Firms pay an increasing portion of the EDI services, about one-third of the total cost with federal and State government sharing the remaining two-thirds. Georgia Tech is a member of the Manufacturing Extension Partnership (MEP), a national network of technical assistance centres that help small- and mid-sized manufacturers. MEP is the largest federal sponsor for EDI. In early 2004, MEP's funding to EDI was cut by 75% because of federal budget reductions leading to the closing of the three regional offices and elimination of service to 300 firms.

Source: Innovation Associates Inc. (2005).

currently operate on a global stage but smaller local businesses that are increasingly able to source goods and services from anywhere and undertake upstream production in distant locations to take advantage of different costs/ environmental conditions. For both types of businesses "immobile" higher education institutions are a means of tying down the global in the local in order to enhance the development of a region. One recent example is Trondheim in Norway which has become "Europe's search capital" when Google, Yahoo and a few smaller start-ups have established their R&D departments. The availability of skilled human resources in the local search community and the proximity of the Norwegian University of Technology are key factors.

Discovering the competitive assets of the region and building on existing strengths is important. While most regional development strategies have a focus on indigenous creation of new industry, upgrading the existing industry and attraction and retention of inward investment may bring a more sustainable solution, at least for most non-metropolitan regions. The focus in most local industry links with higher education institutions, particularly with research-intensive universities, is on high technology sectors/activities. However this does not always have to be the case. In the Castellon province of the Valencia region of Spain a relatively new university has established links to the traditional industry and has helped to transform it into a global leader through improving the absorptive capacity of the region's SME base. (See Box 5.5.)

While the Castellon case has a strong focus on SMEs, evidence shows that the presence of at least one large enterprise can have a beneficial effect on university-industry relations. For example, in a survey of 268 metropolitan areas in the United States, the presence of one large enterprise is seen to have a positive impact on the quality of relations between the university and industrial R&D (Agarval and Henderson, 2002). This is clearly evident in the

Box 5.5. **Upgrading the existing industry base in Castellon, Spain, and North East England**

University Jaume I has contributed to significant restructuring of the traditional ceramic tile production cluster; this comprises 500 businesses, mostly SMEs employing 36 000 people. The links have been mediated by the *Institute for Ceramic Technology (ITC)*, a not-for-profit association formed by an agreement between the University Institute for Ceramic Technology and the Ceramic Industry Research Association. The ITC provides access to the knowledge, skill and expertise of the university in a purpose built premises. It also provides quality certification tests for ceramic products – it is one of only nine laboratories in Europe with a similar service. Both institutions jointly use the facilities, equipment, materials and staff that make up the research infrastructure. There are 23 academic staff, 53 graduates, 27 technicians and 27 support staff in building which includes 8 000 m^2 of laboratories, pilot plant, meeting rooms, offices, etc. The growth of the cluster has been supported by technology transfer, spin-outs and upgrading of existing technologies. The partnership has enabled Valencia to become a global leader in the tile and ceramic industry.

Economic development in the North East of England in the post-World War II period was driven by the attraction of mobile manufacturing investment to the region to take advantage of low land and labour costs and public subsidies. Although much of that investment has been relocated out of Europe, what remains depends on maintaining high levels of manufacturing productivity. *The North East Productivity Alliance (NEPA)* is a regional alliance of industries, academics and government agencies. Established in 2001, the NEPA programme covers work force development, best practice improvement engineering (supported by an industry forum), digital factory design and sponsored engineering fellows linked to higher education institutions. The University of Sunderland delivers 50% of the programmes with participating firms. Critical to its success* is the agreement of Nissan Motor Manufacturing UK to champion NEPA. Nissan is the largest manufacturer in the region, the most productive automobile industry plant in the world and the cornerstone of the region's automotive sector, employing 4 000 people directly and generating GBP 170 million in wages every year. NEPA has spread best practice down the supply chains of other leading firms, providing the opportunity for collective learning experience.

* The outcomes of NEPA include 5000 level 2 National Vocational Qualifications gained by manufacturing staff, 2000 design engineers trained in digital factory tools and techniques and 8 industry-led research projects.

case study from the North East England where the presence of Nissan and its close links to the University of Sunderland are benefiting a cluster-based development, retention of inward investment and general up-skilling of the labour force in the region (see Box 5.5).

Promoting science and technology cities

Innovation requires more than access to the knowledge which can be codified in copyright and patents. It also requires tacit knowledge which can be gained or transmitted through personal experience and interactions. Because of their high population density, cities enable these connections to be made easily. The density of interaction and the likelihood of chance interactions create favourable conditions for a hot-bed of innovation (Burt, 2002). Consequently, many OECD countries have placed a greater focus on cities and city regions in innovation. Examples here come from the UK, Mexico and Denmark (Box 5.6).

The UK has a good record of scientific research endeavour but has been poor in translating research into business opportunities. There are also marked inter-regional variations in innovative performance: many older industrial regions like the North East of England which were the cradles of innovation in the 19th and early 20th century have lost their dynamics. In 2004, the UK Government took a step to address this problem by designating six "Science Cities" in Newcastle, York, Manchester, Nottingham, Birmingham and Bristol in order to link urban/regional policy with science, innovation and higher education policy (see Box 5.6). Science Cities are developed by triple helix partnerships in order to bring industry and universities closer together within the city and to remove physical and institutional barriers to commercial exploitation of science. While the Science City initiative is relatively new and the results to the local economy are not yet visible, in a highly centralised country it is channelling funding to the city level in peripheral parts of the country. In Newcastle it has also enabled the university to win the first UK licence for stem cell research and one of only two national health service R&D centres outside of the "golden triangle" of London, Oxford and Cambridge.

Like in many OECD countries, the Mexican territorial economy is dominated by the capital city region. However, one of the country's most dynamic and entrepreneurial regions, the State of Nuevo León is on the periphery of the national territory on the borders with the USA. The growth of the state is largely dependent on its thriving core city, Monterrey. Here the National Council for Science and Technology is investing in the regional Centre of Knowledge which indicates a readiness to adopt a regional approach to national science and technology policy with a view to exploiting more effectively the university research base for business.

In Jutland, Denmark, where the economy is dominated by SMEs, the University of Aarhus, with the help of local government, has concentrated its ICT research and teaching in an old industrial quarter of the city (IT City Katrineberg). This development includes Computer Science, Computer Engineering, Multi-Media, Information Services, Media Studies, the Schools of Business, Architecture and Engineering and embraces 300 staff and 1 800 students. The university has also created an overarching organisational structure in the form of the Alexandra Institute to link this activity with local and international businesses (Box 5.6).

Box 5.6. **Science and technology cities**

2004, Newcastle upon Tyne, the principal city in the North East region was designated as one of the Science Cities. A partnership was formed between Newcastle University, the City Council and the Regional Development Agency to strengthen the "upstream" links into the research base from the intermediary organisations and to embed business physically and functionally into the core of the university. The aim is to combine local research strength and the critical mass of commercial partners at the regional, national, international level and to build a new economic base through spin-outs, transforming existing businesses and attracting inward investment. Initial domains include Stem cell biology and regenerative medicine, Ageing and Health, Molecular Engineering and Energy and the Environment. *The Newcastle Science City* builds on the experience of establishing the International Centre for Life which aims to transform the mass production pharmaceutical industry in the region into one based around the exploitation of biotechnology developed in the university's medical school and hospital.

Monterrey International Centre of Knowledge is based on a consortium of the three leading higher education institutions in Nuevo León, *i.e.* the Autonomous University of Nuevo León, the Monterrey Institute of Technology (ITSEM) and the University of Monterrey. The Monterrey International Centre of Knowledge promotes the economic development of the city of Monterrey and the state of Nuevo León. A key partner in this consortium is the National Council for Science and Technology, a funding body which supports basic research and postgraduate study on a competitive basis in Mexican universities. Other partners include a research and technological innovation park, an Institute of Innovation and Technology Transfer sponsored by the state government and the Regional Integration Programme of North East States (INVITE) created by the state government to enhance regional competitiveness by fostering cross border relations with Texas in research and innovation. The National Council for Science and Technology is investing in the Centre of Knowledge for example by supporting six new research centres in the state alongside 11 applied

---

Box 5.6. **Science and technology cities** *(cont.)*

research centres created by the universities themselves. The universities are also revising their internal technology transfer operations.

The Alexandra Institute is a research-based limited company, which operates as a matchmaker between researchers and companies in the IT sector. While many Danish companies involve users in the development of new products, they only rarely draw upon the most recent IT research. The Alexandra Institute, however, is specialised in providing a framework for adding research component into the innovation efforts of its public and private sector partners. The Institute has three requirements for engaging in a project: (a) the project must involve users; (b) the project must draw upon IT research of high international quality; and (c) the project must involve at least one private company. Therefore, all projects have not only a research dimension, but also a *developmental component* bringing concrete results to the company (*e.g.* industrial prototypes). Each project also has a project team with researchers, students, company employees, and representatives from the user organisations. Project funding is drawn from a range of sources, companies financing at least half of the project costs.

Co-ordinating local and regional HEI contributions for the benefit of the territorial economy

The OECD study included a number of initiatives that enhance the development of the knowledge-based economy. Higher education institutions can join forces and share assets to improve and diversify their supply of services for local and regional firms and public sector employers. They can attain the critical mass for research and efficient commercialisation of their own innovative activities and increase their comparative advantages. Initiatives which bring together research-intensive universities and polytechnics/community colleges would be particularly beneficial for the enhancement of knowledge-based economy.

The four provinces that form Atlantic Canada have 14 universities which dominate the R&D base of the region. To ensure that this knowledge is mobilised for the benefit of economic development and to embrace the smaller universities that are unable to support a commercialisation function, the Springboard network was established in 2005. It is unique in its identification of indicators for success and pooling the resources of the higher education institutions. A similar type of network has been established in the Öresund cross-border region; it brings together 14 universities in two different countries (Box 5.7 and Box 8.4 in Chapter 8).

Box 5.7. **Higher education networks supporting the growth of knowledge-based economy**

Established in 2004, *Springboard Atlantic Inc.* is a network of university technology transfer/industrial liaison offices that supports the commercialisation of university research in Atlantic Canada. The network is funded by ACOA's Atlantic Innovation Fund, NSERC's Intellectual Property Mobilization (IPM) Program and 14 member universities (*i.e.* Acadia University, Cape Breton University, Dalhousie University, Memorial University, Mount Allison University, Mount Saint Vincent University, Nova Scotia Agricultural College, NSCAD University, St. Francis Xavier University, Saint Mary's University, St. Thomas University, Université de Moncton, University of New Brunswick and the University of Prince Edward Island).

The network offers services and resources to its member universities including; *a)* delivering educational programmes (*e.g.* on intellectual property); *b)* hosting network events for researchers and business people; *c)* facilitating industry sponsored research; *d)* assessing discoveries; and *e)* developing proof of concept projects marketing technologies. The network is sponsored by the Federal Government's regional development agency, the Atlantic Canada Opportunities Agency (ACOA). The network is a gateway to the agency's Atlantic Innovation Fund designed to strengthen the regional economy through development of knowledge based industry.

The Öresund Science Region's platforms seek to link 14 higher education institutions which participate in the cross-national Öresund University. There are nine networks or platforms linked to specific industry/service areas spread across two countries (Denmark and Sweden).* The platforms are thus organised around core competencies in the region. Each platform has built a database of the relevant regional businesses and organisations into its respective core competences, which creates the possibility of directing specific knowledge streams from HEIs to the targeted areas of development. For example, Diginet Öresund, Öresund food network and Öresund IT academy are key sector areas for generating regional development outcomes as they are mainly made up of small firms. Having different platforms under the umbrella of one single organisation also opens up potential to benefit from the economies of scope. Learning advantages and cross fertilisation between different platforms of the Öresund Science Region can be exploited. For example the Öresund food network is linked to the Medicon valley platform and the Diginet Öresund to the Öresund IT academy.

* Öresund Science Region Platforms: Medicon Valley Academy, Øresund IT Academy, Øresund Environment Academy, Øresund Design, Øresund Logistics, Øresund Food Network, Diginet Øresund, Nano Øresund, The Humanities Platform.

Conclusions

HEIs' contribution to business innovation is reflected in new institutional links and a new type of co-operation. These new initiatives utilise a variety of modes of interchange between higher education institutions and business often articulated through multi stakeholder/public/private structures or intermediary organisations. All have a common objective of not only transferring research into business but also supporting indigenous development of local and regional economies, characteristically dominated by SMEs.

Many of the partnerships have evolved through a series of stages utilising time limited public funding. In the process the capacity for joint action between higher education institutions and regional interests has been built up incrementally. Physical proximity of researchers, businesses and intermediary support services is another feature, either built into the partnership initially or added as it matures. In this way knowledge interchange with business becomes more embedded in the customs and practices of the higher education institution, embracing teaching as well as research.

OECD countries have high expectations for cooperation with the private sector in research and innovation and increasing the impact of publicly funded R&D on firms. Science and technology policies have shifted their emphasis to prioritise commercialisation of academic research and cooperation with the private sector. This is evident from the wide range of programmes that target higher education institutions. However, higher education institutions are not always well equipped to play this role and their technology transfer and licensing offices are often in urgent need of further resourcing and not well connected with other knowledge transfer organisations. Higher education institutions also face difficulties in reaching SMEs, especially in regions with low absorption capacity. The cost of research is often underestimated and the revenue generated often disappointing.

Policies could be improved in three ways. First, at the institutional level there is a need to diffuse entrepreneurship culture and willingness to co-operate with the industry. Second, funding for collaborative research is generally not focused on regional firms or linked to regional priorities. Many regions are in short supply of risk capital to finance academic based endeavours.[4] Regional funds for pre-competitive research as well as for venture capital would help to bridge the gap. Third, governments at central and regional level should consider the desirable balance between research for longer term new development and exploitative R&D for the use and dissemination of existing technologies and develop more inter-institutional collaboration and partnerships of a complementary nature. Partnering with firms from the initial phase of R&D programmes reinforces the innovation potential of academic research.

The OECD countries are looking increasingly to higher education institutions to become more entrepreneurial in ways that not only benefit the institution but also contribute to economic development. The above strategies and programmes provide examples of how regional engagement is contributing towards the emergence of more economically proactive institutions where research excellence and business engagement are seen to be mutually compatible. The next chapter reviews how similar processes are in train with respect to teaching and learning in relation to human capital development.

Notes

1. Examples include the Technology Transfer Promotion Act in Korea. Korea has also amended the Industrial Education and Academic Industrial Collaboration Promotion Law (2003) laying the framework for effective university-business collaboration, the introduction of an independent accounting system for higher education institutions and the establishment of school corporations. In Denmark, the university act (2003) has contributed also to extension and development of educational portfolio and profiles to better match the need for new competence and skills. As a result several universities have been awarded the permission to offer degree programmes in order to comply with regional shortage of skills and local needs, for example in engineering (e.g. the University of Aarhus and the University of Southern Denmark).

2. In Japan, national universities have been transformed into National University Corporations. The change has strengthened university autonomy over human and physical resources and links to the SME sector. Enhanced R&D co-operation and mobility between higher education and firms may gradually reduce the dependence on in-house R&D of larger corporations.

3. The cases have been selected because of the potential transferability of experience. However, the importance of the local/regional context both in time and space cannot be over emphasised. Account needs to be taken of the history of economic development, the current industrial and socio-demographic situation, the organisation of local and regional government and the location of the region within the national territory. Equally significant are the evolution of the higher education system within the region in relation to the national system and the length of time partnerships with the region have been in place.

4. Recourse to a private fund might not be easy because private funds will aim to maximise its return on investments. Return on investment in the case of seed and pre-seed venture capital is often difficult to achieve in a relatively short term. In addition a private fund might be more prone to finance spin-offs outside the region or the country because of their stronger potential for competitiveness. Some regulatory framework is often needed to ensure a certain part of these funds to be invested in local and regional spin-offs.

ISBN 978-92-64-03414-3
Higher Education and Regions:
Globally Competitive, Locally Engaged
© OECD 2007

Chapter 6

Contribution of Higher Education to Regional Human Capital Formation: Overcoming the Barriers

This chapter considers the role of higher education institutions in regional human capital systems and in building "learning regions". It presents several examples from OECD countries highlighting the different roles that the higher education institutions play in this domain. First, higher education institutions can widen access to higher education, particularly from remote areas and/or communities with low traditions of participation in higher education e.g. through lifelong and e-learning activities. Second, they can improve the balance between labour market supply and demand through creating improved labour market intelligence, enhancing the links with the employers and supporting new enterprising. Third, higher education institutions can attract talent to the region and help retain it.

The previous chapter examined the ways through which higher education institutions (HEIs) are involved with regional innovation systems. It had a primary focus on the "hard" contributions, such as the inputs to and infrastructure for firm-based innovation, including patenting/licensing activity, consultancy and knowledge transfer and provision of specialist facilities such as laboratories, science parks and incubators. While OECD countries have rightfully pointed the need to focus on the R&D generated by academia, the development of spin-offs and patenting, the approach has sometimes been unbalanced. The focus on the "hard" contributions of higher education ignores what is arguably one of the most effective mechanisms for knowledge transfer, knowledge which is embedded in students and graduates and is subsequently absorbed – via the regional labour market – into the regional knowledge economy (Martin and Trudeau, 1998). This "knowledge transfer on legs" is a critical element of the regional role played by higher education institutions. Thus, this chapter considers the broader significance of labour market processes for the technological and organisational dynamism of regions.

Labour markets are diverse and demand- and supply-side conditions vary significantly within and between OECD countries. The processes that occur at the regional and local level and the articulation between the different instances of governance are important in the success of human capital development. In this sense, analyses of methods for upgrading workforce skills need to be linked to the local labour market (Peck, 1996; Martin and Morrison, 2003). So far only limited attention has been paid to the territorial dimension of skills creation and upgrading (OECD, 2006h). The relationship between geography and skills strategies has recently been acknowledged by some OECD countries (see e.g. DfES, DTI, DWP, HM Treasury, 2003).

Higher education institutions have a key role in building "learning regions". A "learning region" refers to a territory where institutions, individuals and incentives are geared to a continual learning and up-skilling process which maximises not only economic performance, but also individual achievement. It is a special form of human capital system with a set of inter-connected labour markets through which individuals progress during their working lives. Human capital formation is thus driven by individuals seeking learning in response to market demands and to increase their earning potentials and personal fulfilment. Entrepreneurship and enterprise education can help students to be better employed by local businesses, increasing demand for those skills, and stimulating more people to involve themselves with learning. (Lundvall, 1992; Lundvall and Borrás, 1997)

This chapter presents several examples from OECD countries and more specifically from the fourteen regions in the current OECD study highlighting the different roles of the higher education institutions in human capital formation and uptake in the region. Local, regional and institutional responses can reduce the problem of one-size-fits-all approaches that are unsuitable in responding to diverse business and individual needs. However, local solutions do not guarantee policy effectiveness. Practices linked to human capital formation cannot be disconnected from the broader national and supra-national policy framework that governs the fields of education and territorial development. The emphasis given to the regional agenda of higher education institutions by national authorities can act as either a constraining or an enabling factor. Moreover, a lack of involvement on the part of local and regional employers can be a barrier to policy effectiveness and a source of regional variations.

Widening access

Development of human resources is a key element in the enhancement of growth and international competitiveness. Benefits of education include higher employment rates and earnings for individuals, and increased productivity and economic growth for countries and regions. Inequity in education implies that human potential is wasted, and under-educated individuals not only fail to contribute to national prosperity, but also generate social costs. A low level of education attainment is a crucial determinant of being poor. Groups which are likely to suffer from lower levels of education include immigrants, individuals in remote areas and excluded communities, and children of lower socio-economic status (*e.g.* Grubb *et al*, 2006). Increased financial pressures can, however, result in higher education institutions working with those most **able** to participate, which – from the perspective of regional development and equity in education – might not necessarily be the same groups as those which most **need** to secure access to higher education.

Geographical access in higher education systems

National systems have grown considerably during the last decades bringing new groups within the scope of higher education. In some countries the growth has been linked to addressing regional disparities (Chapter 2). The Nordic systems of higher education have traditionally laid a strong emphasis on equity and the main argument behind the expansion has been to include new groups in higher education and to reduce inequalities in gender, place of residence and socio-economic background.[1]

In the Nordic countries, equity in human capital development has been supported by means of free education, generous student support, enhanced geographical accessibility and emphasis on open and further education provided to non-traditional learners. There has, however, been a focus on quantity (in terms of entrance or cost of studies) as opposed to the quality of learning outcomes which may become the key dimension of equity (see Davies *et al.*, 2006).[2] Targeted policy interventions may need to be considered through which individuals are consciously treated differently, as has been done in Sweden in the case of disabled students (OECD, 2008, *forthcoming*).[3]

Some countries have introduced a specific regional dimension to the higher education equity initiatives. (See Box 6.1)

There is pressure in most national higher education systems to establish hierarchies of institutions; entrance to the elite institutions inevitably provides individuals with positional advantage in the labour market often regardless of their personal attributes and home location. In these circumstances individual access to higher education as a means of social advancement from disadvantaged backgrounds may not be possible for students in regions without an elite institution if these students are unable to move away. On the other hand, the expansion of mass higher education into most regions is creating opportunities that did not exist previously and if employment opportunities in regional knowledge economies are expanding, equity objectives will be met. (Compare *e.g.* Brennan and Naidoo, 2007, forthcoming.)

In developing countries, enhancing growth and innovation requires both expanding the higher education sector and widening participation. Mexico

---

Box 6.1. Higher Education Equity Programs in Australia

In Australia, the *Higher Education Equity Program* (HEEP) was reviewed in 2004 as part of the *Backing Australia's Future* initiative to ensure that equity funding remained focused on groups experiencing significant educational disadvantage. It resulted in the launching of two new programmes from 2005, the Higher Education Equity Support Program (ESP) and the Higher Education Disability Support Program (DSP). Allocations to institutions under ESP are driven by enrolments, retention and success of students, from low socio-economic status students, with a weighting to the students from rural and isolated backgrounds. DSP is the scheme that higher education providers may apply for funding the educational support and/or equipment to students with disabilities.

Source: Thematic Review of Tertiary Education (OECD, 2008, forthcoming).

---

has witnessed an explosive growth in higher education; however, participation in higher education remains among the lowest in the OECD countries (Brunner *et al.*, 2006). In Brazil, only 7.6% of the 18-22 year-old age-group enter higher education. There are big regional differences and some evidence that students from higher socio-economic backgrounds benefit from the state universities with lower tuition fees (Box 6.2).

Higher education institutions with diverse cultural foundations respond to particular needs in regions with indigenous and other minorities and are a

---

Box 6.2. **Paraná, Brazil: Higher education expansion driven by the local authority**

Brazil has low educational attainments at all levels. The recent expansion in higher education has taken place in private institutions which have not fully addressed the needs of the labour market. Enrolment in higher-education level technological institutes is low. Brazil has a degree of state-level devolution and higher education institutions in the region are managed through the state Higher Education Co-ordinating Committee, which reports to the State Secretariat for Science, Technology and Higher Education. This council is primarily consultative and faces challenges in channelling the collective views of a highly diversified higher education sector to the State Government.

In northern Paraná, the transfer from extensive grain production towards knowledge-based economy requires the involvement of both public and private universities. The largest state university of Paraná, the State University of Londrina, and several private universities operate in Londrina. Among them, UNOPAR has 12 000 conventional students and 63 000 distance education students mostly from outside Paraná. This institution alone provides 30% of the distance education in Brazil. Still, limited access to higher education remains a critical weakness in the region. The share of the young finding places and able to afford to attend local universities is low.

The State and Municipal governments have interest in increasing the provision and local uptake of short cycle, 2½-year technical courses, which reduce the study costs and increase the employability of students. Public-sector actors in Londrina have developed a number of actions to secure this outcome. These include attracting a new institution, Pontifical university, to the region and granting public land in return for particular course provision Furthermore, the establishment of an extension of the Federal Technological University is helping to guarantee the availability of the short degrees are highly demanded by the labour market. The first programmes to be offered are Food Technology and Industrial Chemistry where special needs were identified.

---

means of raising aspirations in those communities (see Box 6.3). If access to the institutions is not extended to all citizens, they may, however, involve a risk of undervaluing other parts of the culture.

Lifelong learning and distance education

Differences in productivity across countries and regions can be explained by differences in skills and educational attainment. More than a third of working age adults are poorly qualified in the OECD area. Ageing societies depend on older workers as a source of skills and know-how. Due to rapidly changing skill requirements in working life, lifelong learning and skills upgrading are becoming increasingly important. As economies restructure and relocate production in countries with lower labour costs, there is a stronger pressure to upgrade the skills of the local work force so that they can fuel economic growth (OECD, 2006h). The rationale for this investment is supported by modern growth theory, which emphasises the relationship between acquisition of human capital and economic growth. There is a strong linkage between investment in the human capital of the low-qualified workers in a country and labour productivity (Coulombe, Tremblay and Marchand, 2004).

The emphasis on a knowledge-based economy and the need to invest in human capital to increase productivity and competitiveness have significantly raised the profile of adult learning in public policy over the past decade. There are marked differences in the provision of adult learning across OECD

Box 6.3. L'Université de Moncton: A symbol of cultural pride and catalyst of local economic development

The struggle for cultural survival of the Acadian people – numbering some 300 000 in Atlantic Canada – goes back more than three centuries. Traditionally, a people largely dependant on fishery and agriculture, Acadians have emerged as one of the most dynamic elements in Atlantic Canada, with a vibrant entrepreneurial class and strong community leaders. The cultural revival and economic vitality – especially of south-eastern New Brunswick centred on Moncton – have sometimes been referred to as the "Acadian Miracle". The Université de Moncton has been a central player in this development. Incorporated in 1963 – the largest fully French-language university (with regional campuses) outside Quebec – it rapidly became a centre for Acadian artistic life, scientific achievement and community initiatives. The university has produced three Provincial premiers. Some 80% of its graduates have remained in New Brunswick; the percentage is even higher for Atlantic Canada, a sign of the close links between the university and its community.

---

countries and differences in the policy approaches and delivery systems. A large part of the workforce benefits from adult education in the Nordic countries, the United Kingdom, Switzerland and Canada (OECD, 2003c). Other countries show a much lower rate of participation. While some give a prominent role to public institutions in organising and delivering training, others rely on private training providers or transfer responsibility to social partners. Some countries finance training through payroll tax and make training compulsory for workers. Others promote a market-oriented approach. (OECD, 2006h.)

The strategic importance of skills upgrading is felt most urgently at local and regional level and this is also where the majority of initiatives embracing a wide range of stakeholders have taken place (OECD, 2006h). Adult learners, which have established links in a specific locality, are less mobile than younger students. Upgrading their skills will thus have a more direct effect on the region's economic performance. As local initiatives are insufficient, upgrading the skills should become a strategic objective of national governments. In mature higher education systems, access needs to be expanded to include individuals of all ages. In general, higher education institutions are often more strongly oriented to meet the needs of traditional students than those of non-traditional learners. The provision of programmes should be flexible taking advantage not only of work-based learning but also e-learning and distant learning opportunities in order to take account non-traditional learners, those who combine work and study, and the needs of the employers. They also need to allow attendance on the basis of non-formal and in-formal learning. (See Box 6.4, and *Thematic Review of Tertiary Education*, OECD, 2008, forthcoming.)

Some governments have signalled their intention to rationalise their higher education systems through a process of mergers that will lead to a reduction in the number of independent higher education institutions (see also Chapter 3). These mergers have as their main objective to strengthen the national research environment. This trend is motivated not only by the ageing process in the population and the perspective of smaller cohorts of students in the year to come but also by the need to develop internationally competitive and stronger higher education institutions. Scaling down the higher education sector may work against widening participation and geographical accessibility if at the same time distance learning, e-learning and lifelong opportunities are not stepped up.

Conjoint action of higher education institutions to widen access

Within the scope of the current OECD study, there was limited evidence among the higher education institutions and their regional stakeholders of shared commitment to address hard-core problems of a low skills base and

Box 6.4. **Widening access through distance education in remote areas**

In 2002, the four higher education institutions in the sparsely populated northern part of Finland established a consortium entitled *Provincial University of Lapland (Lapin maakuntakorkeakoulu)* with the aim to support the development of the region, to widen access to higher education, to increase co-operation between educational institutions and to foster innovation. The consortium provides degree and non-degree education at bachelor and masters levels reaching out to remote communities with the help of a combination of distance learning and contact education. It has recently expanded its services and now has a portfolio including open education, professional development courses, expert and R&D services as well as foresight and evaluation services. Learning and development needs have been mapped in each of the four sub-regions in co-operation with a wide range of public and private stakeholders. Higher education institutions are engaged in strategy development and implementation at the regional and sub-regional levels. Provision of services and education is based on regional needs which focus on upgrading the tourism industry. The network takes advantage of already existing facilities in the sub-regions and web-based services. Similar initiatives have emerged in other Finnish regions, spurred by the Ministry of Education, and taking advantage of the extensive adult education framework of the higher education institutions and folk institutions.

In 2001, the ITESM – Monterrey Institute of Technology launched *Community Centres of Learning* throughout the state of Nuevo León to serve the geographically isolated areas which lack traditional educational services. Community centres are supported by many partners and draw massive financial support from international foundations and the private sector. Programmes using modern technologies are flexible and interactive. They include basic literacy, IT and other adult learning and programmes for youth which will improve the quality of life of marginalised communities. A website provides academic content and support services. There are now centres not only in every municipality in the State of Nuevo León but also in more than 700 other localities throughout Mexico. The aim to target the poorest micro-regions in Mexico is facilitated by the agreement with the federal Social Development Ministry. With the help of new information and communication technologies Community Centres of Learning are now being emulated in other countries in the wider American region.

> Box 6.4. **Widening access through distance education in remote areas** *(cont.)*
>
> *In Estonia, ane-University consortium,* which works through 10 study centres in remote areas, is targeting people living outside the two university cities. In *Iceland,* the University of Education and the University of Akureyri are dual mode establishments, combining both on-site teaching with distance education. For the University of Education, distance teaching follows a centre-periphery model with national standards being projected into the region. For the University of Akureyri, the distance education works through 8 Life Long Learning Centres, each located in a small community across the country and linked to the university via Internet and video conferencing facilities. 35% of the University of Akureyri's studies take advantage of distance education. See *Thematic Review of Tertiary Education* (OECD, 2008, forthcoming).

inter-related worklessness. The portfolios of higher education institutions did not generally include a systematic approach to raising aspirations and widening access to higher education within the region and its excluded communities. In the North East England, however, the national widening access agenda backed up by funding from HEFCE and the region's low levels of educational attainment have contributed to a collaborative action from higher education institutions (Box 6.5).

Improving the balance between labour market supply and demand

Balancing the aspiration of individuals and the needs of the regional economy poses a major challenge to higher education institutions and regions working to enhance their stock of human capital. In a lagging region with a low demand for graduates higher education can legitimately provide a ladder of opportunity for young people that in the short run inevitably leads them out of the region.[4] On the other hand, gearing teaching and learning towards the needs of established and possibly declining sectors to ensure graduate retention is no service to either the learners or the regional economy unless it is designed explicitly to raise competitiveness of these sectors by up-skilling. The obvious implication of these concerns is that research-based measures designed to stimulate the different categories of business innovation must be linked to teaching-based initiatives designed to enhance the regional skills base.

The impact of higher education institutions on their regional labour markets is significantly affected by the extent to which the knowledge

Box 6.5. **Widening access in the North East England**

The North East of England is below the national average for educational attainment. The performance gap widens at tertiary compared with school levels. The gap is wider in literacy and numeracy, including adult literacy. Historically, the absence of strong labour market demand for graduates has held back rather than driven up demand for investment in higher education (CURDS, 2005).

The five universities in the region support the national widening participation agenda (AimHigher) individually and collectively through building links between different levels of educational institutions in order to change the culture and to raise aspiration in predominantly working class communities and neighbourhoods where going to university is rare. At the same time they seek to persuade the dominant SME part of the private employment sector that graduates can be an asset to their firms.

Different universities employ different techniques to raise their profile with non-traditional learners and their communities. These include: a) partnership with further education colleges; b) non-threatening access and engagement strategies taking advantage of sport and culture; and c) student volunteering participation in community activities that has a direct educational purpose for the students and a community inclusion intent. For example, Teesside, originally a new opportunities university, is leading a longstanding partnership with eight further education colleges known as the Higher Education Business Partnership. It has developed a collaborative strategy to meet the needs of disenfranchised learners in innovative ways, tackling the deprivation of the area.

A special committee of the regional higher education association Unis4NE is facilitating the co-operation in the widening participation agenda. As a result, the universities in the region are able to come together in raising funding streams for this work. For example, as a response to the HEFCE initiative for Lifelong Learning Networks the North East came forward with a single region-wide network proposal in contrast to other regions where local competition between higher education institutions resulted to several individual bids.

developed within students and graduates drawn on and can be applied within the region. There are examples of institutional inertia within higher education institutions. In some cases they prefer to provide courses with relatively low investment costs over expensive but potentially more regionally relevant technology and engineering courses (*e.g.* private higher education institutions in Brazil). The labour market mismatch can often be attributed to the following: First, there may be a lack of labour market intelligence and knowledge gaps between higher education institutions/graduates and regional employers. Second, there may be inadequate co-operation between higher education institutions and employers. Third, there may be inadequate support for new enterprise.

Creating labour market intelligence

Brain drain and skill shortages are not a challenge for lagging regions only. Metropolitan regions often face skill gaps and shortages because of insufficient or maladjusted local skill supply or brain drain. In specific industrial sectors employers cannot find suitably qualified workers. Cities and their higher education institutions can gather intelligence on educational needs and identifying how these needs can be met. They also possess information, expertise and knowledge necessary to anticipate future skill demands which is increasingly needed by the business sector that is willing to settle and expand locally. These demands are likely to increase as city labour markets become more complex and the need for highly skilled workers more crucial.

Graduate databases, graduate progression surveys, alumni surveys, graduate vacancy lists and employability audits are used to varying degrees but are often limited in their scope to the level of a single institution (or discipline) and fail to develop a comprehensive regional picture. The most

---

Box 6.6. **Balancing between labour market supply and demand**

In Toronto, the City has prepared a *Labour Force Readiness Plan* for the period 2001-2010 in partnership with the business community, labour representatives, the education sector and all levels of government. The plan provides an overview of labour market issues in the city region and detailed action plans for three clusters. The labour market forecasts are prepared on the basis of disaggregated data by a team including the University of Toronto.

In the United States *the Great Cities Universities Skill Enhancement Partnership Initiatives (SEPI)* aims at creating a roadmap of educational and training programmes targeted at closing the gap of employees in the technology sector. In the United Kingdom two initiatives from London have similar objectives: *The London Higher Education Consortium* aims at creating a forum and also at providing a body from which higher education representatives can be drawn to serve London's new agencies and boards. *The Thames Gateway London Partnership* is a sub regional alliance of local authorities, universities and the London Development Agency designed to deliver with the private sector the socio-economic regeneration of the Thames Gateway.

---

effective ones develop region-wide graduate labour market systems through creating, disseminating and using the labour market intelligence:

● Creating data on labour market intelligence: undertaking comprehensive regional level surveys of graduates, graduate employment opportunities, graduate employability and employer demands, and matching the demand-side information to the supply-side in terms of the courses offered by institutions in the region;

● Publicising data on labour market intelligence: bringing the data together in a single place so that students can make rational decisions about the choice of subjects given their desired employability outcomes and to help graduates and employers come together and for students to move into employment;

● Using the data on labour market intelligence strategically: analysing the emerging data and to identify regional priorities for development and change, and at an institutional level, responding to that data both in terms of course provision and the provision of employer specified skills.

Improving links with the employers

The supply of skills seldom matches the regional demand of both small and larger firms, thus reducing the innovation potential of the region. Improving and adapting the skills profile of local graduates is therefore a key issue for many OECD countries. The focus of policy here ranges from improving the quality and applicability of the curriculum to regional users, enhancing work-based learning and placement programmes through which students can acquire employability skills and build links with regional businesses, and providing programmes for continuing education and upgrading the skills level of the existing workplaces. The concept of work-based learning has received particular attention from central governments in the OECD countries. (See Box 6.7)

Higher education institutions are under pressure from a range of directions to develop their teaching activities. Some of these pressures can encourage increased regional impact, particularly in ways that generate new income streams. Thus, higher education institutions have designed bespoke short courses for regional businesses or to support regional industrial policy priorities such as clusters or sectors. For example, degree and further education programmes have been designed in the Nordic universities of Karlstad and Jyväskylä to support the development of the paper technology sector in their regions and in Trondheim to support the oil industry.

Many individual institutions are committed to promote graduate employability and use stakeholders in curricular development. They also run alumni networks to gain feedback on their course provision (*e.g.* HEIs in Nuevo

---

Box 6.7. **Work-based learning**

Work-based learning involves a type of "person-embodied transfer" of knowledge between higher education institutions and local firms. In France, a government scheme, *Conventions CIFRE*, supports the recruitment of PhD candidates by private enterprises. The recruited students do their PhD work on an applied topic in enterprises under the supervision of a university or a public laboratory.

In the United Kingdom, the *Knowledge Transfer Partnership* (Former Teaching Company Scheme) provides a grant to cover part of the operation cost to transfer and embed knowledge into a business via a strategic project. SMEs represent about 90% of the industry partners.

The concept of *"cooperative education"* was developed in universities in Canada (*e.g.* the Co-op programme in Waterloo University). It helps students complete work terms in industry as part of their curriculum. Each of these initiatives have been evaluated and judged successful in job creation.

León in Mexico). They operate "Science Shop" arrangements, where firms can come to the higher education institution with potential questions which can be taken forward in student projects. Low threshold knowledge transfer systems have been developed not only in high technology sectors but also in other types of industries and services involving students and businesses. These arrangements include web-based "market places" between enterprises and students, *e.g.* Idea Portal of the Norwegian University of Technology (NTNU) in Trøndelag.

Higher education institutions can also provide structured and targeted teaching and learning programmes that address specific regional development needs and which go beyond responding to demands to upgrade their vocational skills. They also link students and graduates with the local employers. Examples include University Professional Services AB at the Karlstad University which also serves the development in public sector and the Dongseo University's Family Firm System which is mentoring SMEs in Busan, Korea (Box 6.8).

An important labour market interaction between higher education institutions and local firms is the use of local private sector employees as instructors. In Nordic countries, for example, higher education institutions often take advantage of high-skilled personnel from industry and society as part time teachers and adjunct professors. This can have benefits for both the higher education institutions and the firms concerned, but the incidence of this type of relationship is relatively low and the impacts are difficult to assess. The movement

---

Box 6.8. **Targeted development programmes in response to regional needs**

Karlstad University Professional Services AB was established in January 2005 to handle the business side of all commissioned training and education given by the university to companies and public organisations. The company has five staff and organises courses using Karlstad University staff and external experts from Sweden and beyond. The arrangement complements the traditional course delivery within the university and contributes to the general development of more applied and regionally-relevant curricula. It allows university lecturers to make external contacts, giving them experience of other kinds of teaching, and providing them with interesting and well-worked case studies for inclusion in their regular teaching activities. Clients include County Council of Värmland and other public organizations, such as the municipalities of in the region; Paper Province and other non-profit trade associations; companies such as AstraZeneca, Ericsson, MetsoPaper, SkiStar. It also has international clients *e.g.* Jiangxi University and several Norwegian counties. Courses given have the overall goal of strengthening research and teaching. Major areas include culture and learning, management, business and administration; health care, industry, IT and technology. Course examples include Pulp technology; Production management; MBA; Tissue technology, Business administration; Computer vulnerability analysis.

Family Firm System was launched by *Dongseo University in Busan* in 2004 after a 4-year development phase. Under the system, a senior academic mentor is designated to five companies which offer students and graduates internship and job opportunities. The Family Firm system has attracted 556 companies which have benefited from the close co-operation through reduced recruitment and induction costs. The system has enabled the university to: *a)* develop courses reflecting company needs; *b)* effectively utilise internship programmes; *c)* share equipment; *d)* conduct joint projects with business; *e)* increase job opportunities for graduates; *f)* improve the university's reputation; and *g)* improve to university's contribution to the regional community. The existence of the Family Firm System was an important factor in enabling Dongseo University to win five projects from the national New University for Regional Innovation scheme (NURI) competition in 2005.

---

by researchers/teaching staff on a temporary basis to the private sector mainly concerns larger companies that can involve academic staff in development work through formal agreements with higher education institutions. The opportunities for researchers to work in the private sector on a temporary or contract basis varies greatly from country to country. In central and southern Europe mobility is lower. In Spain, studies show that there are few incentives for teaching staff transfer. Transfers are not valued and receive little external recognition. There are also legal barriers which work as strong disincentives.

A number of higher education institutions have taken steps to embed employability and transferable skills and thus mainstreaming regional engagement in their core curriculum. See Box 6.9.

Box 6.9. **Embedding regional engagement in core curriculum**

Project-Organised Problem-Based Learning: Aalborg University was established in 1974 after years of popular campaign to establish a university in northern Jutland, Denmark. The campaign formed the basis for a close dialogue with the surrounding society relying on cooperation with the business sector, trade unions and cultural life. An important early decision was to base research and educational activities on inter-disciplinary integration, problem orientation and group work. In *Project-Organised Problem-Based Learning* study programmes are organised around interdisciplinary project work in groups. Up to 50% of the study work is problem-oriented project work: students work in teams to solve problem areas which have often been defined in co-operation with firms, organisations and public institutions. At any one time there are 2 000 to 3 000 ongoing projects that ensure a high degree of co-operation with the society and private sector. The Aalborg model provides students with transferable skills and authentic work experience; enterprises benefit from a clearer picture of what the university stands for and how the students might fit in as prospective employees; and the university gains feedback and access to instructive cases and ideas for research and teaching.

"Experts in team": The University of Science and Technology (NTNU) in Trondheim, mid-Norway, is the second largest of the Norwegian universities, and was created in 1996 through a merger of two much older institutions, the Norwegian Institute of Technology and the Academy of the Sciences. Its semi-independent Foundation for Technical and Industrial Research (SINTEF) plays an important liaison role, helping NTNU to develop linkages with existing regional industries and to support the development of a new industrial base, *e.g.* the offshore engineering sector following the discovery of North Sea oil in the 1970s. NTNU has introduced an institutional innovation, *"Experts in team"* (interdisciplinary team work) which is a project assignment for all Master's students. It is organised as project work in teams of five students from different disciplines, where the professor operates as facilitator. Each team member ensures that his/her know-how and expertise contributes to the mutual problem-solving process. Many of the projects carried out have a specific regional focus. Between 2001 and 2005 the number of students attending the programme grew from 780 to 1 300. It is the largest pedagogical development project in the history of the university.

Supporting new enterprise formation

As noted in Chapter 5, higher education institutions and regional development authorities have invested heavily to support new enterprise formation. The United States is leading the way with its 400 chairs of entrepreneurship compared to 100 chairs in Europe. For example, Massachusetts Institute of Technology has been developing graduate entrepreneurs for over 40 years. In general, however, there has been only modest success in this area. Limited success may be linked to the nature of entrepreneurship provision which is mainly focused on add-on provision. There is growing evidence (Gibb, 2005; Binks, 2005) that most effective results are achieved when entrepreneurial learning is embedded in the core curriculum.

The most common model is the *self-elected add-on provision* offered through enterprise centres, business start up programmes and networking groups. These programmes provide generic start-up advice and guidance for students from all disciplines. They may also offer a range of services including training, one-to-one advice, legal start-up costs, business competitions and incubation. Higher education institutions have also introduced *entrepreneurship within curriculum through distinct elective modules* on enterprise where students learn about business disciplines such as planning, marketing and finance. This type of provision follows the model of traditional business school enterprise modules sometimes with limited effort to adapt it to the disciplines or to link with the world of practice.

The experience of higher education institutions and regions suggests a shift towards embedding business innovation and new enterprise formation in the heart of the academic endeavour – within the research of individual departments and generic and subject specific education programmes. In such programmes students are offered situated learning experiences and access to in-house learning experiences where students are able to undertake project work to gain knowledge and confidence.

Attracting talent to the region and retaining it

A number of OECD countries have designed policies for attracting various types of talent (students, researchers, IT specialists, research scientists, etc.). These policies have included tax incentives, repatriation schemes and improving the attractiveness of academic careers. Talent attraction of top flight academics, researchers and highly skilled knowledge workers is increasingly replacing inward investment attraction as a key task for regional development agencies (Young and Brown, 2002). In Quebec, for example, the government is offering five-year income tax holidays to attract foreign academics in IT, engineering, health science and finance to take employment

---

Box 6.10. **Enhancing entrepreneurship**

Established in 1993, the *Team Academy* is a special unit at the Jyväskylä University of Applied Sciences in Central Finland. It aims to increase student and graduate enterprise formation, to enhance enterprising attitudes and to help SMEs and other companies to access university expertise in marketing, management and entrepreneurship. It also acts as a learning laboratory, where new learning methods and models for business life are developed (*e.g.* building effective teams, learning organisations and modern marketing). Team Academy offers a special three and a half year educational stream which provides a dedicated intake of students with bespoke education. Each student takes intensive training in leadership and marketing as a member of a team through situated learning and project work. The Team Academy is only open to business students, but the institution has used this resource to develop a set of courses promoting entrepreneurship available to all students, under the title "the path for nascent entrepreneur". During the last ten years, the Team Academy has served the needs of the business life through 1 750 projects. It has provided entrepreneurial education for more than 500 BBA graduates and given birth to 17 companies in addition to the cooperatives that operate during the study time. About 15% of the Team Academy graduates are active entrepreneurs especially in the service sector and consultancy. The Teach Academy has received a number of national awards for its innovative learning methods and its proven track record in the enhancement of entrepreneurship.

The Monterrey Institute of Technology and Higher Education Studies (ITESM) launched a programme on entrepreneurship 20 years ago. It is a compulsory course for all undergraduate students provided by the Directorate of Entrepreneurial Leadership within the Entrepreneurship Development Centre. *The Entrepreneurial Development Centre* also embraces a Directorate of Company Incubation which promotes the creation and development of nationally and internationally competitive companies with high growth potential and social commitment. The incubator has two sections – one devoted to technological projects based on university research and the other for all other projects. In addition to the development of generic entrepreneurial skills the university ensures that promising students and ideas are supported through the critical initial incubation stages.

in the region's universities. In Finland, Nokia invests in the cultural adaptation of foreign IT workers as a way to improve productivity, but also to help to retain this talent (OECD, 2004). The policies need to be carefully developed as the different categories of migrants respond to different types of incentives. Regional policy makers need to work closely with local higher education institutions to formulate the appropriate package to attract high potential individuals or groups of academics. Further, the attraction policy needs to be customised for each country and region. Since the key industry clusters tend to be territorially based, talent attraction initiatives may be better designed by regional bodies that have strong industrial connections and knowledge of the local labour market.

Higher education institutions are increasingly investing in their alumni organisations which have also designed targeted projects to attract alumni to return to the region. In some cases, institutions have also taken steps to provide work-based learning experience for high potential graduates in order to retain talent in the region. The Saxion University of Applied Sciences in the Twente region has organised an educational trajectory "Fast Forward" for high-achieving graduates who undertake an educational track which includes a strong component of work-based learning, (see Box 6.11 below).

Strategic co-ordination of the regional human capital system

The emergence of a regional human capital system as distinct from a number of disconnected components requires some degree of co-ordination and steering, not least between different stages of education. In many countries each stage is managed by a different level of government with varying degrees of input from employers. There are also variations in

---

Box 6.11. **Fast Forward high potential management development programme**

Fast Forward is a separate post-graduate programme provided by Saxion Universities of Applied Sciences in Twente in the Netherlands to retain high potential graduates in the region. Over a two-year programme the Fast Forward trainees receive tailored management training and undergo three eight-month work assignments in different local or regional companies and organisations. High potential graduates are matched with organisations which need innovative staff that are able to contribute from day one. For a graduate, Fast Forward provides a personal development project with self-awareness training, peer development, continuous assessment and feedback from peers and coaches.

In six years, more than 200 Fast Forward apprenticeships have been completed with about 100 different employers. The programme is successful in retaining graduates in the region: 95% of Fast Forward graduates – now highly qualified – have stayed in the region and work there. The programme has also encouraged new graduates to move to Twente from other regions in the Netherlands.

---

responsibility between "academic" and "vocational" pathways. Typically, the pattern of higher education programmes is nationally regulated by government or the professions; intermediate or vocational education may have a regional or sub-regional dimension while the education of young people up to the age of 16 or 18 is a local responsibility with all levels operating within a national framework. Finally, continuing professional development either at the initiative of the individual or the employer is typically unregulated, operating in a highly competitive market place. Ensuring that there are progression pathways into higher education and out into the regional labour market allowing easier up-skilling can present a major challenge for higher education institutions. As a consequence there can be a range of barriers which may hinder higher education institutions from fully contributing to human capital formation in the region.

These barriers manifest themselves in many ways. There may be a direct mismatch between the courses offered by higher education institutions and the regional skills needs. There may also be poorly developed progression pathways, including access from secondary/lower tertiary institutions and for non-traditional (distance, mature, lifelong) learners. Divisions of activity and territory between institutions may block progression pathways and create course overlap and gaps in provision. Competition between institutions within a region for students may undermine effective co-operation, specialisation and building critical mass. There may be a failure to engage with and integrate regional businesses into the design and delivery of curricula, and a failure to identify potential employers for graduates, to work with them and willing students in order to increase the aggregate skills levels of regional businesses. Finally, the impacts may be restricted to traditional students and graduate users which does not allow for a transformation increasing the openness of higher education and the knowledge intensity of the regional economy.

The strategic co-ordination between institutions can maximise the regional uptake and benefit of their educational activities. This inter-institutional co-ordination activity involves progressing towards managing the overall regional human capital system with higher education institutions consolidating their strengths and collectively identifying and addressing market failures and system faults. Different types of higher education institutions play different roles in human capital formation. As the World Bank (2002) points out, "the diverse and growing set of public and private tertiary institutions in every country forms a network of institutions that support the production of the higher-order capacity necessary for development".[5] Co-operation and co-ordination between universities and polytechnics/community colleges are increasingly viewed in many countries as a means to develop synergies and improve the offer of services for regional clients, while collaboration with community colleges or secondary education seems less commonplace.

In regions with a diverse set of institutions, co-ordination can maximise the number of pathways, allowing progression between institutions, and focus on core markets without neglecting hard-to-reach regional student groups, such as remote, distance or part-time students. Where there are similar institutions within one region, co-ordination will allow specialisation between institutions, sharing of best practice and avoidance of harmful competition. In any regional arrangement, co-ordination will also allow the development of institutional capacity between higher education institutions. Co-ordination between higher education institutions can contribute to:

● Critical mass: given increasing inter-regional competition, dialogue between higher education institutions allows for the identification of regional strengths – not necessarily congruent with particular institutional educational strengths – which could be used for talent attraction.

● Multiple pathways: in regions with low levels of educational attainment, the presence of multiple institutions with well-co-ordinated transfer routes and accreditation allows non-traditional students the easiest access to the most appropriate forms of higher education.

● Shared learning: collaboration between higher education institutions could facilitate best-practise sharing and development of supportive regional higher education system to address particular human capital problems.

● Problem solving: where there are identified omissions in higher education provision, partnerships between higher education institutions could work to fill gaps in provision and to better meet the needs of regional stakeholders.

● The development of coherent voice for higher education institutions. (See Chapter 8 for higher education regional associations.)

Conclusions: managing the regional human capital system

Depending on the retention rates of graduates in the region, higher education institutions can provide crucial human capital inputs for regional and local labour markets. By supplying knowledge in the form of educated people, higher education institutions increase the region's capacity for generation and absorption of knowledge and innovation. The presence of an educated labour force is instrumental in nurturing a specialised labour pool and helping to attract and retain firms. For this purpose, the demand orientation of higher education should be improved not only through full time courses, but also work-based learning and further education which helps to repair the educational deficit resulting from brain drain and low education participation especially in less advanced regions. Appropriate fiscal incentives could make business more eager to obtain adjustments in the higher education provision reflecting regional needs. It could also help higher education institutions diversify their funding streams. Given that one-third of working age adults have low skills, a particular challenge is up-skilling and lifelong learning.

National governments have an important role to play in facilitating regional co-operation. The functional separation is a critical challenge for regional engagement of higher education institutions. In many instances, higher education institutions in the region have to work around functional stovepipes of national regulations which create inconsistent timescales, spatial boundaries and output measures.

Notes

1. In Norway, the expansion of higher education has been used to help preserve the geographical distribution of the population and to increase tertiary education in the non-urban regions, especially in the northern part of the country. Sweden has had a distinct regional dimension to higher education which has brought higher education institutions to each county. Despite the increase in enrolment, regional differences remain between rural and urban areas and at the municipality level. Finland has doubled its higher education sector through the establishment of polytechnics.

2. For example the Finnish comprehensive education system has been successful in producing good learning outcomes and little variation in performance between and within schools. It has been particularly successful in its ability to prevent students from falling behind. (PISA). Differences, however, start to show in transition to upper secondary education and tertiary education. As individuals progress up the system, the processes that create inequality become more visible: students from families with higher incomes and higher parental education levels are more likely to enrol in higher education where universities are the more preferred option. Polytechnics were created in the early 1990s to provide greater choice in higher education and to open access to non-traditional students. The ability of vocational students to apply to higher education institutions has also expanded access to higher education. At the national level, this channel was used in 2004 by 28% of polytechnic's new students and 5% on new students at universities. These figures show remarkable scope for improvement.

3. In Sweden, each higher education institution must use 0.3% of the public funding it gets (except for doctoral training) to provide support to disabled students (*e.g.* sign language interpretation and help with taking notes). In addition, the State contributes additional funding for expenses not covered by the ear-marked funds.

4. In the long run these graduates may return with enhanced skills and financial capital to contribute to the regional economy or, if they remain, contribute to a skills pool that attracts inward investors operating in tight national or international labour markets.

5. Research-intensive universities influence regional development through the recruitment of graduates and postgraduates and increasingly foreign students.

They also have a key direct role in upgrading the skills of both large firms and SMEs through student placements and industrial fellowship schemes. When regions are urbanised, retention effects (for students) are stronger but relatively variable. Polytechnics or new universities have usually a more local recruitment base and higher retention rates. They also provide dedicated degrees and certification courses to suit the needs of local employers and R&D services. Technical colleges provide vocational courses as well as generic training. Their role in helping local firms is often underestimated. For example, they provide training for technicians, an employment category with an important role in innovation (Rosenfeld, 1998).

ISBN 978-92-64-03414-3
Higher Education and Regions:
Globally Competitive, Locally Engaged
© OECD 2007

Chapter 7

Contribution of Higher Education to Social, Cultural and Environmental Development: Overcoming the Barriers

Regional development is often thought of in economic terms only, and with a focus on technology-based development. The current OECD project briefing notes, however, suggested a wider interpretation. This chapter looks to the wider community engagement of higher education institutions. Through case studies it reviews the attitudes and practices of higher education institutions in relation to the social, cultural and environmental development of the region, not only as means to economic progress but also as ends in themselves. It identifies three key drivers in this domain: first, beneficial framework conditions, second, existence of networks for sustained co-operation and, third, local conditions which create a sense of urgency.

Social, cultural and environmental developments have demonstrable if indirect economic as well as intrinsic benefits. They offer benefits underpinning and stabilising economic growth, as well as direct benefits in terms of community health and welfare, social cohesion, a diverse cultural and community life, and a clean, healthy, sustainable and self-renewing natural and man-made environment with robust and serviceable institutions including higher education institutions themselves. The costs of social and cultural exclusion and impoverishment can be calculated in the breakdown of law and order and the bill for law enforcement, lack of earning power of the under-educated and unemployed, the cost of health services and welfare benefits to the sick on sink estates and in economically collapsed areas. The same principle applies to environmental damage, where quantifiable measures may be closer to reach, and impact statements have become more common. (See *e.g.* OECD 2006i; OECD, 2007d, forthcoming.)

The idea that higher education institutions belong to and are at the service of their communities dates at least from the mid-19th century in the case of the United States Land Grant institutions. Despite the different missions and histories, most higher education institutions see social and cultural contribution as part of their role. They contribute to urban and rural area regeneration, health and social care, library services, research for community benefit as well as cultural, and environmental development. Their staff and students play civic and voluntary roles serving in local government and leading and participating in community associations, adding to the region's stock of human and social capital. Some fields of study, especially medical, social work and teacher training, lend themselves to student activities which make a contribution to the social good, sometimes voluntarily or *pro bono*, sometimes as part of work placements. This may include direct provision of medical and clinical facilities and services; other examples can be found as in law, with legal aid to those in need and poverty.

Higher education institutions can play an important role in the vitalisation and regeneration of cities and regions. Regions can regenerate themselves through the complementary and cumulative efforts of formal and informal learning, economic actions, social measures and cultural/intercultural practices which work in reciprocal movement. Accordingly, the cumulative effect takes place if measures are taken not only for creating an attractive environment for economic activity and inward investment but also for wealth distribution, social cohesion and the removal of barriers to learning opportunities and raising aspirations. (Bélanger, 2006). Figure 7.1 below attempts to describe a model for regional regeneration.

The current OECD study draws attention to a number of activities linked to the social, cultural and environmental role of the higher education institutions. Whilst many of the initiatives were excellent in their own right, they often remained marginal endeavours. The primary focus of concerted efforts was clearly on business related competitiveness and measurable outcomes related to this. There is, however, evidence that concentrating solely on business, competitiveness and technological advancement involves a risk of reduced sense of belonging on the part of people in the remote areas and in the fringes of the society as well as under-optimal use of human resources. Arguing the social, civil and sustainability case in specific economic terms may, however, be a necessary expedient to take social, cultural and environmental issues up the agenda.

Health and welfare

Higher education institutions often have a strong emphasis placed upon health and welfare services including neighbourhood renewal and community development. These forms of public service involvement represent a massive part of the business of the higher education and the region, but the scale of work of higher education institutions is often overlooked. The research-based work carried out in medicine and health illustrates that high quality international level research is not jeopardised by regional co-operation and application.

Figure 7.1. **Regenerating the region adapted from Barnley's model**

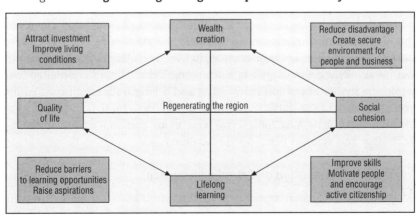

Source: Belanger, 2006.

Higher education institutions contribute to health, safety, physical fitness and general social well-being of the regions residents through their learning programmes, research, services and infrastructure. Examples include Busan, Korea, where there is a number of activities in the medical, health and social welfare fields including a range of special programmes for different groups in need. The role of university medical schools in contributing to community health is strengthened by voluntary community service groups, free medical services and special outreach activities. In the North East of England, which lags behind in many health indicators, the region's Public Health Observatory is housed at the Durham University and works with the Regional Development Agency to turn regional data into information which is useful for carrying out successful health policies. The work of the Wolfson Research Institute on Queen's College Stockton campus of the University of Durham focuses on research on medicine, health and wellbeing of people and places with particular emphasis on analysing these issues in the North East of England. It has turned the region into a laboratory for university research. Newcastle University's Cancer Unit has become part of the regional health system. In Denmark, higher education institutions are working in close collaboration with the public health system, *e.g.* Alexandra Institute in Aarhus is carrying out R&D projects for user-driven ICT-based innovation in hospitals and public health.

Most OECD countries are faced with a rapidly ageing population. There is a need to keep the ageing population – which often has low skills – active in working life and also to support the functional independence of the elderly in order to decrease the costs of social and health care services. In the current OECD study the emphasis on this challenge was evident *e.g.* in Finland and Korea, both experiencing exceptionally rapid demographic change. While the Jyväskylä region in Finland had already taken steps to mobilise higher education in this agenda in a more systematic manner, Busan did not yet show evidence of integrative development strategy in the so-called "Silver Industry" in which higher education institutions could be centrally involved. The difference may be attributed not only the small size and the limited number of higher education institutions in Central Finland, but also to the fact that in Jyväskylä gerontology has a strong multidisciplinary knowledge base within the higher education institutions and a long tradition of community level intervention. The public authorities, regional and local, have played a key role as facilitators because their social services are potential customers for the technology and systems being developed (Box 7.1).

Community regeneration and rural development

In declining urban areas, higher education institutions can have a positive impact through their campuses and other property assets for the provision, for example, of low-cost student accommodation and low-cost

Box 7.1. **Jyväskylä conjoint effort to respond to the challenges of ageing population**

Finland has one of the fastest ageing populations among the OECD countries. Central Finland has particularly pronounced regional disparities in this field. For example, the small community of Luhanka in the southern part of Central Finland is the "oldest" in the country in terms of its population: 33% of population is over 65 years old whereas for Central Finland the corresponding figure is 17%. In addition, the Jyväskylä region in the core of the region is one of the fastest growing city regions in the country. Due to rapid structural change it lags behind the national average in terms of long term and youth unemployment rates, as well as the share of the population receiving social assistance. The demographic and structural changes are closely linked to the social and health care provision.

Good practice of collaboration between higher education and regional and national stakeholders include the WIRE *programme* which seeks to enhance the life quality and social inclusion of the long-term unemployed. The Jyväskylä University of Applied Sciences is working with a wide range of stakeholders to bring the long-term employed back into working life. The programme has been running over a ten year period using a range of physical and social rehabilitation measures, in part through a Rehabilitation Service Clinic which is a student training centre of the University. A wide range of partners is involved across public, private and third sectors. The WIRE approach has proved a success in empowering the long-term unemployed, encouraging them to acquire new skills and getting them back into employment; in 2000-2004 it contributed to the re-employment of 800 persons who no longer generate social cost but instead contribute to the regional and national prosperity. WIRE has been recognised as the best practice by the National Research and Development Centre for Welfare and Health (STAKES). Its methods are being embedded into the service systems of the municipalities in Central Finland. WIRE is also one of the best practice cases linked with the European EuroHealthNet which aims at decreasing health inequalities in Europe.

In the 1990s, Jyväskylä Science Park launched a special programme for the development of the new emerging Wellness industry combining education and research in the university. During the following ten years, the region developed a system to translate leading-edge research in health and physical activity amongst older people into products and services that could benefit an ageing population served by the municipal authorities. Activities are based on the strong multidisciplinary knowledge base in gerontology and basic research which is funded by the Academy of Finland. An independent foundation, *Gerocenter*, has been established with a representation from civil society and funded by Finland's Slot Machine Association (RAY) to underpin the development of systems and services to support active ageing.

Box 7.1. Jyväskylä conjoint effort to respond to the challenges of ageing population (cont.)

Translation of research into products is facilitated by the Wellness Dream Lab. Practice-based applied research in hospitals and community services, and practitioner training are undertaken in the Jyväskylä University of Applied Science. There is also a flow of practitioners into the research programmes in the University of Jyväskylä to undertake higher degrees. A Human Technology Forum has been established so that actors in the system meet and exchange knowledge and experience. A building (Viveca), owned and managed by the Science Park, houses selected parts of the above chain, including spin-off companies.

---

student transportation initiatives. When linked in with the local and municipal authority, the higher education institutions can add to the general amenity of the town centre, for example parks and gardens, safety, recreation. The contracting out of HEI catering, cleaning, financial and other services can add to the employment based of depressed urban and rural areas in which the campuses are located.

Higher education institutions can also target part of their core functions, i.e. research and teaching, to regenerate disadvantaged geographical communities. For example, in Twente (Netherlands) the redevelopment of the Roombeek estate in Enschede involves a partnership between two higher education institutions and the community sector. It provides research support, including student dissertation projects, in the rebuilding of a suburb devastated in an industrial disaster in 2000. The partnership approach to integrative regeneration is already judged a success and being emulated elsewhere. The case is unusual in being triggered by a particular disaster and concerned with the regeneration of a poor urban area.

The North East of England has witnessed a rapid decline in traditional industries. The University of Sunderland, the public authorities and private donors have engaged in the regeneration of the Wearside area devastated by shipbuilding collapse while the Durham University is working in the deprived are of Stockton through the new Queen's College. In Newcastle, the two universities are engaged in the regeneration of the deprived West End and other parts of the city and the wider region.

The University of Mount Allison in Canada offers a Rural and Small Town Programme which prepares people and organisations for developing sustainable rural communities and small towns. The programme links research and action by generating and sharing new knowledge, developing self-help tools and providing information and educational services.

Networks for rural regeneration led by higher education institutions have been established for example in Central Finland, Twente in the Netherlands and the North East of England. A rural enterprise initiative of the University of Twente (Kansrijk Eigen Baas or KEB) supports innovation and enterprise in declining agricultural settings, working with a local bank to access small loans. Newcastle University is leading the Northern Rural Network bringing together more than 600 researchers and rural development practitioners from businesses, public agencies and the voluntary sector in the region the neighbouring regions of Cumbria, Lancashire and North Yorkshire to help rural and regional development. It has operationalised a model of locally centred rural development. Almost 400 firms have benefited from students' work. The approach is unique in the way it copes with the low base of aspiration of the micro enterprises and the voluntary sector. The free membership has more than doubled over the past three years.

Culture and creative industries

Culture as an agent of development takes three forms:

● culture as an end in itself, enhancing the quality of life;

● indirect economic benefit in attracting and retaining the creative classes which drive the knowledge society;

● direct contribution to the creative industries through enterprise formation, growth, productivity and employment.

Higher education institutions can make a contribution to the cultural foundation of a region and to the quality of life of the community. They can do this through culturally-based learning programmes and research projects that increase awareness, provide policy advice and services for culturally diverse groups. Higher education institutions can engage with cultural groups to help build their capacity to better serve their members. They can also make available for public access a wide range of culturally-specific infrastructure, such as museums, libraries, galleries, orchestras, auditoriums, sporting facilities, community radio and television stations. They may also sponsor cultural festivals and performances, offer specialist expertise and take part in specific cultural initiatives and events.

Richard Florida (2002) has proposed that a booming economy is driven by the presence of "creative class", who are attracted to cities characterised by talent, tolerance and technology. Higher education institutions help to connect city-regions (and nations) to global flows of knowledge and talent, thereby enhancing regional competitiveness. Furthermore, higher education institutions can build social inclusion and cohesion by creating more diverse, multicultural and tolerant communities (see *e.g.* Gertler and Vinodrai, 2004). Through this process, they internationalise their regions and act as anchors for creative thinking and activity and have a positive effect on inward investment. There is often, however, no overall strategy to link the internationalisation of the higher education institution to the region building to make the region a more diversified and culturally developed place, interesting and attractive to people and business. Active measures are not taken to link the international students and the faculty with region and its working life. There is also a lack of effective use of the higher education institution's international linkages and alumni.

The creative class is closely linked to human capital and business formation. Evidence comes from the United Kingdom where the creative industries are the fastest growing sector of the economy: between 1997 and 2002 it grew at around twice the rate of the rest of the economy at an average of 6% per annum. It contributes about 8% towards UK GDP and employs almost 2 million people. Exports have grown by an average of 11% per annum during the same period, contributing over GBP 11 billion to the balance of trade, more than the construction, insurance and pensions industries and twice that of the pharmaceutical sector. Graduates from creative arts, design and media courses are entrepreneurial and about one third of all self-employed first degree graduates come from these disciplines. The sector is one of the most highly educated with around 43% having degrees of higher level qualification, compared with 16% of the workforce in total. (DCMS, 2006).

Creative sector is also a major economic driver globally: it accounts for 7% of GDP and is growing at 10% per annum. A number of countries, regions and cities, *e.g.* Queensland, New Zealand, Hong Kong and Singapore, have developed their strategies for Creative Industries emphasising the sector's economic impact. Also China is making heavy investments in the Creative Industries and applying a broad definition of creativity. (DCMS, 2006).

Some regions in the OECD study aim to reinvent themselves as "creative places" with the help of their higher education institutions: In Trøndelag, Norway, the vision of Trondheim as a creative city has been developed by local and regional authorities. State of Nuevo León has launched Regia Metrópoli project which aims to highlight historical and cultural heritage of the region. Busan in Korea seeks to brand itself as "Dynamic Busan" with a revived cultural centre which will attract inward investments and human capital. The Busan International Film Festival is more than ten years old and Asia's largest film festival, supported in different ways by several higher education institutions in a concerted attempt to recreate a strong cultural identity for Busan. Examples of longstanding collaboration in the arts arena include *e.g.* the cross-border region Öresund where the Cultural Bridge Fund for strengthening cultural cooperation has been an important tool for building a more integrated culture across the Strait. There was also evidence of collaborative efforts between higher education institutions and their cities and regions to create a new location for collaborative cultural activity (*e.g.* Twente Music Quarter, Aalborg, Denmark and to a smaller scale in Jyväskylä).

In general, however, the stakeholders inside and outside of the higher education institutions had not yet fully recognised the potential for collaboration, partnership and advocacy in culture and creative industries. Examples from across the UK show that development of the cultural sector can lead directly to regeneration, increased investment and growth in city regions. For example, commercial businesses have been attracted by the development of cultural and creative hub in Manchester's Northern Quarter and Quayside in Newcastle. The North East England example demonstrates the importance of flagship projects in mobilising the region building. It also highlights the importance of collaboration between higher education institutions and regional stakeholders (Box 7.2).

While culture and creative industries may be perceived as elitist, sport can provide opportunities for all social groups. Many higher education institutions provide sports activities and facilities for their own students and staff but there is only limited evidence of using sports strategically as a means of region building. In the North East of England sport is, however, regarded as a great leveller in facilitating knowledge sharing between higher education institutions and their communities. Sport is used in helping address disparities, in retaining a well-rounded and educated workforce, promoting social equity and impacting positively on the daily lives of the communities.[1]

Environmental sustainability

Higher education institutions can contribute to sustainable environmental development in their regions in many ways, for example by:

- generating human capital in the region through their learning and further education programmes in areas of sustainable development;
- acting as a source of expertise through research, consultancy and demonstration;
- playing a brokerage role in bringing together diverse regional actors and elements of capacity to the sustainability process;
- demonstrating good practice through on-campus management and development activities, strategic planning, building design, waste minimisation and water and energy efficiency practice, responsible purchasing programmes and pursuing good citizen type initiatives like a "green campus";

Box 7.2. **Cultural and creative industries in region building**

Newcastle-Gateshead's joint bid to be nominated European Capital of Culture for the United Kingdom attracted attention to the role of culture in the city regions. Although ultimately unsuccessful, the bidding process provided a concrete goal upon which a wide range of public, private and community partners including the higher education institutions could work together. In the long run, the Capital of Culture bid represents only an episode within a range of high-profile cultural development projects and networks within the region including the Year of the Visual Arts in 1996 and the development of the Culture 10 strategy.

The universities in the North East have recognised the potential for collaboration, partnership and advocacy in culture and cultural industries which are seen as a major source of growth for the region. They collaborate to drive the renaissance of local culture and *e.g.* support the two major developments on the Tyne: The Baltic Contemporary Arts Centre and the Sage Gateshead Music Centre. Each university has its own strengths to drive the cultural agenda. For example, The Centre for Cultural Policy and Management of Northumbria University provides advice, project development and research in relation to cultural policy and is working closely together with the range of cultural stakeholders in the region. Newcastle University in partnership with Sage Gateshead Music Centre and the region's other universities a national Centre of Excellence in Teaching and Learning in Music which *inter alia* uses music as a pathway from the community into a wide range of academic programmes. The University is also leading a partnership of local bodies to establish a Cultural Quarter which will transform the space where the city and the university meet into an area of social and cultural activity. The higher education regional association and its special committee for culture have a brokerage role in all these projects.

- offering recognition and reward incentives for staff to be involved in sustainable development leadership groups in the regional community.

Higher education institutions are not only consumers of non-renewable energy and generators of CO_2, they are also sources of technological and organisational expertise in this field. At the heart of this global challenge is the link between the opportunities arising from technology-based research (*e.g.* the exploitation of geothermal energy sources) and its incorporation into the actions in the wider community where regional and local agencies such as local government can play a key role, for example through the land use planning systems. Students and alumni as future responsible actors and opinion formers could also be critical members of regional as well as global learning systems. Embedding sustainability into study programme can thus have long term effects on the working life through "knowledge transfer on legs" i.e. students and graduates shaping the working life. This requires articulation from within the region outside the higher education institutions as well as inside the institutions.

At the first Earth Summit in 1972 in Stockholm, education was identified as fundamental to the successful achievement of sustainable development. Since then progress has been patchy. A necessary injection of urgency was given in 2005 when the United Nations adopted a Decade of Education for Sustainable Development. An essential part of the subsequent strategies for Europe/North America, Australia/Asia and Africa is the requirement to develop national education for sustainable development policies. Some countries like the Netherlands, the United Kingdom, and to some extent the Nordic countries have these in place already.

Many higher education institutions have introduced or are in the process of introducing sustainability development policies, statements and visions. Some have developed estate management systems and supplier policies which are geared towards minimising energy use and are also working to reduce the "travel foot print" of their staff and students. There is also a wide range of R&D activities and consultancy services available to facilitate and embed environmental management systems into local businesses. For example, in Nuevo León, Mexico, the Monterrey campus of the ITESM has a Centre for Environmental Quality which has since 1961 provided a broad range of teaching, research, consulting, laboratory services, extension courses and continuing education in environmental quality. In Central Finland, the approach of the two higher education institutions to environmental development is an example of complementary work between polytechnics and universities with broad indirect and direct community involvement to support the aim to make the region free from fossil fuels by 2015. In the Canary Islands, the Forum for Sustainable Development is bringing together higher education institutions and a range of governmental and other agencies in a situation where the two universities often seemed to be at loggerheads and the region has yet to find a way of harnessing their energies effectively in the region's interest.

Sunshine-Fraser Coast: Building on local assets

In the Sunshine-Fraser Coast the higher education sector provides education for local students and also aims to attract external students whose fee income provides institutional stability. The University of the Sunshine Coast has chosen to do this through building a critical mass in subjects which are of local interest and for which the local environment provides an interesting "laboratory" or case study. The university has developed courses in coastal studies, marine tourism, and plant/marine biotechnology. It has also developed partnerships with local businesses and created an infrastructure which gives it a competitive edge in delivering these courses with local applicability. The Institute for Sustainability, Health and Regional Engagement (iSHARE) has provided an institutional framework for this work. (See Box 7.3.)

In general, however, the OECD study revealed only limited conjoint action in the domain of environmental sustainability. International experience in this field shows that individual university approach cannot work alone and what is needed is an approach that targets education systems complemented by organisational change of institutions in that system. This is happening for example in the United Kingdom through the Sustainability Integration Group (SIGnet) a body made up of all the organisations that plan, fund and regulate the higher education sector, facilitated by Forum for the Future. In addition, there is a need for a strategic partnership between the higher education institutions and their region. This can play a key role is environmental sustainability generally and global warming in particular.

Box 7.3. **Institute for Sustainability, Health and Regional Engagement (iSHARE)**

The Institute for Sustainability, Health and Regional Engagement (iSHARE) of the University of the Sunshine Coast provides a research platform for the interface between environment and health disciplines. A regional advisory board brings community, business leaders, and researchers together to engage in identification of priorities. There is also an international benchmarking group to provide input and feedback. An example of collaborative research under the administration of iSHARE is The Fraser Island Research and Education Facility, developed in co-operation with the Kingfisher Bay Resort and Village.

This teaching and research laboratory on Fraser Island, along with an environmental camp, provides a base for advanced environmental and eco-tourism research and education. The significant level of private sector support for this facility from the Kingfisher Bay Resort, as well as the interaction between the university and the Resort in identification of relevant research and education projects, makes this facility a model of collaboration. As a result of this initiative, the university research capacity has been enhanced and the eco-tourism offerings through Kingfisher Bay Resort have been strengthened.

The case of Nuevo León in Mexico

In Nuevo León the community development agenda is driven by the state government which has included an entire programme in its State Development Plan aimed at transforming the urban image of Monterrey's metropolitan area through a series of projects with the different municipalities and through building up an urban centre using a series of symbols embodied by cultural and recreational, educational, religious and leisure centres.

Underpinning the efforts is a social commitment and responsibility which is facilitated by the federal government's requirement of mandatory student social service as a graduation requirement. While there are national concerns about the way social service is operationalised, it has potential for much impact in Mexican society and has generated good results in mainstreaming community service activities into the core business of the higher education institutions (Box 7.4) (see also OECD, 2006).

The programmes developed by individual higher education institutions are notable for their partnership and their capacity to work across all sectors in sustained commitment. There is, however, limited evidence of systematic inter-institutional co-operation between different institutions. Mandatory social service is not underpinned with specific incentives or monitoring of results. More could be achieved with conjoint action and for example opening the well-developed cultural and sport services to the people.

Conclusions: from entrepreneurial university to the socially engaged university

While the wider contribution of higher education to community development and cultural change seem to be relatively under-developed in many regions, there are notable exceptions where higher education institutions have embraced the role of "good regional citizenship". There are three key drivers which facilitate active engagement of higher education institutions in this area:

● beneficial framework conditions created by the government, *e.g.* legislation and funding;

● existence of networks for sustained co-operation;

● local conditions creating a sense of urgency.

These key factors were present to a varying degree in two cases of the current OECD study. In Mexico, mandatory social service for higher education students coupled with the local conditions provides a framework for enhanced community service. This is a national approach and Mexico thus gives an interesting model for countries seeking to mobilise their higher

---

Box 7.4. **Mandatory social service for higher education students in Mexico**

Mexican students in public (and some private) institutions are required to perform public service. Established in the 1940s, to assist marginal rural and urban communities it has expanded to productive sector and public, municipal, state and federal entities using collaboration programmes and inter-institutional agreements. Social service lasts between 6-12 months but the duration is in no case less than 480 hours. The concept of Student Social Service as a graduation requirement in higher education has the potential for much impact in the society. While it provides a powerful mechanism for region building it often remains paternalistic and aid-based rather than aligned with the community development objectives. To take a full advantage of the social service closer links between social service programmes and local development efforts need to be created. There is also need to incentivise this work and monitor the outcomes.

The University of Monterrey's Center for Solidarity and Philanthropy enables the university community to take part in community work programmes designed to empower people and enhance social growth. Courses in Mexican Reality, Ethics and Social Responsibility and Social Community Development are linked with social service projects in the field. The University of Monterrey has twenty years' experience in working with low income communities and is involved with more than a hundred collaborative programmes with social work institutions.

---

education to strengthen a social contribution through teaching and assessment channels. In the North East of England the existence of a long-standing higher education regional association and a shared experience of a struggling rustbelt area remote from the centre of power and lagging on many socio-economic indicators work towards the same end. In this case the context is regional, but in both, higher education institutions, despite their different identities and histories, see community engagement as part of their mission and work. The form that it takes depends on the character and location of the institution and on the particular socio-economic and regeneration needs of the city or region.

In general, however, the softer and longer term community development and cultural issues remain relatively under-developed. This can be attributed to national policy environments and to the pressures on and behaviour of higher education institutions in this environment. The problems of measurement of impacts and limited resources, including absence of incentives for institutions and staff members influence all the wider aspects of development. Funding for regional development is typically project-based, short term and tightly focused on an economic task. Staff promotion is usually dependent on publication, not on engagement in the 3rd task activities. Narrowly defined output targets within short time frames to which higher education institutions' income streams are tied militate against building the social as well as economic infrastructure on which sustainable (and measurable) development is based. By virtue of using comparative and often competitive indicators for national purposes they also militate against the kind of regional diversity built on different endogenous strengths and assets which provides an underlying logic for decentralisation.

To take this agenda forward, there is a need for higher education institutions to undertake and disseminate an audit of their engagement in the social, cultural and environmental development of the region, highlighting examples of good practice locally as well as elsewhere.[2] This should be followed by a preparation of joint strategies between the higher education institutions and the appropriate public bodies who should use their resources to underpin selective programmes of action within the higher education institutions.[3] However, until governments at national and regional levels (and indeed at European Union and other international agency levels) include social, cultural and environmental dimensions into the agenda, this aspect of regional development including higher education partnership will continue to struggle.

Finally, the public good implies access to the reservoir of knowledge generated in higher education, how that knowledge is used to the benefit of the wider society, not just the academy and last but not least the role of the society in the co-production of this knowledge. The Council of Europe (2002) has argued that it is higher education's responsibility to foster the commitment of citizens to sustain public action aimed at the wellbeing of society at large rather than just individual benefits. It should promote the values of democratic structures and processes, active citizenship, human rights and social justice; environmental sustainability and dialogue. While these are abstract and global aspirations, the word "citizen" does have a specific territorial connotation. Many of the goods and bads of modern society become transparent at the city and regional level and public discourse around them leading to action can and should be mobilised by higher education institutions working with their regional partners. The capacity of these partnerships to enter into such mature dialogues is the subject of the next chapter.

Notes

1. The Directors of Sport of the five universities in the North East of England have come together to build innovative sporting engagement with local communities. The universities draw on the resources of a student population; students are now working alongside young people in the local communities to help develop leadership and life skills, as well as sporting capability. The partnership is in the process of building on the concept of Sport Universities to develop more inclusive partnering with local communities.

2. Higher education staff and students lead community associations and serve in local government positions, adding to the region's stock of human and social capital. Systematic mapping of the links and networks of their staff was carried out only in a few higher education institutions. There is generally a lack of comprehensive information on "who" is engaged with "what" as a way to achieving more systematic regional engagement by the higher education institutions.

3. There are different ways of exploring this complex, multi-stranded area. Different types of typologies may help higher education institutions to address holistically their regional social, cultural and environmental engagement: 1) Classifying between the social, cultural, and economic in a scorecard way to appraise institutional success; 2) Distinguishing different processes and methods of nurturing social, cultural and environmental contributions to identify the effective or deficient modes of self-development, outreach, partnership and delivery; and 3) Distinguishing activities that are mainstreamed into regular programmes of teaching and research from the add-ons.

ISBN 978-92-64-03414-3
Higher Education and Regions:
Globally Competitive, Locally Engaged
© OECD 2007

Chapter 8

Building Capacity for Co-operation between Higher Education and Regions

Interactions between higher education institutions and the region in which they are located can be beneficial to both parties. For this interaction to take place bridges have to be constructed based on firm pillars on both sides. This chapter seeks to identify the elements for developing the capacity for joint working between regional actors and agencies and higher education institutions in the round, not just particular institutions or parts of institutions. These are the building blocks for the pillars and the spanning techniques for bridging the gap to enable the traffic to flow from one side to the other. In regions where there is more than one higher education institution and a number of sub-regions this implies developing the capacity of the region as a whole.

The higher education pillar

Institutional autonomy and leadership

Strong institutional leadership embraces issues of strategic direction and operational management of the institutions. Some structures of governance set constraints on what a higher education institution can plan and do. These include the traditions whereby academic leaders are chosen from and return to the ranks of the professoriate after a short spell in office. There are two dimensions to this: the higher education institution needs autonomy in relation to central government and the institutional leadership needs authority in relation to the faculties. Where the central authority of the higher education institution is weak and the faculties remain strong, the reach and scope as well as the time-span for leadership may be curtailed.

If the administration has not been modernised for example in terms of human resources and financial resources management and this has not been underpinned by effective IT systems, the capacity to secure and monitor effective action is further limited. This sets constraints to the institutional capacity to plan for and enter into sustained partnerships. The constraints are particularly prominent in regional development as the mission of regional engagement is less familiar and therefore more likely to encounter greater academic resistance than efforts to enhance conventional teaching and research.

Countries wishing to see the shifts of culture and direction that entrepreneurial activity and regional engagement requires will need to consider the legal and regulatory changes necessary to enable strong leadership of higher education institutions to emerge. This involves strengthening the autonomy of higher education institutions by increasing the responsibility over the curriculum and the use of human and financial resources. It may extend to changes in the ownership of real estate, and other capital investment that underpins capable leadership and the institution's ability to invest in place making.

Strong leadership means also reforming discipline-based structures that prevent engagement with the trans-disciplinary problems of the region and the "real world". This report has earlier referred to the management of younger higher education institutions (Chapter 3). The external mechanisms which mobilise such institutions to support the region are often better developed than those of the older institutions, for example through the use of a variety of performance measures. This is the case for example with many polytechnics in Finland. (See Box 8.1.)

Developing leadership skills

What practical steps can be taken to ensure that leaders have the necessary skills to undertake the challenging boundary spanning tasks? The European Universities Association and the OECD have long recognised the need for leadership development, and more recently programmes for senior management in higher education are being established in several OECD countries. For example the Leadership Foundation has been established by the Higher Education Funding Council for England. It aims among other things to deliver a programme relevant to leadership in regional engagement. New post-graduate and executive programmes on the business school model are

---

Box 8.1. Higher education management at the Jyväskylä University of Applied Sciences: supporting regional engagement

Jyväskylä University of Applied Sciences (formerly Jyväskylä Polytechnic) in central Finland has a set of engagement activities which help the institution to respond to local needs as well as to bring local stakeholders into the institution to help with the delivery of education. One of the institution's past challenges involved the integration of seven constituent vocational colleges into one higher education institution which meets the needs of the regional businesses and working life in general. This merger process has strengthened the institution's capacity to develop new cross- and multi-disciplinary courses and educational trajectories in existing and emerging disciplinary areas to meet the needs of firms.

The institution is particularly well equipped to work with the SMEs which form the backbone of the regional economy in Central Finland. It has defined nine multi-disciplinary Centres of Expertise which respond to regional needs. Each school has an external board as well as a regional/business development office. Most significantly, it also maintains a sophisticated management information system which tracks the performance of each individual school. Of 29 Balanced Scorecard indicators, 8 are specifically linked to regional engagement. The school-based indicators are regularly monitored by the central management team. Strategic planning is implemented as part of the elaboration and annual revision of the three-year Agreement on Objectives set with the Ministry of Education. The planning process translates these objectives into school-, team- and personal-level goals and actions. Strategies are brought into practice through the Balanced Score Card.

---

making an appearance. In addition to the soft skills of leadership, such programmes need to focus on the generic issues regarding regional development and engagement and the facts regarding their own region (such as powers and responsibilities of external actors and agencies, and the dynamics of the regional economy).

Some of the knowledge and expertise necessary to advise leaders may reside in their own institutions. In the current OECD study, several self-evaluation reports include contributions from research groups within the higher education institution specialising in different aspects of regional engagement and/or higher education/management.[1] While many of these groups are actively involved in providing advice to regional agencies, they are not always used by the academic leadership to guide institution wide policy and practice in this domain.

Management of regional engagement

Influencing and managing the external environment of the higher education institution is a time consuming task. This includes making and sustaining strategic regional partnerships and assuming real and shared responsibility for the prosperity and development of the region. Modern higher education institutions find the scale and scope of top leadership too much for any one person and devise means of dividing this between key people. Another approach is to retain a single institutional head, but to delegate almost the entirety of internal management and development to a fully empowered deputy.

For managing its regional interface the higher education institution may need to establish a regional office. This has happened *e.g.* in the Purdue University (Indiana, USA) and the University of Newcastle upon Tyne (UK). Regional offices are helpful when scaling up the institutional capacity from individual good practice cases to a well developed system. A systematic approach will require focus on the following tasks: co-ordination and management of regional links; provision of input to strategic planning; contribution to the marketing of the institution; development of frameworks for engagement and regional understanding within the institution; and maintaining pressure for mainstreaming of regional engagement through the normal channels of the institution (OECD, 1999). (See also Chapter 5.)

The regional office needs to retain close links to the head of the institution. While it is desirable to have a senior (second tier) person heading this office and exercising responsibility and oversight for all 3rd task policy and activity, it is essential that this does not separate it from teaching/learning and research. The third task means permeating and transforming much of the teaching and research strategy and practice of the higher education institution. Managing, monitoring and developing engagement, regional partnership and development require consistent interrogation of all academic and administrative activities.

Mobilising the institution to regional engagement

Regional engagement is not only the task of the top leadership and management. Higher education institutions wishing to mobilise their staff in support of this agenda need to ensure that it is taken into consideration in the recruitment, hiring and reward systems as well as human resources development. Leadership requires underpinning with tangible rewards and incentives that make it possible to change behaviour and ultimately attitudes and values. Employment and human resources management practices need to allow greater segregation of roles among academic staff, with different kinds of workloads and reward systems. Reward systems have been developed for example in Australia, in the University of the Sunshine Coast (Box 8.2).

One of the key factors of success in regional partnerships is the presence of facilitators who act as gate keepers between the different networks and organisations. If higher education institutions wish to mainstream the regional agenda, they will require a number of staff with knowledge of regional development including: a) structure of the organisations involved in regional development; b) central, regional and local government powers and responsibilities; c) different time scales and drivers influencing these organisations; and d) overlaps between organisations and how these can be used to mutual advantage. A tailored human resources development programme for

---

Box 8.2. **Rewarding staff for regional engagement**

In 2005, after extensive consultation with key stakeholders, a new Promotion Policy was developed in the University of the Sunshine Coast, Australia, to improve alignment between the university's mission and this fundamental component of the university's recognition and reward system. The new policy defines, clarifies and reinforces the behaviours expected of academic staff. Applicants are required to demonstrate performance and achievement in teaching, research and service, which are valued equally. Service includes regional engagement. Regional engagement is perceived as scholarly practice, which derives from teaching and research and through which worthwhile social, civic and professional functions are achieved as academics apply their specialist knowledge and skills to consequential problems in the world beyond the University. Promotions have been made on the strength of applicants' regional engagement.

---

facilitators also needs to include the following know-how aspects: *a)* management of change; *b)* building and managing networks; *c)* facilitation and mediation; *d)* working with different organisational cultures; *e)* project planning and implementation; *f)* raising financial support; *g)* supervision and personal support techniques; and *h)* organisational politics and dynamics. These facilitators can mobilise the higher education institutions individually and collectively to a dialogue about the regional role of higher education. (OECD, 1999).

Collaboration between higher education institutions

Regional engagement of higher education requires co-operation and also division of tasks between the individual institutions. An important aspect of governance is that of co-ordination among higher education institutions and promotion of a "common higher education vision" to policymakers. While co-operation between higher education institutions allows for critical mass and provision of more diverse services, the intensity of collaboration remains uneven. Co-operation has thrived in some countries such as the United Kingdom leading to successful initiatives (see Knowledge House in Chapter 5). Although competition for funding has sometimes slowed down the development of inter-institutional collaboration, the trend has been encouraged by central government measures and the awareness of the benefits that can be drawn from speaking with one voice to regional agencies. Some regions have a longer history of collaboration among higher education actors and/or stronger "social capital". However, in many countries and regions, due to a lack of funding, weak interest and/or difficulty to agree on a clear division of tasks, clustering of higher education institutions and inter-institutional co-operation remains limited.

The current OECD study suggests that connectivity often needs to be planned and the local or central government can lay the groundwork for such initiatives. In this regard, there are two main types of programmes: *a)* experimental initiatives targeting a broad set of issues but requiring some level of inter-institutional co-operation or *b)* more specific programmes designed to counter the fragmentation of the tertiary education system in certain countries and as a consequence to remedy its weak ability to collaborate with the private sector. Also supra-national organisations, such as the European Union, have facilitated this type of work (see Box 8.3).

Closer higher education collaboration may require an establishment of a one-stop-shop to systematise regional engagement. This joint liaison office would have a matchmaking, co-ordination and quality assurance role and would provide a visible and single access point to the resource base of the higher education institutions in the region (see Box 5.4 in Chapter 5). Less

---

Box 8.3. **Regions of Knowledge**

In the EU, the Regions of Knowledge pilot initiative, introduced in the 2003 Community budget by the European Parliament, aims to support experimental actions at the regional level, to improve co-operation between universities and research at this level and to stimulate the integration of regions in Europe. The indicative budget for this initiative is a modest EUR 2.5 million which shows that it is mainly focused on facilitation and organisational issues (setting up networks). Within this framework, the University Driven Actions for Regional Development (UDARD) focus on the capacity of higher education institutions to provide expertise; to perform an advisory role for local companies and public institutions; to stimulate technology-creation and uptake by creating spin-off companies and incubators in a regional, trans-regional, and trans-national context.

---

radical option would be setting up a first-stop-shop, *i.e.* separate, but co-operating liaison offices in each higher education institution.

In some countries higher education institutions have made tentative steps to address the challenge of closer co-operation by establishing regional associations of higher education institutions. These have been based on initially top-down initiatives as in the United Kingdom where higher education regional associations have been established. The Öresund University is an even more ambitious association insofar as it transcends national boundaries and brings together higher education institutions in both Denmark and Sweden (Box 8.4).

Universities for the North East England and Öresund University both have their own support staff funded by subscriptions from the member higher education institutions and/or overheads charged on collaborative projects. They are characterised by *a)* pragmatism based on incremental approach to facilitate capacity building in complex situations with many stakeholders each with different short term targets; *b)* relationship maintenance to guarantee system management; *c)* long-term commitment to provide the groundwork for more strategic management of the human capital system; and *d)* external linkages which can be used to revitalise the partnership to sustain the momentum. They have a valuable role in representing the higher education institutions collectively to regional stakeholders. Nevertheless, they remain associations and their chief executives are not empowered to commit individual institutions beyond the collaborative operational projects that they have collectively signed up to. Core areas of teaching and research where the institutions often compete are "off limits". Major investments in structural

Box 8.4. **Higher education regional associations supporting regional development in the North East of England and Öresund region**

Higher Education Regional Associations (HERAs) were created in England as a means of encouraging research, teaching and access at regional scale. HERAs are increasingly seen as brokers for the allocation of funds for HEIF and linking learning networks in regions. In England, *Universities for the North East (Unis4NE)* is the oldest higher education regional association in England. Its precursor the Higher Education Support for Industries in the North was founded in 1983. Unis4NE works for the universities in the region, the Open University being an affiliate. Its board is made up of the Vice Chancellors of the higher education institutions. By virtue of the funds that it handles including the throughput of Knowledge House, its budget exceeds that of each of the other eight regional associations in England, despite being the smallest in membership. Unis4NE has several committees playing a brokerage role in collaboration between higher education sector and the region. These include Sports Committee, Culture Committee, Knowledge House, Aim Higher, Health Committee, Music Committee, European Committee, Research and Knowledge Committee and Academic Development Committee. It also serves as a vehicle for join resource bids for example to Whitehall, HEFCE or the European Union.

The Öresund University alliance was established at the time of the opening of the Öresund Bridge. It is led by Lund and Copenhagen universities and involves 12 other institutions of higher education in both Denmark and Sweden. The 14 universities (150 000 students) regrouped in the Öresund University Association aim to work together to consolidate the cross-border region, enhancing its dynamics, setting up sectoral organisations and organising forums and training for regional clusters. It is a mechanism for co-operation and interface between industry and society and a way of branding and enhancing the attractiveness of this cross border region. The alliance encourages the development of joint teaching programmes and research projects, PhD co-operation and student mobility. It supports networking university services (*e.g.* International offices, libraries, European funding, student counselling, marketing) as well as networks with regional authorities. The alliance also supports the Öresund Science Region, an umbrella organisation and incubator for a number of regional industrial clusters facilitating organisations and projects. It seeks to foster networking amongst researchers and firms, provide strategic advice to business and government, to contribute to branding and inward investment, promote new technologies, spin offs and the diffusion of innovation.

change such as new research institutes, teaching programmes and property have to be dealt with directly between the individual institutions and external stakeholders be they regional or national.

Mapping, monitoring and evaluating engagement

The collective working of higher education institutions for the region requires a systematic mapping and monitoring of the regional and external links in terms of teaching, research and third stream activities. Higher education institutions should establish collective mechanisms to track students' origins and destinations on a longitudinal basis including their careers as alumni and use this intelligence to guide the shaping of academic programmes. Similarly, the geography of the collaboration with the users and beneficiaries of research and the contribution of the higher education institutions to regional public affairs (staff participating in politics, the media, the voluntary sector, the arts and culture and other educational institutions) should be mapped. Documenting the present linkages and publicising them within the region and within the institutions itself will raise the profile of higher education as region builder (OECD, 1999).

This mapping should be followed by a self-evaluation of the higher education institutions. The template guiding the self-evaluation process of the current OECD study asked higher education institutions to critically evaluate with their regional partners and in the context of national higher education and regional policies under four major headings, *i.e.* contributions under research to regional innovation; the role of teaching and learning in the development of human capital; contributions to social, cultural and environmental development; and contributions to building regional capacity to act in an increasingly competitive global economy (Annex A). The regions and their higher education institutions which participated in the current OECD review project have – depending on the regional and national context – benefited from enhanced partnership working in the regional strategy process and implementation, generation of new funding streams from the local businesses, stronger branding for the institution(s) and the region and greater impact on national policies.

In most countries, there is no formal process of monitoring the outcomes and assessing the impact of the policies linked to the regional engagement of higher education institutions. In the United Kingdom, some Regional Development Agencies have set up regular programmes of strategic meetings between agency directors and vice chancellors of universities in order to regularly assess the progress made. In addition, the central government assesses some aspects of regional involvement through annual report in its HEIF funding from each university and through the annual collection of data on business and community engagements. In Finland and Sweden, knowledge institutions have been mapped in certain regions including evaluation of knowledge infrastructure. There has, however, been a number of evaluations and studies about limited aspects of regional engagement often identifying good practices. For example, Finland has a systematic evaluation template for the regional impact of polytechnics, and evaluations are carried out at regular intervals.

With regard to the policy support to technology transfer or creating networks, the evaluations refer to the number of business ideas screened and to the number of development products generated, but also stress the need for complementary initiatives. In the case of business start-ups, incubators and science parks, indicators include the capacity of the programme to establish large partnerships and to gain access to private funds, which are usually intended to take over public funds after a few years. The number of higher education institutions involved in the enterprise and job formation is often quoted as elements of success. More sophisticated analysis, such as using questionnaires addressed to customers or cost benefit analysis of programmes, is rare. Evaluation practices seem more widely spread in some countries than in others *e.g.* Germany, Finland, Sweden, the United Kingdom or the United States. In the UK, the Higher Education and Business Community Interaction Survey provides a number of indicators on research collaboration, consultancy, intellectual property exploitation, spin-off firms, study engagement and participation in regional partnerships. The survey published in 2005 notes an improvement in the quality of interaction between university and business. 89% of universities are now offering a single point of enquiry for business and 79% are assisting SME to identify what resource they need. There has also been an increase in job creation as a direct result of university spin-offs.

There is a need for higher education institutions to collectively construct an overall monitoring and evaluation system, covering all the regional development issues. This has to be supported by coherent and informative systems of indicators for the measurement of the regional contribution of institutions. The system should be able to gather information at the organisational level, the institutional level and the regional level.

Regional higher education systems

There is a marked difference between OECD countries in how higher education systems are steered at the regional and national level and what weight is given to the regional dimension.

For example, in the more market-oriented systems there is an increasing tendency to expect higher education institutions to be entrepreneurial, to create partnerships and raise funds from many sources, especially the private sector and private fees. This may encourage them to work closely with regional partners, possibly across all sectors, to diversify income streams. On the other hand it may militate against regional engagement which does not promise obvious profit. *Pro bono* public good may have little chance when balancing the books is the principal imperative. Thus regional engagement and development may stand in opposition to and be disadvantaged by the new entrepreneurialism. However, by setting priorities and channelling public funds, central governments can incentivise and persuade some or all higher education institutions to make regional development an attractive part of their central business – for example as a means of widening access to higher education or engaging with SMEs.

A critical choice for governments and higher education institutions is where and how in a mass system diversification takes place. One option is to expect most institutions to undertake all forms of academic activity including research, teaching and community service. Another is to designate some as mainly or only teaching institutions and to concentrate research in a few "world class" research-intensive institutions that enjoy much higher status. Many countries are striving to create world-class centres of excellence. In the global research context, building a world-class international centre of excellence is a difficult challenge for an individual country let alone individual institutions. The bias towards cutting-edge science needs to take account of the evidence that most innovation is incremental in character and also relies on non-scientific knowledge such as design, marketing and tooling-up. A balance therefore needs to be achieved between supporting basic and applied research within each major region of a country. Research, teaching and regional development feed one another and need to go together in a virtuous development cycle.

Extensive and flexible diversification among higher education institutions may provide countries with a wider capacity to address varied national and regional needs. The solution to a dichotomy between world-class research and heavily engaged regionally oriented institutions, however, lies in developing regional higher education systems in which there is strong interdependency, with role specialisation. All institutions are then made responsible together for meeting agreed and required targets across research, teaching and community service roles. Open regional network systems are a logical deduction from the needs, problems and pressures in the regions. Effective regional development, especially in terms of a labour market with fast-changing skill needs and mobile populations, requires a repertoire of youth and adult learning opportunities with functioning pathways and co-operation, not a disjointed set of provisions.

The regional pillar

Building regional partnerships

Successful partnerships between higher education and the region cannot be built on one pillar. They will also depend on regional leadership and collaboration. A key feature of the methodology developed in this OECD review was the establishment of a regional steering committee composed of higher education institutions and a wide range of regional stakeholders. In some regions this was already in place, for example Busan and Jutland-Funen but often with a focus on one aspect of the development process, usually business innovation.

Populating and finding a chair for a new grouping can be problematic where the leadership in the public and private sector is weak. Higher education leaders are often confronted with a multiplicity of regional agencies and partnership structures requesting their input and specific outputs in return for time-limited funding. There can be tensions between different parts of the region, between different agencies and even within single agencies which have multiple objectives – for example in a local authority between town planners required to conserve historic buildings and those charged with encouraging new investment. The fragmentation of local government, the issues of who speaks for the private sector and the role of different parts of central government in the region are common issues.

The same general point holds in federal systems, whether the province or state is also the region or the region is a smaller or larger entity than the political region. In all cases the region may have the potential to function more or less well, depending on a variety of issues such as history and path dependency, the rationality of its geography, economy, political life and setting and personnel.

In Canada the Atlantic Canada Opportunities Agency (ACOA) is a regional development agency that reconciles central financing and accountability with regional control. Its unique character lies in its position within Canada's government structure. It has direct access to the upper echelons of political power while at the same time ensuring its autonomy as a regional agency (Box 8.5).

Whatever the space to manoeuvre, resources and degree of devolution, it is essential for the region to create the means whereby its governing and administrative duties and opportunities can be exercised well, with horizontal communication as well as effective links to local authorities. In some countries there is a long tradition of regional government; in others the attempt to devolve powers is very new. Elected and appointed personnel have to learn to assume responsibility, liaising across the region's different

---

Box 8.5. **Atlantic Canada Opportunities Agency (ACOA)**

Founded in 1987, ACOA is the principal instrument of the Canadian Federal Government for promoting the economic development and entrepreneurial culture in the Atlantic Provinces. It is a separate ministry with its own responsible minister – elected from the region – ensuring that the region's voice is heard in Cabinet. Its status allows it to develop distinct policies adapted to the region with high degree of flexibility. ACOA's head office is located in the region where final decision-making power resides, advised by a local board, in accordance with the normal rules of ministerial consent and parliamentary accountability.

ACOA aims to make more people aware of opportunities for business creation and support, thereby helping to increase both the rate of small business formation and their likelihood of success. It offers programmes and services for futures entrepreneurs, business owners and managers, non-commercial organisations, communities and higher education institutions throughout the region. Education is seen as an important means of developing entrepreneurial skills and changing mindsets. ACOA has created programmes aimed at schools and higher education institutions.

ACOA's longevity has allowed it to experiment and to establish its credibility as an essential partner across the region. A number of measures have been developed over the years to increase the contribution of higher education institutions to regional development. These include the Atlantic Innovation Fund which has proven to be a key catalyst in encouraging partnerships among businesses and the research community, including higher education institutions. The Export Internships for Trade Graduates programme is another initiative involving higher education institutions. The Agency, in partnership with Atlantic Canadian post-secondary institutions, places university students who have completed formal training in the area of trade with companies actively pursuing new export markets. The programme provides hands-on, trade-related work experience for students, while contributing to the export performance of the region by providing SMEs with in-house trade expertise. ACOA also works with universities in the region to support their international recruitment efforts, and is considering ways of strengthening the role that the higher education institutions in the region play with regard to immigration and the retention of international students.

portfolios but also managing changing relations with central government. In short higher education's contribution to regional development requires effective regional governance. Without this, the full potential of higher education will not be realised.

Regional strategies

One way of tackling these challenges is through the preparation of overarching regional development strategies which focus on regional strengths and opportunities and address weaknesses and threats and which highlight the role higher education can play.[2] In several regions participating in the OECD study such as the Atlantic Canada and the North East of England research groups within the higher education institutions have played a key role in shaping strategies which embrace the contribution of higher education. Such strategies usually cover business, people and places and highlight the contribution that higher education can make in each of these areas. Specific action lines include:

- knowledge creation through research and its exploitation (spin-outs, intellectual property rights, business advisory service);
- knowledge transfer via teaching (worked-based learning, graduate recruitment, professional development/continuing education);
- cultural provision and campus development contributing to vibrant places that attract and retain creative people;
- social inclusion embracing different communities (urban, rural, ethnic);
- marketing the region nationally and internationally (via student recruitment, research links, alumni linkages, conference activity);
- sustainability.

Strategies and regional plans need to elaborated as a shared task between governments, higher education institutions, research centres and the business sector. This should translate into better links between the expertise of the higher education institutions and the strategic priorities of the region. It could also coalesce various sectoral plans often designed at the regional level (technology, health, labour market, etc.). Some regions have initiated such approaches, but many are still inactive. The strategic plans should help to diagnose comparative advantages and to build vision based on dynamics of local and regional economies. They should be transparent with regard to the stakeholder's commitment. They would contribute to shape different roles of higher education institution, including but not restricted to technology issues. While research intensive universities often give insufficient priority and investment to activities that are not technology or R&D intensive (*e.g.* service related activities), environmental management, tourism, transport services, culture, sport and leisure can offer new possibilities for higher education institutions to develop joint activities with the business sector. Related action plans should be prepared specifying individual tasks, responsibilities, timelines, resources and performance measures if they are to drive the

---

Box 8.6. **Examples of strategic co-operation in regions**

Strategy making: In the Netherlands, the Innovation platform Twente, originally established by the Province of Overrijssel and Network City Twente, involves representatives from industry, local governments and major higher education institutions contributing to the development of the region. It elaborates a vision for an innovative Twente region and publishes a delivery plan. It has identified key innovative actors and projects that could be harnessed to boost innovation in five key domain clusters. The delivery plan aligns funding from municipalities, the province, the RDA behind existing activities and should help to develop more of integrated multi agents projects across the five regional clusters.

Building infrastructure for collaboration. In Denmark, in the wake of the local government reform that came into effect in 2007, Regional Growth Forums have been established with representatives from the newly created regions, municipalities, local trade and industry, the institutions of education and research and the parties of the labour market. Regional Growth Forums are expected to monitor local and regional opportunities for growth and to formulate regional development business strategies which can be fed in into the development plans of the regional councils. The success of this reform and the forums is dependent on the financial resources that will be devoted to the new regions and to their ability to influence national and local policy making.

Joint strategies. In Finland, the Ministry of Education has requested higher education institutions to jointly devise regional strategies for areas that are larger than a municipality or a county (*maakunta*). At the same time each regional council elaborate a four year regional programme for its *maakunta*. Though higher education does not belong to the matters governed by the regional development legislation, *the maakunta* specific implementation plans list a number of expectations regarding universities and polytechnics.

---

regional agenda forward, be accountable and be comprehensively evaluated on a regular basis.

Putting the bridge in place

Funding conjoint action

Many national systems have allocated limited resources to the regional engagement of higher education institutions. There are, however, some national initiatives which have been set up to drive the regional agenda of higher education. Examples of top-down initiatives involving central government thrust include the US University Centre Programme, the

Canadian Federal Government's Atlantic Innovation Fund which supports universities in the four Atlantic provinces seeking to undertake R&D projects with local businesses (Box 8.7) and the already mentioned Korean New University for Regional Innovation Fund (NURI). (See Chapter 3, Box 3.1.)

Box 8.7. **Central government initiatives supporting the regional agenda of higher education institutions**

In the United States, the Economic Development Administration, EDA (US Department of Commerce) launched long ago a *University Centre Programme* which aims to partner with higher education institutions to improve the economies and economic development capacities of their service areas with emphasis on economically distressed communities. The programme funds proposals for a three year period with most regional offices providing funding on a year to year basis depending on performance and the availability of funds. University centre projects provide management and technical assistance services to communities, counties, districts, non profit development groups and technology transfer assistance to firms. The programme co-finances 69 centres housed by universities in 45 States and Puerto Rico with a budget of USD 7.7 million. A recent evaluation has examined a number of programme features, including centre effectiveness, distressed-area targeting, and utilisation of university resources.

In Canada, the Atlantic Investment Partnership was announced in 2000 as a five-year, CAD 700 million initiative delivered by ACOA and designed to build new partnerships that will increase the capacity of Atlantic Canadians to compete in an increasingly global, knowledge-based economy. Through the Atlantic Investment Partnership, the Government of Canada targeted major investments in the areas of innovation, community economic development, trade and investment, and entrepreneurship and business skills development. The main component of the overall initiative was the CAD 300 million *Atlantic Innovation Fund* which is designed to strengthen the economy of Atlantic Canada by accelerating the development of knowledge-based industry. The Atlantic Investment Partnership was renewed in 2005 for another five-year period with a similar level of funding and with the Atlantic Innovation Fund remaining as its main programme element. The AIF has proven to be a key catalyst in encouraging strong partnerships among businesses and the research community including higher education institutions. Its objectives are to: *a)* build capacity for innovation and research and development (R&D) that leads to technologies, products, processes or services that contribute to economic growth in Atlantic Canada; *b)* increase the capacity for commercialisation of R&D outputs; *c)* strengthen the region's innovation capacity by supporting research, development and commercialisation partnerships and alliances

---

> **Box 8.7. Central government initiatives supporting**
> **the regional agenda of higher education institutions** (cont.)
>
> among private sector firms, universities, research institutions and other organisations in Atlantic Canada; and d) maximise the region's ability to access national R&D funding programs. The Atlantic Innovation Fund focuses on R&D projects in the area of natural and applied sciences, as well as in social sciences, humanities, arts and culture. Assistance is provided to eligible projects, specifically up to 80% of total eligible cost for non-commercial projects and up to 75% of total eligible costs for commercial projects. Contributions to the private sector are conditionally repayable based on commercial success. Contributions to non-commercial organisations such as research institutes in universities, are non repayable.

In most countries the absence of national funding supporting regional engagement of higher education institutions places greater onus on regional stakeholders, drawing on national and international resources where appropriate. One possible solution would be the creation of a single pot of public funding contributed to by a range of stakeholders which higher education institutions could draw on against an agreed set of deliverables which are regularly monitored. Not all higher education institutions in the region would be expected to do everything. Rather they could select from a portfolio of programme possibilities to suit their own missions and academic profile. In many instances programmes are, however, likely to transcend several institutions and modes of engagement (teaching as well as research) and may require the establishment of Special Purpose Vehicles to ensure delivery. Such local actions may persuade national ministries of education who have laid external engagement duties on higher education institutions without appropriate support to enter into match funding arrangements.

Accountability and impacts

Working in partnership for regional development requires: a win-win situation, the capacity to commit to specific short-term decisions with a clear product and delivery date and sustainability, institutional memory supported by modern knowledge management system that transcends changes of personnel and policy orientation, and formal arrangements for evaluation and programme enhancement.

One of the challenges of partnership working is that of accountability. Each of the partners in the higher education/regional development nexus have different accountabilities and expectations. Job generation and placemaking is not a responsibility of higher education, nor is higher education a responsibility of local government and only in certain countries of regional government. Impacts of engagement are difficult to measure. It is virtually impossible *ex post* to determine how much any improvement in regional economic performance or reduction of inequalities is due solely to interventions by higher education institutions working in partnership with regional agencies.

Notwithstanding the difficulties in measuring impacts, there is a need to invest in a rigorous machinery to undertake baseline analyses specifically designed by partners to address regional weaknesses, build on strengths, contain threats and exploit opportunities. Baseline studies need to be followed by regular monitoring of outcomes. This process will require external peer review. It will require input from all of the stakeholders to ensure their individual accountabilities are taken care of in the analyses.

Realising the potential of higher education to contribute to regional development

The preceding discussion has implicitly accepted a network model for moving towards higher education and regional development systems. It has not advocated a centralised steering approach whereby the national government directs individual higher education institutions to undertake particular tasks in specific locations. Nor for reasons partly related to the problem of appropriate metrics has a market driven model based on performance or output measures been proposed. Rather the emphasis has been on a bottom-up approach of collaborative working where all the partners appreciate the mutual benefits of coming together. Insofar as steering occurs the approach favoured has been of peer learning through sharing of good practice.

To succeed such regional collaboration needs a national framework consistent between the domains of higher education and territorial development which facilitates or permits conjoint action at the sub-national level. There is some evidence that national governments are moving away from strictly prescribing tasks for regional or local governments and what higher education institutions should do where. Movements towards greater direct participation of citizens and businesses in the affairs of state locally and nationally and in the co-production of knowledge are reinforcing these tendencies and thus assisting with the building of bridges between regional institutions and higher education institutions. While the extent of local and regional empowerment and the extent to which it embraces higher education vary significantly from country to country, without this empowerment it is difficult to see how the potential for higher education institutions to actively contribute to regional development can be realised. With the right conditions regional engagement can become a crucible within which more dynamic and open higher education institutions can be forged, both responding to and shaping developments in the wider society.

Notes

1. These centres include the Centre for Higher Education Policy Studies (CHEPS) at Twente University, the Centre for Urban and Regional Development Studies (CURDS) at Newcastle University (North East England), the Leslie Harris Centre of Regional Policy and Development at Memorial University (Newfoundland, Atlantic Canada), the Institute for Sustainability Health and Regional Engagement (iSHARE) at the University of the Sunshine Coast, and the Centre for the Study of Higher Education Management (CEGES) at the Technical University of Valencia.

2. Higher education institutions are well placed to provide regions and communities with numerous services. They have the expertise to analyse future challenges from a multidisciplinary perspective and identify policy options and scenarios for the future. They are a reservoir of ideas and innovations and can be valuable contributors to the regional development policy process. While foresight and visioning exercises are mainly used at the national level, it has only started in some countries to trickle down to regions and sub-regions.

ISBN 978-92-64-03414-3
Higher Education and Regions:
Globally Competitive, Locally Engaged
© OECD 2007

Chapter 9

Pointers for Future Development

This final chapter draws together pointers for future development for actors at three different levels: central, regional and institutional level. The recommendations emphasise the facilitating role of the central government in creating beneficial framework conditions and incentives. The recommendations highlight the importance of partnership building between the higher education institutions, and between the higher education institutions and regional stakeholders. Finally, they emphasise the need for more active role of higher education institutions.

Central governments

There is a need to acknowledge across government the key role that higher education institutions can play in joining up a wide range of policies at the regional level. These policies include science and technology, industry, education and skills, health, culture and sport, environmental sustainability and social inclusion. If countries wish to mobilise their higher education system or part of it in support of regional development, the higher education policy which embraces teaching, research and third strand activities should include an explicit regional dimension. There should also be an acknowledgement that the varying regional contexts within which higher education institutions operate and the national policies, especially funding regime for higher education, have differential regional impacts. The recommendations to the central governments include the following:

- Create more "joined-up" governance (Finance, Education, Science & Technology, and Industry Ministries, etc.) to co-ordinate decisions on priorities, resources and strategic items in regional development.

- Make regional engagement and more specifically its wide agenda for economic, social and cultural development explicit in higher education legislation and encourage higher education institutions to address regional engagement in their mission statements and strategies.

- Further strengthen institutional autonomy of higher education institutions by increasing their responsibility over curriculum and the use of human, financial and physical resources and provide incentives to exercise these responsibilities through developing long-term core funding for higher education institutions to support regional engagement and providing additional strategic incentive-based funding schemes.

- Strengthen higher education institutions' accountability to society by developing indicators and monitoring outcomes to assess the impact of the higher education institutions on regional performance; require governance of higher education institutions to involve regional stakeholders and encourage the participation of higher education institutions in regional governance structures.

- Mobilise the joint resources of the higher education institutions for the preparation and implementation of regional and urban strategies and encourage genuine partnerships where higher education institutions are not only technical advisers for regional strategy making but also actors in the process and genuine stakeholders.

● Provide a more supportive environment for university-enterprise cooperation: regulatory and tax environment and accountability regimes that do not place an undue burden on higher education institutions and businesses.

● Continue to focus on the development of human capital through developing highly skilled graduates for the national and regional labour market and up-skilling the local labour force; Improve educational opportunities through distance learning, lifelong learning and e-learning.

● Support collaboration between universities and other higher education institutions in the region through joint degrees, programmes, research programmes, strategies and one-stop-shops for industry collaboration to improve the supply and delivery of higher education services for regional firms.

Regional and local authorities

For many public authorities operating at the local and regional level, the higher education and the individual institutions remain a "black box". What drives academics as teachers and researchers, the way in which the institutions are governed and managed, the mechanisms of central government funding are seldom understood. This understanding needs to be supported by detailed knowledge of the research and teaching portfolio of the higher education institutions, so that when opportunities arise, the development agencies can identify the appropriate institutions or part of it to be engaged in the negotiation process. The recommendations to the regional and local authorities include the following:

● Establish a partnership structure of key stakeholders from local and regional authorities, business, the community and the higher education to provide a focus for dialogue with higher education in relation to its contribution to regional development and identify and develop leaders within the public and private sectors to populate this partnership structure.

● Mobilise the resources of higher education institutions in the preparation and implementation of regional and urban strategies for economic, social, cultural and environmental development.

● Invest jointly with higher education institutions in programmes which bring specific benefit to regional businesses and the community (*e.g.* translational research facilities, advisory services for SMEs, professional development programmes, graduate retention programmes, cultural facilities and programmes); Support higher education institutions in bids for national and international resources for activities that will enhance their regional impact (co-investment/leverage); Ensure that resources provided to higher education institutions facilitate regional engagement building capacity in a sustainable (multi-annual) basis and are more than a collection of short term *ad hoc* projects.

- Ensure a fully functional human capital system with pathways between different levels of education.

Higher education institutions

The scope and extent of regional engagement of a higher education institution are largely dependent on the role the institution chooses for itself and the leadership role it adopts. Some institutions are more entrepreneurial than others not only because they develop more spin-offs, but because they have established long-term relationships with their regional stakeholders and because they have embarked on a process of institutional adjustment strengthening their management core and creating professional management systems and outreach activities. Better results can be achieved through enhanced co-operation and co-ordination between the higher education institutions in the region. The recommendations to higher education institutions include the following:

- Map the regional and external links in terms of teaching, research and third task activities of higher education institutions individually and collectively and carry out a self evaluation of institutional capacity to respond to regional needs.

- Adopt a wide agenda of regional engagement considering the whole range of opportunities for engagement whether economic, social or cultural and then engage in continuous improvement of these activities and monitoring of results.

- Acknowledge that regional engagement can enhance the core missions of teaching and research (*e.g.* the region as a laboratory, a provider of work experience for students and a provider of financial resources to enhance global competitiveness). Enhance transversal mechanisms that link teaching, research and third task activities and which may cut across disciplinary boundaries (faculties and departments).

- Develop senior management teams able to deliver the corporate response expected by regional stakeholders but without disincentivising entrepreneurial academics.

- Establish a regional development office to mainstream the regional agenda and to scale up the individual case studies to a system; Develop facilitators who act as gate keepers between the different networks and organisations.

- Ensure that units established to link the higher education institution to the region (*e.g.* science parks, centres of continuing education, knowledge transfer centres) do not act as barriers to the academic heartland or provide an excuse for detachment.

- Establish modern administration with human resources and financial resources management systems; Review recruitment, hiring and reward systems to include regional engagement agenda.

- Establish partnership organisations with their own staff and resources which link all higher education institutions within the region and which are able to undertake substantive collaborative projects and programmes that address regional needs and opportunities.

ISBN 978-92-64-03414-3
Higher Education and Regions:
Globally Competitive, Locally Engaged
© OECD 2007

ANNEX A

OECD Project on Supporting the Contribution of Higher Education Institutions to Regional Development
Self-evaluation Report: Issues to be Addressed

This document suggests a structure for the regional self-evaluation report, and gives examples of the questions that it might cover. This is not a questionnaire and it is not intended that responses be given to every item. Its purpose is rather to act as an aide-memoire, illustrating the range of topics and information that might be covered.

Chapter I: Overview of the region (about 10 pages)

The geographical situation

1. What is the position of the region in relation to the national territory in terms of accessibility to the national capital and other major centres of economic and cultural activity?

2. Where does the region fit in terms of the national hierarchy of cities and regions? Has its position been improving or deteriorating in the past 20 years?

3. What are the key features of the internal settlement structure in terms of: 1) pattern of urban centres; 2) intra regional accessibility; and 3) urban/ rural linkages?

4. Where is higher education provided in relation to the settlement structure (campus locations and distance learning provision)?

The demographic situation

5. What are the key demographic indicators for the region and how have they changed over the last 20 years? Please include the following:

- age structure of the population
- emigration and immigration
- health and wellbeing
- levels of deprivation

6. What are the participation levels of the local population in higher education by social group and by gender and where do students attend for this purpose (within and beyond the region)?

The economic and social base

7. What is the economic and social base of the region compared to the national average? Please include the following:

- industrial structure by sector
- the importance of knowledge intensive sectors within the regional economy
- the leading export sectors
- the occupational structure of employment (manual, technical,. clerical, professional, etc.)
- ownership structure of enterprises (*e.g.* balance between SMEs and MNCs)
- level of public and private R&D
- indicators of entrepreneurial activity (*e.g.* rates of new business formation)

8. What are the distinguishing social and cultural characteristics of the region?

9. What is the economic impact of the higher education sector in terms of: 1) numbers employed; and 2) multiplier effect of HEIs and staff and student expenditure?

10. What are the key labour market indicators? Please include the following:

- unemployment
- economic activity rates
- levels of educational attainment of the population including the proportion proceeding to
- and with tertiary level of educational qualifications
- origin and destination of graduates

11. How has the region performed over the last 20 years in relation to the nation in terms of the following key indicators: (1) GDP per capita; (2) GVA per capita; (3) unemployment; and (4) share of employment in growing sectors?

Governance structure

12. What is the structure of central, regional and local government in the region? Specifically, who is responsible for the following:

- resourcing public services (balance between local, regional and national taxation)
- economic development
- education (primary, secondary, tertiary, vocational)
- health and welfare
- cultural provision

13. What powers are available to local and regional authorities in relation to economic and social development? Please include the following: 1) acquisition of land and property; 2) financial inducements to business; and 3) provision of vocational education.

14. What influence, if any, do local and regional authorities have over the provision of tertiary level education **and** research and development?

15. What influence, if any, do local and regional authorities have over national policy with regard to tertiary level teaching and research?

16. What are the principal drivers in relation to national territorial development policy as these impact on the region and what place does higher education have in these policy developments?

Chapter II: Characteristics of the higher education system (about 10 pages)

Overview of the national system of higher education

1. What are the dominant characteristics of the national higher education system? Please include the following:

- What is the overall size of the higher education system (number of students, participation rate)? How has the overall size of the system changed over the last ten years, and in which parts of the system has any growth been concentrated?
- What data analysis has been performed at a national level to establish the demand and supply of different types of higher education "product"?

- Outline the basic governance of and regulatory framework for the higher education system (*i.e.* funding mechanism and institutional autonomy) including the major legislation that applies to it.

- Describe briefly the major national agencies responsible for developing tertiary education policy, for financing the system, and for assuring its quality, and their mandates. Outline how national higher education policies are developed.

- What characterises inter-institutional relationships – co-operation, competition, market-led?

2. To what extent is there dialogue between government ministries concerned with territorial development, science & technology and those sponsoring higher education? What mechanisms exist to co-ordinate and attune the policies and measures taken by the different ministries?

Regional dimension "inside" the national higher education policy

3. To what extent does national higher education policy have a regional dimension? In answering this, the following questions could be taken into consideration:

- Have regional development (economic, social, cultural) considerations played a prominent role in decisions on where to locate and build up new institutions?

- Have funding arrangements been altered to reward institutions for regional engagement or to make this engagement possible?

- Is regional engagement imposed on institutions by government as a formal requirement?

- What policy initiatives have been taken by various actors (*e.g.* central governments in different policy domains, regional authorities) to foster the regional role of HEIs and to stimulate regional collaboration between HEIs, industry, government and civil society?

4. To what extent do these considerations have a differential impact upon different types of higher education institutions? (*i.e.* universities *vs.* non-university HEIs)

5. Does an emphasis upon a regional role for HEIs involve any policy tensions? For example, is there a conflict between regional commitment and the strive for quality and international competitiveness in higher education? If so, how are these resolved?

Regional higher education system and governance

6. Outline the basic profile and character of HEIs in the region: universities, non-university HEIs.

   ● What are the historic links between the HEI and the region and how have these developed? How has the institution evolved over the last ten years in terms of: 1) staff and student numbers; 2) faculty mix; 3) place of the institution in the regional and national higher education systems; 4) balance between teaching and research functions; and 5) territorial focus.

7. To what extent does the financing and management of HEIs occur at a regional level?

8. Are there regional organisations that have strategic responsibility over funding and management of HEIs?

Chapter III: Contribution of research to regional innovation (about 15 pages)

Responding to regional needs and demands

1. Does HEI research policy have a regional dimension?

   ● To what extent do HEIs draw upon the characteristics of the region to develop research activity?

   ● What other regional partners are drawn into this process? How have such research links established?

   ● Do the technology transfer offices have a regional as well as an international and national role?

2. How is provision made to meet specific regional technology & innovation needs and demands, such as those from SMEs? Is such provision undertaken in collaboration with other regional innovation and technology actors such as public labs and research institutes? What is the relationship between these innovation and technology actors other than HEIs and business in the region?

3. What mechanisms exist to reward and acknowledge regionally-based research (i.e. the application of the established knowledge for the local/ regional community as opposed to the generation of "basic" knowledge for the national/ international academic community) which has been traditionally outside of peer review processes such as academic journals?

Framework conditions for promoting research and innovation

4. Does the national legal framework (*e.g.* Intellectual property law) support the role of HEIs in research and innovation (including research and innovation partnerships with industry)? What are the incentives and barriers in HEI-industry relationships both for HEIs and for industry?

5. Describe the ways in which HEIs help to stimulate innovation and knowledge transfer between researchers and industry (both larger enterprises and small and medium-sized enterprises). Do national or regional policies exist to encourage HEIs to play such a role?

6. Do policies or funding programmes exist to encourage co-operative research between HEIs and industry or the exchange of research staff between the two?

Interfaces facilitating knowledge exploitation and transfer

7. What mechanisms have been developed to commercialise the research base of the HE sector and to promote technology transfer between the HEI and regional stakeholders? Please include the following:

   ● research contracts, collaboration and consultancy ;
   ● intellectual property (IP) transactions ;
   ● promotion of spin-offs, incubators, science parks; and clusters ;
   ● teaching/ training and labour mobility.

8. How have HEIs and other regional stakeholders been promoting these mechanisms described above?

   ● What are the respective roles of the central government, regional authorities, HEIs, regional research institutes, and business in creating such mechanisms?
   ● Are there any specific mechanisms that have been created within or between higher education institutions?

9. Are there structures in place in the region that enable the HEIs to more widely disseminate its R&D and innovation initiatives beyond its contractual industry partners (*i.e.*, exhibitions, competitions, regular demonstrations, media, regional web page entry points, etc.)?

Conclusions

10. Collaboration between regional stakeholders related to *contribution of research to regional innovation*: 1) between the universities in the region; 2) between universities and non-university HEIs; and 3) between HEIs and other regional stakeholders (*i.e.* business, local government, research labs & institutions, etc.);

11. Strengths, weaknesses, opportunities and threats related to *contribution of research to regional innovation* in the region.

Chapter IV: Contribution of teaching and learning to labour market and skills (about 15 pages)

Localising the learning process

1. How do HEIs draw upon the specific characteristics of a region to aid learning and teaching?

   ● Are there any courses which meet regional needs?

   ● In what ways are learning programs tied to reflecting and finding creative solutions on regional issues over the medium to long term rather than not simply to meet the short term need for training students for existing known skill number gaps?

   ● Are there learning programs within the HEIs that enhance the capacity of students to be enterprising with the skills to put in place entities and initiatives to take advantage of regional issues and opportunities?

2. What is the role of the careers service in the process of localising learning?

3. How are students integrated in the region, in terms of course placements, accommodation, volunteering activities?

4. What mechanisms exist to monitor/accredit extra-curricular activities?

5. To what extent is postgraduate activity – which can be an effective tool of technology transfer to the region and a way of embedding highly skilled graduates in the regional economy – geared towards meeting regional needs (*i.e.* Ph.D industrial programme in Denmark; Teaching Company Scheme in the UK; external associate professorship from local industry, etc.)?

6. Do the HEIs in the region facilitate voluntary associations and coalitions of regional expertise and knowledge around key regional strategic priorities?

Student recruitment and regional employment

7. What are HEIs' policies concerning regional recruitment? What mechanisms are in place to increase this? Are there any collaborative partnerships or quota arrangements among regional HEIs to manage regional recruitment?

8. To what extent do HEIs recognise themselves as part of a regional education supply chain?

9. What mechanism exists to create pathways between regional HEIs and regional firms, especially SMEs?

10. To what extent is labour market information gathered to monitor the flow of graduates into the labour market? Does this process involve other regional stakeholders?

11. Are there any specific initiatives or practice to support graduate enterprise (i.e. the Cambridge MIT initiative in the UK) in an effort to retain graduates in the region and recruit alumni to return to the region?

Promoting lifelong learning, continuing professional development and training

12. How is continuing education and continuing professional development activity organised? (i.e. adult liberal education; tailored and specialist continuing professional development)

13. Have external or independent enterprises (i.e. separate and independently-run business school) been established within HEIs to extend professional education provision to the region?

14. Is such provision undertaken in collaboration with other regional stakeholders?

15. Which regional partners are involved in meeting regional training needs?

16. What mechanisms are in place to increase access to learners in the region who have been traditionally under-represented in higher education? (i.e. ethnic minority, returning adult learners, those with disabilities)

Changing forms of educational provision

17. What mechanisms exist for promoting flexible education provision such as satellite campuses, accreditation networks, on-line courses and outreach centres?

18. How do HEIs maintain institutional coherence in the light of this multi-territorial educational provision?

19. Are regional HEIs drawing upon new forms of ICT-based course delivery to enhance educational opportunities to a wider group?

20. What are the tensions between place-based and virtual forms of education provision?

Enhancing the regional learning system

21. To what extent is there a coherent vision of an education system existing at the regional level? Do HEIs acknowledge the need to develop education on a regional basis?

22. What data analysis has been performed to establish the demand and supply of different types of higher education "product" within the region?

23. Are procedures in place to support regional collaboration between HEIs in this respect?

- Is there a credit transfer system between education institutions and what links exist between the university and non-university higher education sector?

24. What measures exist to promote gender equity in participation in higher education in the region?

Conclusions

25. Collaboration between regional stakeholders related to *contribution of teaching and learning to labour market and skills*: 1) between the universities in the region; 2) between universities and non-university HEIs; and 3) between HEIs and other regional stakeholders (*i.e.* business, local government, research labs & institutions, etc.);

26. Strengths, weaknesses, opportunities and threats related to *contribution of teaching and learning to labour market and skills* in the region.

Chapter V: Contribution to social, cultural and environmental development (about 10 pages)

Social development

1. Do the HEIs provide community access facilities and expertise support for services such as health and medical, welfare advisory, cultural exchange, indigenous support, religious?

2. Do the HEIs engage in partnership with the community in the provision of social services?

Cultural development

3. Do the HEIs provide facilities, expertise and learning programme support for cultural groups?

4. Do the HEIs encourage sporting development?

5. Do the HEIs support the arts through its infrastructure, programmes and services?

6. Have HEIs established mechanisms through which their stock of cultural facilities can be jointly managed and marketed to the regional community?

Environmental sustainability

7. Are the campus of HEIs a practical demonstration of best practice to address environmental issues of concern to the regional community?

8. Are there joint initiatives between the university, the regional community and others to demonstrate environmental sustainability possibilities for the region?

Conclusions

9. Collaboration between regional stakeholders related to *social cultural and environmental development*: 1) between the universities in the region; 2) between universities and non-university HEIs; and 3) between HEIS and other regional stakeholders (*i.e.* business, local government, research labs & institutions, etc.);

10. Strengths, weaknesses, opportunities and threats related to social, cultural and environmental development in the region.

Chapter VI: Capacity building for regional co-operation (about 15 pages)

Mechanisms to promote HEI-regional involvement

1. What formal and informal mechanisms exist to identify regional needs? Has the catalyst for regional engagement been internal or external to HEIs?

   ● Are their formal processes such as signed agreements that bind those in the engagement relationship?

2. Have government and/or regional authorities undertaken an audit of the knowledge resources of the region in terms of: 1) the expertise, skills and experience of people in the regional population; 2) the research places and spaces; and 3) the accessibility of research and learning infrastructure for new innovative knowledge generating and dissemination initiatives?

3. Does the region's strategic plan include the role of the HEIs as a key element?

4. What resources are made available to HEIs by government and other organisations to support regional engagement? How are these distributed? What incentives and support are provided to support regional engagement of HEIs?

5. What processes are in place to regularly review current engagement arrangements between the HEIs and the region so as to build an element of ongoing improvement into the relationship?

- How do government and/or regional authorities evaluate the success of HEIs in regional engagement? Have government and/or regional authorities identified any good practice in respect of regional engagement of HEIs and if so how has this been disseminated?

6. What formal and informal mechanisms exist to co-ordinate the activities of HEIs in regional engagement both within HE sector and with those of other participants?

7. Do the HEIs make use of existing regional community infrastructure for its operation? Also, does the community access HEI infrastructure for its day to day needs (i.e., testing laboratories, libraries, sporting and cultural facilities, transport, accommodation for students, etc.)?

Promoting regional dialogue and Joint marketing initiatives

8. What mechanisms exist to promote communication and dialogue between HEIs and regional stakeholders?

9. What groups are part of the dialogue of regional engagement? How are the regional interests of various sectors of interest such as HE, industry, the private, public and voluntary sectors represented?

10. What is the extent and nature of HEI staff representation on public/private bodies in the region? What are the reasons for such representation and what is their role? Is such representation monitored?

11. What role do external bodies play in decision making within HEIs?

12. Are there joint HEI/ regional promotion and marketing initiatives or a "buy local" purchasing program within the HEIs in the region?

Evaluating and mapping the impact of the regional HE system

13. Have HEIs, collectively and/or individually, undertaken an audit of their (its) impacts on and links with the region? (i.e., Direct economic impact of the institution; Contributions to local economic development; Social and cultural impact).

14. How are such impact statements used and distributed to the region and further afield to promote the HEIs and the region?

15. Do mechanisms exist to raise awareness of the role of HEIs in the region? What is known about the contribution that higher education makes to the region?

[For Each HEI in the Region]

Institutional capacity building for regional involvement

1. To what extent has academic leadership and central management been altered to engage with regional needs?

2. Does the institution's strategic plan include its relationship with the regional community as a key strategy for enhancing viability?

3. What are the main channel of communication between regional stakeholders and the institution (senior managers, committees, etc) and who is responsible for regional decisions in the institution?

4. What internal mechanisms exist for co-ordinating regional activities within the institution especially in relation to funding issues and what new posts/offices have been created with an explicitly regional local remit?

5. Does the institution use adjunct appointments to add expertise to its capacity?

6. In what ways is the institution responding to regional ICT infrastructure and is it adopting new technologies to restructure their own management structures?

Human and financial resources management

7. How is the regional dimension incorporated into the human resources policy of the institution?

   - What training is given to staff with regional responsibilities? How is staff rewarded for regional engagement?

8. How are regional and national funding streams managed? What are the possibilities of financial decentralisation within the institution?

9. How does the institution embed new devolved financial responsibilities into academic life?

10. How are new resources for regional engagement and activity generated? Who pays for the regional role of the institution?

11. What new regional funding streams are emerging which the institution can tap into? What mechanisms are being established to tap into these sources?

Creating a new organisation culture

12. Are there any significant cultural obstacles to adopting greater regional engagement within the institution (i.e. the connotations which regionalism has with parochialism, newness, and unsophistication)? What efforts have been done to overcome these obstacles?

13. Is regional engagement part of the institution's mission? Has regional engagement become part of the academic mainstream of the institution? If so, how far this has influenced mainstream teaching and research?

Chapter VII: Conclusions: moving beyond the self-evaluation (about 5 pages)

1. Lessons to be learned from the self-evaluation process. Please include the following issues:

   ● Which practice and methodologies seem to be the most promising for strengthening regional capacity building, and what factors make for their success?

   ● What synergy is there between the aims and objectives of institutions and regions? Are there conflicting interests?

   ● What incentives are there at institutional, departmental and individual level for HEIs to become more engaged?

   ● What are the main challenges facing the different sets of decision-makers?

2. The potentialities and problems, opportunities and threat for increasing the contribution that HEIs make to the region.

3. The way forward: the discussion of the region's vision for future policy.

ANNEX B

Selected OECD Countries' Characteristics and Innovation-based Policies Targeting at the Regional Engagement of Higher Education Institutions

Table B.1. **Selected OECD countries' characteristics and innovation-based policies targeting at the regional engagement of higher education institutions**

Country	HE research % of GDP 2004	HE research financed by industry 2004	Number of HEIs	Policy focus	Policy issues	Main programmes[1] (central or federal level)
Australia	0.48%	5.7%	37 public and 3 private universities + 4 other HEIs	Working against university fragmentation; Promoting innovative universities	Increasing critical mass in research universities; Setting up single points access for research projects; Enhancing co-operation between HEIs and the private sector	Collaboration and Structural Reform Fund; Australian Research Council; Linkages project; Australia Regional Partnership programme; CRC; Cooperative Research Centres
Austria	0.59%	4.5%	14 universities	Regional cluster policy	Coordination between federal and Länder level	A+B Academic Business Spin-Off Programme; Centres of Excellence; REG+; FH
Belgium	0.41%	11.6%*	15 universities	Tackling the bottlenecks in knowledge and innovation systems	Improving knowledge absorption capacities in regions	*Flanders*: TETRA fund for traditional industries; Financial support to Science Parks; IOF for university research with industry applications *Brussels*: Industrial research subsidy *Wallonia*: FIRST
Canada	0.70%	8.2%	157 public universities, 175 recognised public community colleges and technical institutes	Commercialisation of HE research	Aligning HE research with market needs; Improving the system of intellectual property rights; Setting up single points of contact for business in HEIs	Atlantic Innovation Fund; Chairs of Research Excellence; Centers of Excellence; NRC-IRAP; Canada Foundation for Innovation; NSERC collaborative programme; NSERC Ideas to Innovation; IMAC
Denmark	0.61%	3.0%	12 public research universities, 55 other HEIs, and ca. 20 cultural institutions	Regional Innovation Platform	Implications of the creation of five regions	Regional Centres of Excellence; Regional Knowledge Pilot programme; Trade and Industry Partnerships

1. See below more details on each country's programmes.

Table B.1. **Selected OECD countries' characteristics and innovation-based policies targeting at the regional engagement of higher education institutions** (cont.)

Country	HE research % of GDP 2004	HE research financed by industry 2004	Number of HEIs	Policy focus	Policy issues	Main programmes[1] (central or federal level)
Finland	0.68%	5.8%	20 universities, 27 polytechnics	Broadening the scope of regional innovation system	Adaptation of HEI expertise and services to SME needs	Centres of Expertise; TULI programme; Cluster programme; Technology clinics
France	0.41%	2.7%	85 universities plus numerous Grandes Ecoles	Increasing regional innovation performance	Weak university R&D; Limited co-operation with firms; Low participation of innovating SMEs in regional innovation systems	Poles of Competitiveness; Industrial and commercial services in HEIs; Technology platforms; Entrepreneur Houses
Germany	0.41%	13.2%	350 universities and Fachhochschulen	Learning regions; Development of Eastern Germany	Stimulating entrepreneurship; Bundling competencies	Innoregio; EXIST; Innovative Regional Growth Poles; Innovation Competence; INNOPROFILE NEMOS
Italy	0.36%		77 universities	North-south divide	Instilling R&D and innovation in districts and clusters	Technological districts; joint labs; ICT action plan; incubators
Japan	0.43%	2.8%	716 universities and 478 colleges	Improving creativity of HEIs in science and technology	Enhancing competence building functions of HEIs; Promoting local co-operative centres and regional HEI consortiums	Knowledge cluster programme; Industry cluster programme; Support to approved technology licensing offices
Korea	0.28%	15.9%	135 four-year universities and 106 regional colleges	Balanced regional development; Improving the governance of regional innovation systems	Increasing co-operation between HEIs; Facilitating partnerships between sub-national governments and HE institutions;	New University for Regional Innovation (NURI); NRL; Industry-Academia co-operation groups; Technical Innovation Centres
Mexico	0.16%*	2.0%*	1 892 HEIs including 713 public institutions	Integration of research in the productive efforts of region and the country	Strengthening the collaboration between HEIs, federal laboratories and the industry; Building Regional Innovation Clusters	COEPES; Mexican Knowledge and Innovation Programme (KIP); AVANCE; CIMO
Netherlands	0.50%	6.8%*	13 research universities, 45 HBOs, open university	Transfer of knowledge	Connecting SMEs with HEIs	Lectors; Knowledge circles; Knowledge Vouchers; RAAK regulation

1. See below more details on each country's programmes.

Table B.1. **Selected OECD countries' characteristics and innovation-based policies targeting at the regional engagement of higher education institutions** (cont.)

Country	HE research % of GDP 2004	HE research financed by industry 2004	Number of HEIs	Policy focus	Policy issues	Main programmes[1] (central or federal level)
Norway	0.48%	5.0%*	6 universities, 5 specialised university institutes, 25 university colleges, 2 arts academies	Coherence between innovation and regional policies	Fostering involvement of universities in clusters; Monitoring govt innovation strategies based on research, transfer and commercialisation of knowledge	FORNY; MOBI; SIVA innovation centres; VS 2010, ARENA; Centres of Expertise
Spain	0.31%	7.5%	48 state-funded universities (incl. 1 distance learning HEI) and 23 private universities	Discrepancies between regional innovation system support	Improving co-ordination between HEIs and firms; Improving the access to public funds	Regional authorities programmes; PETRI programme; Projects to encourage the transfer of research results with industrial applications
Sweden	0.87%*	5.5%*	14 state universities, 22 state university colleges and 3 private institutions	Regional Innovation Systems; HEI- industry interface dominated by a small number of multinational enterprises working with 8 oldest universities	Increasing the number of HEI-based start-ups	University-SME co-operation; VINNVÄXT regional growth programme through dynamic innovation systems; Öresund Contract
Switzerland	0.67%	8.7%	15 universities, 12 universities of applied sciences (Hautes Écoles Spécialisées)	Bridging the gap between research and innovation	Specialisation of HEIs; Accelerating knowledge transfer	Competence building in universities of applied sciences; Promotion of start-ups and entrepreneurialism in HEIs
UK	0.40%	5.1%	169 universities and HE colleges (+ further education colleges), some private colleges	Better tap into HEIs' innovation potential	Absorptive capacity in peripheral regions	HEIF2; Knowledge Transfer Partnerships; Regional Innovation Fund

* Reflects figures for 2003.

1. See below more details on each country's programmes.

Source: OECD, *Main Science and Technology Indicators*, December 2006.

Australia

Majority of funds for the HE sector are derived from the Commonwealth Government. The **Collaboration and Structural Reform Fund** (CASR) promotes structural reform in the HE sector and business-HEI collaboration. Budget: AUD 51 million in 2005-2010. There is also a potential for HEIs with strong regional engagement practices for several **Australian Research Council (ARC) programmes** in particular linkage funds (collaborative research). Budget: AUD 76 million in 2002. **Regional Partnerships Grants** are administered by Area Consultative Committees which have representation from business and key economic sectors in regions. Finally the **Cooperative Research Centres (CRC) programme** supports application to establish CRCs which bring together researchers and research groups from universities, government research laboratories (federal, State and Territory) and the private sector into long term cooperative relationships. 145 CRCs proposal have been approved since the start of the programme in 1990. A AUD 148 million budget was devoted to this programme in 2002/2003.

Austria

A+B: Academia-business networks of regional partners compete for national support for start-up centres (participation of Academia in projects is compulsory). Budget: EUR 20 million in 2002-2009 for the first two calls. The aim is to incubate 200 firms in 5 years. Evaluation is ongoing. **REG+** aims at increasing the performances of technology and innovation centres, strengthening the regional innovation systems and enhancing co-operation with HEIs. It has involved 240 partners. Budget: EUR 10.8 million in 2000-2006. Positive evaluation. **FH+** aims to enhance competencies in Fachhochschulen. Budget EUR 7.5 million in 2002-2015. Positive evaluation based on the growing involvement of the Fachhochschule-sector in national and international consortia. **Seed financing:** Budget: EUR 38 million.

Belgium

Brussels capital region: Industrial research subsidy programme. This programme focuses on increasing firm R&D and on strengthening linkages with the research base. Budget: EUR 5 million. No evaluation.

Wallonia: FIRST programmes aim to increase the science and technology potential of university research **(FIRST higher education)**, encourage HEI researchers to study the conditions for the commercial exploitation of research results **(FIRST spin-off)**, promote research within the framework of a partnership with firms **(FIRST enterprise)** and encourage international mobility **(FIRST DEI)**. **Feasibility study for university-based technical support** for a firm.

Budget: EUR 9.5 million. Favourable evaluation and evidence of increasing demand. **University-Industry Interfaces Programme.** It supports hiring of supplementary personnel. Budget: EUR 1 million in 2000-2003. **Mobilising Programmes** are opened to university laboratories fostering research in strategic areas. Budget: EUR 180 million for 1991-2004.

Flaunders: IOF is an industrial research fund for universities to develop research relevant to industry. Budget: EUR 12 million in two calls. **Poles of Excellence** have an annual budget of EUR 100 million. Evaluation results are often positive. **Support for industrial estate and science parks.** TETRA funds provides assistance for university technology transfer. Budget: EUR 6 million for 23 projects in 2004. The goal of **research mandates** is to help researchers in the commercialisation of research results.

Canada

The Federal government is the principal supporter of university research and innovation. Component of the new strategy include the **Canada Foundation for Innovation** (CFI), the 21 **Chairs of Research Excellence** (budget: CAD 300 million per year) and the network of **Centres of Excellence**. The federal government funds also university research through research granting councils, such as the National Science and Engineering Research Council (NSERC), the Social Sciences and Humanities Research Council (SSHRC) or the Canadian Institutes for Health Research (CIHRC). Among main programmes for SMEs are the **NSERC Collaborative Research Development Grant**, National Research Council Industry and Research Programme **NRC-IRAP** or **NSERC Ideas to Innovation**. Universities received CAD 2.2 billion in 2005-06 from NSERC, SSHRC, CIHR, CFI and IC. There are also special innovation funds such as the **Atlantic Innovation Fund** (AIF) through which CAD 370 million has been awarded in three rounds to knowledge-based development projects involving industry and HEIs. The **Innovation Management Association of Canada** (IMAC), which has representation from the high tech sectors and R&D industries and universities, works to expand the commercialisation of innovation.

Denmark

Regional Knowledge Pilots enable SMEs to employ academic staff. Budget: DKK 17.5 million for the two last years. **Centres of Expertise** focus on regional competencies and act as intermediaries with SMEs. **Centres of Excellence** (6-10 planned) aim to strengthen the collaboration between research and industry. These initiatives are recent and have not yet been evaluated. **Incubators**: eight university incubators have been approved by the Ministry of Science, Technology and Innovation. The **Trade and Industry Local Partnerships Programme for IT** has been developed initially in four regions.

Finland

The **Centres of Expertise Programme** aims to ensure rapid transfer of latest knowledge from research centres and HEIs to companies (co-operation mandatory). The investment of EUR 52.5 million (1999-2006) has levered in EUR 578 million of total funding and created over 13 000 new knowledge-intensive jobs, preserved 29 000 jobs and led to the formation of 1 300 companies. The **Cluster programme** (budget: EUR 100 million) has been successful in the public sector, while the participation of companies remains a challenge. **Improving use of research results** (budget: EUR 2.3 million in 2003; no evaluation). **Technology Clinics** (budget: EUR 4 million) aim to improve technology transfer to SMEs. 15-20 clinics are operating. Evaluation results stress the need for more effective marketing. The **TULI programme** (budget: EUR 2.6 million in 2005) aims to promote the exploitation of research results and promising ideas. TULI projects are run by local technology transfer companies and co-ordinated by the Finnish Science Parks Association (TEKEL). The flexibility of the programme is recognized. Its mediator network in research institutions is considered as its major strength.

France

Poles of Competitiveness. This programme supports locally or regionally based networks of firms and HEIs which have been selected through a call for tender. Budget: EUR 1.5 billion in 2005-2007 for projects presented by 66 selected poles. **SAIC (Industrial and commercial business services)** aim to concentrate the promotion of HEI industrial and commercial activities into a single structure. Through several calls for participation, public funding has been channelled to universities to fund these structures. Since 2001, 22 SAICs have been created. **Regional Incubators Structures.** They support the co-operation between public research bodies and enterprises. National public funding represents 50% of the incubation expenses. Budget: EUR 46 million from Ministry of Research and EUR 8 million from the ESF. **Technology Platforms (PFT)** aim to develop the third mission of HEIs and other training institutions and to enhance the links between SMEs and HEIs. In 2004 there were 70 platforms. Budget: EUR 0.22 million. **Entrepreneurship Houses** in HEIs: six projects selected in 2004. Budget: EUR 250 000. No evaluation so far.

Germany

Innovation Growth Poles supports regionally and thematically focused bottom-up innovation initiatives in the Eastern Länder, bringing together SMEs, research organisations/universities and other actors. Until 2007, 28 Poles were funded. Budget: EUR 150 million until 2009.

Centres for Innovation Competence establish research centres with innovation competence and attractiveness for young researchers. Until 2002, 6 centres are funded with EUR 73 million. *InnoProfile* promotes since 2005 young research groups at research centres addressing concrete innovation-related questions of the SMEs in their region and co-operating with them. Budget: EUR 150 million until 2012.

EXIST selects networks based on a competition. Since 1997, 200 universities with 109 projects participated in the programme. About 550 innovative start-ups have been established in the 5 EXIST model regions. Budget 1998-2005: EUR 45 million. **Networks of Competences** support regionally concentrated networks between science, education and business in order to generate innovation. 102 of these networks have been established in 32 regions. Budget: EUR 2 million for marketing and management. The **Learning Regions** programme brings together supply and demand in education within a region and tries to find optimal solutions for lifelong learning. Budget: EUR 120 million in 2000-2007 from the Ministry and the European Social Fund. **NEMO**, Management of Innovation Networks for East German SMEs, provides support for the networks of SMEs and R&D organisations . The 1st round: 23 networks, the 2nd round: 15 networks. Budget: EUR 6 million in 2005. The **High Tech Start-up Fund** promotes spin-offs from public research and universities. Budget: starting amount of EUR 142 million (average funding: EUR 0.5 million for project).

Italy

Joint labs aim to foster the co-operation between industry and research centres in the Mezzogiorno. Participation of universities is compulsory. Budget: EUR 212 million. Eligible costs include equipment, training, external expertise and labour cost. 22 centres were created following the previous call. **Technological districts** in six locations enhance the Italian district model. Districts are co-financed by the private sector and have participation of venture capital fund, but no funding from the government. The **Incubators for start-ups** programme provides high level technical assistance, training, consultancy and logistic support to enterprises in the start-up phase. Budget EUR 23 million in 2005-2007. Universities and research institutes are eligible for funding. **ICT action plan** provides grants, guarantees, subsidised loans and tax incentives for the diffusion of ICT to firms especially SMEs and promotes technology transfer from public research institutes including universities.

Japan

In 2004, 90% of the national universities were engaged in co-operative research or commissioned research. In 83% of the cases the partner institutions were private sector businesses; in 29% they were SMEs. Under the 1998 *Law for Promoting University-Industry Technology Transfer* the right to obtain patents was transferred to University Technology Transfer Offices (TLOs). *Approved TLOs* receive state assistance until the business is established. Following the 2004 reform, it has become possible for the National University Corporations to have shares in the start-ups. Details about the *cluster programmes* are given in Chapter 5.

Korea

The *New University for Regional Innovation programme (NURI)* is a government-funded initiative to strengthen the capability of HEIs outside the Seoul metropolitan area, to promote curricula alignment to the characteristics of the regional economy and to establish triple helix collaboration system between HEIs, local governments, research institutes and corporations. Budget: KRW 1 420 billion in 2004-2008 (112 universities). *Brain Korea 21 (BK21)* aims to create trained workforce through programmes that establish research-focused graduate schools, educate graduates to meet the demand of the job market and develop local universities. Budget: KRW 200 billion per year since the end of the 1990s. The government also supports over 444 *National Research Laboratories (NRL)* across the country: 278 are in Academia. Budget: USD 250 000 for five years. There are also 38 *Technological Innovation Centres* in universities in different regions. Since 1995, the Ministry of Science and Technology has provided funding for 59 *regional research centres in academia*. Budget: KRW 133 billion for 8 years.

Mexico

Mexico has designed a set of educational policies that aim to improve greater decentralisation. A State planning agency, **COEPES,** manages tertiary education planning at the regional level. The SEP (Secretariat of Public Education) and CONACYT (The National Agency for Science and Technology) have established a range of programmes to stimulate the research qualifications of teachers in tertiary education, to expand the quality of graduate programmes and to increase productivity and output of HEIs. The *Knowledge and Innovation Programme (KIP)* aims to strengthen the linkages between HEIs, industry and society to pursue opportunities in technological innovation. It is instrumental in the decentralisation of the national innovation system. The *Programme for Integral Quality and Modernisation (CIMO)*, run by the Ministry of Labour, provides technical training to local firms and brings together networks of researchers from across universities and public and private institutions. Elements of government–industry matching funds for collaborative research exist in the form of the CONACYT Programme for the Creation of New Businesses Based on Scientific and Technological Development **(AVANCE).** CONACYT Programmes of mixed federal and state funds help to improve strategies that support cluster development and address the gaps in the innovation support infrastructure.

Netherlands

Since 2001, there has been a policy of appointing a growing number of **lectors and knowledge circles** at the institutions of higher professional education. Lectors and knowledge circles aim at improving the external orientation of HEIs especially with regard to SMEs. The networks of knowledge circles consist of companies and relevant organisations in the field. Budget: EUR 38.4-50 million per year in 2006-2007. **Knowledge Vouchers** (see also Chapter 5) are an incentive to companies that buy services from knowledge institutes. The **RAAK-regeling** (Regional Action and Attention for Knowledge Innovation) aims at strengthening the relationship between HEIs and the SME sector. It offers financial support to co-operation projects in the field of knowledge development and knowledge exchange between HEIs (including also regional education and training centres) and SMEs. Budget: EUR 5-8 million.

Norway

Key initiatives with explicit regional orientation include FORNY, MOBI, SIVA, VS 2010, ARENA and the Centres of Expertise. The **FORNY** programme has a focus on the commercialisation of higher education sector's ideas and on intellectual property. A part of the **MOBI** programme funds R&D projects involving university colleges and firms located in the same region. **SIVA** is a co-owner of more than 60 innovation centres, including science and research parks, knowledge parks, business gardens, as well as venture capital and seed financing institutions. Budget: NOK 300 million (about USD 50 million). Participants include more than 1 000 private investors, industrial corporations, HEIs and other R&D institutions. **VS 2010** encourages companies to collaborate with researchers in organisational development and innovation processes, triggering internal- and network-based innovation potential in companies, especially at the regional level. This is emphasised through a focus on union/employer federation participation and development coalition, both in network- and regional partnerships. **ARENA** contributes to increased innovation and wealth creation through co-operation between firms, knowledge providers and the public sector. The programme is intended for regional clusters of firms and knowledge institutions. The **Centres of Expertise (pilots)** aim to increase regional and national competitiveness through strengthening core competences in the regions and through encouraging formal triple helix collaboration. HEIs' external relations and externally-oriented activities have been established through a specific framework ("randsonevirksomhet") which provides HEIs with tools to become proactive in external project acquisition and to create revenue related to such activities.

Spain

Most national programmes have no specific regional dimension apart from the **PETRI** programme which encourages the transfer of research results generated in universities and public research institutes to companies, particularly SMEs.

Sweden

The **VINNVÄXT *regional growth programme*** aims to stimulate strong innovation systems with qualified environment for R&D as well as dynamic networks. A few selected regions receive funding for ten years within specific areas of growth. Triple helix co-operation with actors from the public sector, academy and business is mandatory. Evaluation is ongoing. **Öresundskontrakt:** The programme aims to strengthen the competitiveness of the Öresund cross-border region through enhanced collaboration between the research centres and universities in Sweden and Denmark. Projects are co-financed. Budget: EUR 1.8 million. Evaluation: co-operation has improved cross-border connections but the long term collaboration remains a challenge. The ***University and SME Co-operation scheme*** focuses on new forms of co-operation between small businesses and HEIs. Seven universities have been selected to implement and try out experiences that can generate knowledge about entrepreneurship at universities. Six other universities have been chosen to disseminate the results of the first round. Budget: EUR 3.5 million in 2004-2007.

Switzerland

Competence Building in the Universities of Applied Sciences (UAS or "Hautes Ecoles"). The Innovation Promotion Agency (KTI) supports joint projects between UAS and private sector through funding the salaries of UAS researchers and/or co-financing professional consultancy services. This benefits not only SMEs, but also UAS institutions which gain expertise through participating in a competence network that draws from different regions and disciplines. Budget: EUR 73.6 million in 2004-2007. Evaluation: progress has been made in telecommunications. ***Knowledge and Technology Transfer (KTT)*** promotes technology transfer from public science institutions including universities to private firms through five consortiums consisting of KTT service centres. The five regionally focused consortiums link KTT offices at

HEIs and the federal Institute of Technology at a regional level. Budget: EUR 6.5 million in 2005-2007. No evaluation so far. The **Promotion of start-ups and entrepreneurial spirit** aims to develop a culture of innovation and to enhance the way from idea to market. The programme supports labour cost, infrastructure and equipment. Budget: EUR 23.7 million. It has created 750 jobs and 67 start-ups which are still in business.

United Kingdom

Higher Education Innovation Fund (HEIF) embeds the third mission to encourage universities to work with industry and the wider communities alongside teaching and research. HEIF builds co-operation in English universities for knowledge transfer and commercial sector activities with a focus on co-operation with the regional community. Budget for the two last academic years: EUR 279 million. A 2005 evaluation showed limited impacts with regard to university-industry connections indicating a need for long term scale between developing capacities and delivering businesses. **Knowledge Transfer Partnerships** aim to increase interactions between universities and companies. Graduates are recruited to work in a company for two years in close co-operation with a university. Total government spending: EUR 35.4 million in 2004-2005. Each GBP 1 million of government support has generated 47 new jobs, GBP 2.5 million annual increase in profit and GBP 1.3 million investment in plant and machinery. 80% of companies considered that the placement had considerably extended their knowledge base.

ISBN 978-92-64-03414-3
Higher Education and Regions:
Globally Competitive, Locally Engaged
© OECD 2007

Bibliography

Agarval and Henderson (2002), "Putting Patents in Context: Exploring Knowledge Transfer from MIT". *Management science*, January 2002.

Aghion P. and P. Howitt (1998), *Endogenous Growth Theory*, The MIT press, Cambridge.

Arbo, P. and P. Benneworth (2007), *Understanding the Regional Contribution of Higher Education Institutions: a Literature Review*, OECD Education Working Paper, No. 9, OECD, Paris, *www.oecd.org/edu/workingpapers*.

Asheim, B. and M. Gertler (2005), "The Geography of Innovation", in J. Fagerberg *et al.* (eds.), *Oxford Handbook of Innovation*, Oxford University Press, Oxford.

Audretsch, D. B. and M.P Feldman (1996), "Innovative Clusters and the Industry Life Cycle", *Review of Industrial Organization*, Vol. 11, No. 2, pp. 253-273.

Bachtler, J. (2004), "Innovation-led Regional Development: Policy Trends and Issues", Paper presented at the OECD Conference on Innovation and Regional Development: Transition Towards a Knowledge-based Economy. Florence, Italy, 25-26 November 2004.

Bélanger, P. (2006), "Concepts and Realities of Learning Cities and Regions", in C. Duke, L. Doyle and B. Wilson (eds.), *Making Knowledge Work. Sustaining Learning Communities and Regions*, National Institute of Adult Continuing Education (NIACE), Asford Colourpress, Gosport.

Bender, T. (1988), Introduction in Bender, T. (ed.), *The University and the City, from Medical Origins to the Present*, Oxford University Press, New York/Oxford, pp. 3-10.

Best, M. (2000), "Silicon Valley and the Resurgence of Route 128: Systems Integration and Regional Innovation", in J. Dunning (ed.), *Regions, Globalization, and the Knowledge-Based Economy*, Oxford University Press, Oxford.

Binks, M (2005), *Entrepreneurship Education and Interactive Learning,* National Council for Graduate entrepreneurship (NCGE) Policy Paper No. 1, *www.ncge.org.uk/downloads/ policy/Entrepreneurship_Education_and_Integrative_Learning.doc*.

Birch, D. L. (1987), *Job Creation in America: How Our Smallest Companies Put the Most People to Work*, Free Press, New York.

Brennan, J., R. Naidoo (2007), "*Higher Education and the Achievement of Equity and Social Justice" in* Higher Education Looking Forward (HELF), European Science Foundation: Forward Look, forthcoming.

Brunner, J. J., P. Santiago, C. García Guadilla, J. Gerlach and L. Velho (2006), *OECD Thematic Review of Tertiary Education. Mexico. Country Note*, OECD, Paris, *www.oecd.org/dataoecd/22/49/37746196.pdf*.

Brusco, S. (1986), "Small Firms and Industrial Districts: The experience of Italy", in D. Keeble and E. Wever (eds.), *New firms and regional development in Europe*, Croom Helm, London, pp. 184-202.

Burt, R. (2002), "The Social Capital of Structural Holes", *New Directions in Economic Sociology*, Russel Sage, New York.

Christensen, JL., B. Gregersen and A. Rogaczewska (1999), "Vidensinstitutioner og innovation" (Knowledge Institutions and Innovation), DISKO project, Report No. 8, Erhvervsudviklingsraden (Council for the Development of Economic Life), Copenhagen.

Centre for Urban and Regional Development (CURDS) (2005), *OECD Territorial Review of Newcastle and the North East*, OECD, Paris.

Clark, B. R. (1998), *Creating Entrepreneurial Universities: Organizational Pathways of Transformation*, Pergamon-Elsevier Science, Oxford.

Clark, (2006), OECD, *Thematic Review of Tertiary Education. Country Report: United Kingdom*, OECD, Paris, *www.oecd.org/dataoecd/22/3/37211152.pdf*.

Cook, P. (2004), "University Research and Regional Development", European Commission, Research Director-General.

Coulombe, S., J.-F. Tremblay and S. Marchand (2004), "Literacy Scores, Human Capital and Growth Across 14 OECD Countries", *Statistics Canada*, Ottawa.

Council of Europe (2006), *Declaration on Higher Education and Democratic Culture: citizenship, human rights and civic responsibility*, Strasbourg, 22-23 June 2006, *http://dc.ecml.at/contentman/resources/Downloads/Declaration_EN.pdf* (accessed January 2007).

Crawford, E., T. Shinn and S. Sörlin (1993), "The Nationalization and Denationalization of the Sciences. An introductory essay", in E. Crawford, T. Shinn and S. Sörlin (eds.), *Denationalizing Science. The Contexts of International Scientific Practice*, Kluwer, Dordrecht.

Davies, J., T. Weko, L. Kim, and E. Thustrup (2006), *Thematic Review of Tertiary Education: Finland Country Note*, OECD, Paris, *www.oecd.org/dataoecd/51/29/37474463.pdf*.

Department for Culture, Media and Sport (DCMS) (2006), *Developing Entrepreneurship for the Creative Industries. The Role of Higher and Further Education*, DCMS, London.

DfES, DTI, DWP, HM Treasure (2003), *21st Century Skills: Realising Our Potential (Individuals, Employers, Nation)*, The Stationery Office, London.

Drabenstott, M. (2005), *Review of the Federal Role in Regional Economic Development*, Federal Reserve Bank of Kansas City.

Etzkowitz, H. and L. Leydesdorff (2000), "The Dynamics of Innovation: from National Systems and 'Mode 2' to a Triple-Helix of University-Industry-Government Relations", *Research Policy*, Vol. 29, No. 2, pp. 109-123.

Felsenstein, D. (1996), "The University in the Metropolitan Arena: Impacts and Public Policy Implications", *Urban Studies*, Vol. 33.

Florida, R. (2002), *The Rise of the Creative Class and How It's Transforming Work, Leisure, Community and Everyday Life*, Basic Books, New York.

Florida, R. (2005), "The World is Spiky", *Atlantic Monthly*, Boston.

Forum for the Future (2006), Forum for the Future website, *www.forumforthefuture.org.uk*, accessed 12 January 2007.

Friedman, T. (2005), *The World is Flat: A Brief History of the Twenty-First Century*, Farrar, Straus and Giroux, New York.

Fundación Conocimiento y Desarrollo (2005), *Informe CYD 2005: La contribución de las universidades españolas al desarrollo*, Fundación CYD, Barcelona.

Gertler, M. and T. Vinodrai, (2004), Anchors of Creativity: How Do Public Universities Create *Competitive and Cohesive Communities?*, Department of Geography, University of Toronto.

Gibb, A. (2005), Towards the Entrepreneurial University: Entrepreneurship Education as a Lever for Change.

Gibbons, M., C. Limoges, H. Nowotny, S. Schwartzman, P. Scott and M. Trow (1994), *The New Production of Knowledge: The Dynamics of Science and Research in Contemporary Societies*, Sage, London.

Goddard, J., D. Charles, A., Pike, G. Potts and D. Bradley (1994), *Universities and Communities: a Report for the Committee of Vice-Chancellors and Principals*, Centre for Urban and Regional Development Studies, Newcastle University, Newcastle.

Goddard, J. B. and P. Chatterton (2003), The response of universities to regional needs, in F. Boekema, E. Kuypers, R. Rutten (eds.), *Economic Geography of Higher Education: Knowledge, Infrastructure and Learning Regions*, Routledge, London.

Goddard, J. B. (2005), "Supporting the Contribution of HEIs to Regional Developments Project Overview", Paper presented to OECD/IMHE Conference, Paris, 6-7 January 2005.

Goldstein, H. and M. Luger (1993) "Theory and Practice in High-Tech Economic Development", in D. R. Bingham and R. Mier (eds.), *Theories of Local Economic Development: Perspectives from across the Disciplines*, Sage Publications, Newbury Park.

Grubb, N., H. M. Jahr, J. Neumüller, S. Field (2006), *Equity in Education. Thematic Review. Finland Country Note*. OECD, Paris, *www.oecd.org/dataoecd/49/40/36376641.pdf*.

HEFCE (Higher Education Funding Council for England) (2006), *Widening Participation: a Review*, Report to the Minister of State of Higher Education and Lifelong Learning by the Higher Education Funding Council for England, *www.hefce.ac.uk/widen/aimhigh/review.asp*.

Innovation Associates Inc. (2005), *Accelerating Economic development through University technology Transfer*, based on Report to the Connecticut Technology Transfer and Commercialization Advisory Board of the Governor's Competitiveness Council, *www.innovationassoc.com*.

Joaquin B.J, P. Santiago, C. García Guadilla, J. Gerlach, L.Velho (2006), *Thematic Review of Tertiary Education: Mexico Country Note*, *www.oecd.org/dataoecd/22/49/37746196.pdf*.

Kaldor, N. (1970), "The Case for Regional Policies", *Scottish Journal of Political Economy*, Vol., 17, No. 3, pp. 337-348.

Kline, S. J. and N Rosenberg (1986), "An Overview of Innovation", in R. Landau and N. Rosenberg (eds.), *The Positive Sum Strategy: Harnessing Technology for Economic Growth*, National Academy Press, Washington, D.C., pp. 275-304.

Laursen, K and A. Salter (2003), "The Fruits of Intellectual Production: Economic and Scientific Specialisation among OECD Countries", Paper No. 2, Danish Research Units for Industrial Dynamics, University of Aalborg, Aalborg.

Lawton Smith, H., J. Glasson, J. Simmie, A. Chadwick and G. Clark (2003), *Enterprising Oxford: The Growth of the Oxfordshire High-tech Economy*, Oxford Economic Observatory, Oxford.

Lester, Richard K. (2005), *Universities, Innovation, and the Competitiveness of Local Economies: A Summary Report from the Local Innovation Systems Project–Phase I.* MIT IPC Local Innovation Systems Working Paper 05-005 | IPC Working Paper 05-010, *http://web.edu/lis/papers/LIS05.010.pdf.*

Locke, W., E. Beale, R. Greenwood, C. Farrell, S.Tomblin, P-M. Dejardins, F. Strain, and G. Baldacchino (2006), *OECD/IMHE Project, Supporting the Contribution of Higher Education Institutions to Regional Development, Self Evaluation Report: Atlantic Canada, www.oecd.org//17/12/37884292.pdf.*

Lundvall, B. Å. (ed.) (1992), *National Systems of Innovation: Towards a theory of Innovation and Interactive Learning*, Pinter Publishers, London.

Lundvall B. Å. and S. Borrás (1997), *The Globalising Learning Economy: Implication for Innovation Policy*, The European Communities, Luxembourg.

Malmberg, A. and P. Maskell (1997), "Towards an Explanation of Regional Specialization and Industry Agglomeration", *European Planning Studies*, Vol. 5, No. 1, pp. 25-41.

Martin, F. and M. Trudeau (1998), *The Economic Impact of Canadian University R&D*, AUCC publications, Ottawa.

Martin, R. and P. Morrison (2003), "Thinking about the Geographies of Labour," in R.Martin and S. Morrison (eds.), *Geographies of Labor Market Inequality*, Routledge, London, pp. 3-20.

Mathiessen, Christian Wichman, Annette Winkel Schwarz and Søren Find (2005), *Research Output and Cooperation: Case Study of the Øresund Region: An Analysis Based on Bibliometric Indicators*, University of Copenhagen, Copenhagen.

McClelland, C. E. (1988), "To Live for Science: Ideals and Realities at the University of Berlin", in T. Bender (ed.), *The University and the City. From Medieval Origins to the Present*, Oxford University Press, New York/Oxford, pp. 181-197.

Morgan, K. (1997), "The Learning Region: Institutions, Innovation and Regional Renewal", *Regional Studies*, Vol. 31, No. 5, pp. 491-403.

Myrdal, G. (1957), *Economic Theory and Under-Developed Regions*, Gerald Duckworth, London.

OECD (1999), *The Response of Higher Education Institutions to Regional Needs*, OECD, Paris.

OECD (2001a), *Cities and Regions in the Learning Economy*, OECD, Paris.

OECD (2001b), *Managing University Museums*, OECD, Paris.

OECD (2003a), *Funding of Public Research and Development: Trends and Changes*, OECD, Paris.

OECD (2003b), *OECD Territorial Reviews: Öresund, Denmark/Sweden*, OECD, Paris.

OECD (2003c), "Upgrading Workers' Skills and Competencies", *OECD Employment Outlook*, OECD, Paris.

OECD (2004), *OECD Territorial Reviews: Busan, Korea*, OECD, Paris.

OECD (2005a), *OECD Territorial Reviews: Finland. OECD*, Paris.

OECD (2005b), *Economic Surveys: Korea*, OECD, Paris.

OECD (2005c), *Economic Surveys: Mexico*, OECD, Paris.

OECD (2005d), *Economic Surveys: The Netherlands*, OECD, Paris.

OECD (2005e), *Economic Surveys: United Kingdom*, OECD, Paris.

OECD (2005f), *Reviews of National Policies for Education: University Education in Denmark*, OECD, Paris.

OECD (2006a), "The Contributions of Higher Education Institutions to Regional Development: Issues and Policies", GOV/TDPC(2006)22, OECD, Paris.

OECD (2006b), *Economic Surveys:Australia*, OECD, Paris.

OECD (2006c) *Economic Survey of Brazil*, OECD, Paris.

OECD, (2006d), *Economic Surveys: Canada*, OECD, Paris.

OECD, (2006e), *Economic Surveys: Denmark*, OECD, Paris.

OECD (2006f), *Economic Surveys: Finland*, OECD, Paris.

OECD (2006g), *Building a Competitive City-Region: The Case of Newcastle in the North East*, OECD, Paris.

OECD (2006h), *Skills Upgrading. New Policy Perspectives*, OECD, Paris.

OECD (2006i), *Measuring the Effects of Education on Health and Civic Engagement* (Proceedings of the Copenhagen Symposium), OECD, Paris, available in *www.oecd.org/edu/socialoutcomes/symposium*.

OECD (2006j), *Main Science and Technology Indicators*, OECD, Paris.

OECD (2007a), Supporting the Contribution of Higher Education Institutions to Regional Development, project website, *www.oecd.org/edu/higher/regionaldevelopment*.

OECD (2007b), *Economic Surveys: Sweden*, OECD, Paris.

OECD (2007c), *Economic Surveys: Spain*, OECD, Paris.

OECD (2007d), *Understanding the Social Outcomes of Learning*, OECD, Paris, forthcoming.

OECD (2008), *OECD Review of Tertiary Education. Final Report*, OECD, Paris, forthcoming.

OPDM (Office for Deputy Prime Minister) (2004), *Competitive European Cities, Where Do the Core Cities Stand?*, *www.communities.gov.uk/pub/441/CompetitiveEuropeanCitiesWhereDoTheCoreCitiesStandFullReportPDF444Kb_id1127441.pdf*.

Paytas, J., R. Gradeck and L. Andrews (2004), *Universities and the Development of Industry Clusters. Paper for the Economic Development Administration*, US Department of Commerce, Centre for Economic Development, Carnegie Mellon University, Pittsburg, Pensylvania.

Peck, J. (1996), *Workplace: The Social Regulation of Labor Markets*, Guildford Press, New York and London.

Piore, M. J. and Sabel, C.F. (1984), *The Second Industrial Divide. Possibilities for Prosperity*, Free Press, New York.

Porter, M. E. (1990), *The Competitive Advantage of Nations*, MacMillan, Basingstoke.

Porter, M. E. (1998), "Location, Clusters and the New Economics of Competition", *Business Economics*, Vol. 33, No. 1, pp. 7-17.

Porter, M. E. (2003), "The Economic Performance of Regions", *Regional Studies*, Vol. 37, No. 6/7, pp. 549-78.

Rosenfeld, S. (1998) *Technical Colleges, Technology Deployment and Regional Development*, draft stock-taking paper prepared for the OECD, Regional Technology Strategies Inc, Chapel Hill, North Carolina.

Rothwell, R. and W. Zegveld (1982), *Innovation and the Small and Medium-Sized Firm*. Frances Pinter, London.

Scott, A. and M. Storper (2002), "Regions, Globalization and Development", *Regional Studies*, Vol. 37, pp. 579-593.

Simmie J., J. Sennett, P. Wood and D. Hart (2002), "Innovation in Europe, a Tale of Networks, Knowledge and Trade in Five Cities", *Regional Studies*, Vol. 36, pp. 47-64.

Smith, T and C. Whitchurch (2002), "The Future of the Tripartitite Mission: Re-Examining the Relationship Linking Universities, Medical Schools and Health Systems", *Higher Education Management and Policy*, Vol. 14, No. 2, OECD, Paris.

The Finnish Higher Education Evaluation Council (2006), The Finnish Higher Education Evaluation Council website, *www.kka.fi/english*, accessed 3 January 2006.

Vestergaard, J. (2006), "HEIs and Their Regions – an Innovation System Perspective", paper presented to OECD/IMHE Project Task Group, 10 April 2006, Paris.

Wittrock, B. (1993), "The Modern University: the Three Transformations", in S. Rothblatt and B. Wittrock (eds.), *The European and American University Since 1800. Historical and Sociological Essays*, Cambridge University Press, Cambridge, pp. 303-362.

World Bank Group (2002), *Constructing Knowledge Societies: New Challenges for Tertiary Education*, http://www1.worldbank.org/education/tertiary/cks.asp.

Young, S. and R. Brown (2002), "Globalisation and the Knowledge Economy", in N. Hood, J. Peat, E. Peters and S. Young (eds.), *Scotland in a Global Economy: The 20:20 Vision*, Palgrave Macmillan, Hampshire.

OECD PUBLICATIONS, 2, rue André-Pascal, 75775 PARIS CEDEX 16
PRINTED IN FRANCE
(04 2007 07 1 P) ISBN 978-92-64-03414-3 – No. 55653 2007